FIND IT FAST

FIFTH EDITION

*How to Uncover
Expert Information
on Any Subject
Online or in Print*

Robert I. Berkman

HarperResource
An Imprint of HarperCollinsPublishers

HarperCollins books may be purchased for educational, business, or sales promotional use. For information please write: Special Markets Department, HarperCollins Publishers, Inc., 10 East 53rd Street, New York, NY 10022.

FIFTH EDITION

Library of Congress Cataloging-in-Publication Data has been applied for.

ISBN 0-06-273747-3

00 01 02 03 01 10 9 8 7 6 5 4 3 2

To Sol, Pat,
Budd, and Don

Contents

Contents

PART II: EXPERTS ARE EVERYWHERE

Acknowledgments

I'd like to express my gratitude to the people who in one way or another played a big part in making this book come to pass.

Mary Walsh gave me encouragement at the most critical moments—without it, this book would not have been written. George Finnegan has been a true mentor. I'll always be thankful for the chance to work for him and receive a once-in-a-lifetime learning opportunity. Janet Goldstein, my editor at HarperCollins, believed enough in the book to give it a chance, and always gave me her support and great ideas.

I'm grateful to Nancy Brandwein, Ken Coughlin, and Lilli Warren, all of whom provided critical insights, suggestions, and critiques of the final manuscript.

I also want to thank Sandy Gollop for her assistance, knowledge, and kindness; my colleagues at PIN for their encouragement and interest in the book; Debbie Cohen for her hard work and sharp eye for detail; and Ginny Fisher, Leigh Woods, Hella Rader, Cindy Pereira, and Pam and Jeff Goodman for so generously helping me out in the final stages. Trisha Karsay put in a lot of hours and top-notch work—her enthusiasm for the book meant a lot to me and is genuinely appreciated.

A special thank-you goes to everyone in the Norris family up in Cape Cod for providing me with such a beautiful and relaxing spot to think and write.

And finally, thanks to my parents and brothers for their love, support, and invaluable ideas.

Preface to the Fifth Edition of *Find It Fast*

The previous edition, written in 1996 and published in 1997, discussed how the Internet was changing, well, *everything* for information gatherers. Now, a few years later, it's clear that the Internet—for better or worse—*has* changed everything. In fact, doing research has virtually become synonymous with searching the Net. What does this mean for information gatherers today?

There's no question that the Internet has proven to be enormously beneficial for researchers. There are now mountains more facts, data, and information easily and quickly available. These days, from the convenience of your own home, you can find out, literally in a matter of seconds, facts and answers ranging from Antarctic expeditions to careers in zoology. And the U.S. government, which is one of the largest publishers in the world, has been moving rapidly to make more and more of its mother lode of data available over the Internet, making it easier than ever to find and obtain information from all the federal agencies.

The Internet has also benefited researchers by lowering the price of information. Some sources that had been quite expensive are now available on the Net for much less—some are now even free. For example, breaking news stories from newswires like AP and Reuters were accessible only to media outlets and cost a fee to access in the pre-Internet world. But these sources are now available over the Internet to anyone—*and* for free. The same is true for certain kinds of business information, such as directory data and even the financial filings of public companies.

There's also no doubt that the virtual communities and support groups that populate the Internet are of tremendous help, particularly to researchers looking for information or advice from those who have knowledge of a specific topic or will share their own experiences. These groups are especially helpful for those seeking medical and health-related information. While you naturally have to be very careful in assessing the reliability of this kind of information (chapter 9 is devoted to evaluating sources), there's no question that people *are* being helped with health-related issues. I, for example, had an occasion to take advantage of the Internet's power in this area. My aunt had just been diagnosed with an eye disease called Anterior Ischemic Optic Neuropathy (AION) and her doctors were at a loss to tell her what she could do about it. I did some searching on the Internet and located a bulletin placed by the press office of a medical school on its home page announcing the finding of one of its researchers. The researcher found a statistically significant difference in the recovery rate of a group of AION patients that had been treated by a certain drug, which in the past had only been used to treat a different ailment. I e-mailed this report to my aunt, who then showed it to her doctor. Her doctor was surprised and a bit taken aback—he had not heard about the study. He checked his latest journals and found a confirming report. He subsequently prescribed the drug for my aunt, whose condition improved, apparently at least partially due to the drug.

In this case, the benefit of the Internet was not in finding an anecdotal report in a support group, but in zeroing in on some newly released official data *before* it was widely published in the medical journals. The fact that authors and researchers can now disseminate their findings instantly on the Net, rather than waiting for a scholarly journal to publish them, is, in fact, causing a reexamination of the entire traditional scholarly peer review process.

The Internet has also proven to be a godsend to anyone who has an obscure interest or hobby and wants to find like-minded individuals. I have a small collection of antique typewriters. Before the Internet, it was almost impossible to find other people with a similar interest, and certainly not within my own geographical area. But on the Net, I've found more than one site that's devoted to people who have the same passion. And these sites allow me to buy and sell machines, read about the history of typewriters, view pictures of unusual models, learn of upcoming meetings, ask questions, and so on. That's an example of the kind of "virtual community" you may have heard of.

The Internet, of course, is changing many other aspects of our lives, beyond how we research. It is impacting how business is conducted ("e-commerce") and the way we teach and learn—distance learning over the Net, for example; it's changing journalism, how we communicate with each other, and more. But this book is about research and information gathering, so our discussion of the Internet will be focused on these activities.

Now, there has been something of a price to pay for getting all these goodies. As they say, you can have too much of a good thing—in this case, too much information. Those who venture onto the Internet often find themselves overwhelmed by the sheer amount of data returned from a typical search. Who has time to look though the 12,478 Web pages just retrieved by a search engine? Some call it information overload, others data deluge or infoglut. Whatever you call it, it's a problem, and it's a problem that has been getting worse and is going to get even worse.

And, of course, the other issue, once you've chosen what to look at, is how to decide whether what you are viewing is trustworthy and credible. When people began using the Web as a source of information in the mid-1990s, they were, perhaps, so impressed and grateful to be able to find *anything* of substance that they did not question the data's origins and validity enough. By now we've all heard the stories of misleading and bad information circulating online, and the pendulum has swung in the other direction—so much so that some people automatically disparage information if it was obtained over the Internet. But this approach is also overly simplistic.

In sum, the Internet has been of enormous benefit to information gatherers, but it has also caused a great deal of frustration. One critical reason for that frustration is that many Internet users lack adequate instruction. What do you really know about what happens when you go on the Internet? Do you know how much of the world's knowledge is really available through the Internet? What kind of knowledge is available and what kind is not? Which search tool is best to use for which search? Of the information that *is* on the Internet, how much of it is a search engine really able to find? And how do you fine-tune a search to find just what *you* need? These are all critical questions that a serious researcher needs answers for. As the need becomes more obvious, one of the buzzwords you're likely to hear to describe the solution is "information literacy."

The Internet does represent an unprecedented, powerful tool for the researcher. But unless you learn how to use it, it's like being handed a treasure map with an X marked on it to signify the treasure chest, but no path marked leading to the prize. I hope that this book serves to provide you with the directions you'll need to mine the lode of good data and information that resides on the Internet, and also shows you how to access information at your library, from the government, and from experts.

Finally, the Internet's impact on information, research, and information-intensive institutions has larger implications and will bring about change in other parts of our lives. For instance:

- What is going to happen to our libraries? A good chunk of chapter 1 is devoted to the exciting intersection of libraries and the Internet, and I discuss why the Internet has not, by any means, meant that it's no longer necessary to visit your library to do research. But at the same time, as more people do their research from PCs, the Internet is forcing libraries to reexamine how they carry out their mission and how they remain relevant and important to their communities.

- What is going to happen to journalism? As more people get their news from the Web, the question arises as to who is a journalist in the age of the Internet. The higher purpose of journalism as a profession is to provide the information necessary for self-governance and participation in a democracy. Though this has not always been the case with traditional print and broadcast journalism, what will the Internet's impact be here?

- The Internet may be changing the balance of power between the patient and his/her physician. At no other time is the aphorism "information is power" more true than when consumers obtain medical and health information on the Internet. As people go onto the Net and empower themselves with knowledge, they are going to take more decisions about their health and medical treatments into their own hands.

- What does it mean when fewer of our questions go unanswered? One task the Internet performs exceedingly well is to act as a giant question-answering machine. Not only does it provide answers to factual queries—How far is Pluto from the Sun? or What is the capital of Zimbabwe?—but it can also solve nagging questions that previously would have been almost impossible for us to track down. Who was the guest star in that episode of the *Lost in Space* TV series? Where is my old high school buddy today? How do other adult adoptees feel about the adoption process?

The Internet even provides explanations for problems or concerns that may have stumped you for years—Aha! I see now that my sister acts this way because she may suffer from borderline personality disorder! Perhaps you've always wondered about a quaint French village where a certain movie was filmed. So you find the name of that village from a film database, learn what's it like today from a French tourism site, and discover how to get there from a mapping site. Before the Internet, you'd not likely ever uncover these answers.

The sum total of all of our knowledge and thoughts, in fact, is increasingly being made public, linked, and accessible. And if you are interested in something, chances are there are many other people that are as well. I think that this is an interesting phenomenon—kind of the old "global brain" sci-fi scenario coming to pass. All sorts of artifacts of knowledge are being digitized, made searchable and available—not just books and articles, but other information like music, movies, and even museum objects. There are still, though, various technical barriers that prevent all electronic sources, all storehouses of knowledge, from being searched simultaneously in a giant single database. But it's being worked on . . .

Of course, the Internet will never answer the deepest human questions ... or will it? And finding answers to one set of questions allows for, and even compels, the emergence of a new set . . . and so our questioning will surely continue.

> *We shall not cease from exploration.*
> *And at the end of all of our exploring, will be to arrive where we*
>   *started.*
> *And know the place for the first time.*
>   T. S. ELIOT

I always enjoy hearing from readers—if you have thoughts on any of the above, or other comments about research, the Internet, or this book, feel free to e-mail them to me at rberkman@aol.com.

Introduction
Taking Advantage of the
Information Explosion

It may come as a surprise to you, but for virtually any subject, facts and information are out there—by the truckload. Whether it is moviemaking, the wine industry, real estate investments, or baseball statistics, information and expertise is available—at no or low cost.

Perhaps you're a market researcher digging up forecasts on the growth of the computer software industry, a college student studying the latest advances in genetic engineering, a writer who needs facts about a new form of dream research, an entrepreneur interested in starting a health food store, or an activist investigating the pornography industry. Whatever your particular situation, this book will provide the knowledge, information sources, and strategies you need in order to quickly find top-quality advice and answers. With this know-how, you'll be able to get the kind of information that's normally available only to a select few.

As everyone knows, we are living in the age of information. Every day, book and periodical publishers, government agencies, libraries, professional associations, conventions, private companies, research centers, and museums are adding to our store of knowledge. Unfortunately, most of us have little idea how to find the specific information we need, when we need it. And when it comes to searching the Net, all too often the gems we find are buried in an avalanche of Web pages that are trivial, irrelevant and of questionable credibility.

In this book you'll discover where to go and what to look for in pinpointing information on any subject, whether it's from a traditional print source, on the Web, or given by a live expert. First, *key resources*, including many little-known information gold mines, are identified and described, and for each of these an address, phone number, Web site, or other specific contact information is given.

Second, you'll be shown how to go beyond the written and electronic sources and learn from the experts themselves. Most people would assume that experts don't bother to talk to a lay information seeker. But that's untrue. This book will show you not only how to find experts—the sources behind the sources—but also how to get them to freely share their knowledge with you.

Finally, this book will help you learn how to conduct an information search from beginning to end. You'll discover what the various steps of an information-finding project are—all the way from defining your problem to receiving a final expert review of your finished project. This process is summarized in chapter 12, "A Researcher's Road Map."

WHY THIS BOOK

Some years ago I found myself in a new position for which I had to learn how to find information on many subjects—fast. I had landed a job at McGraw-Hill, Inc. and my duties were to research and write in-depth analyses and reports for businesses and government agencies on a wide range of technical subjects—from cutting energy costs to selecting the best computer. With each of these projects, I'd start off knowing absolutely nothing about the topic. But in the course of a few short weeks I needed to turn out an accurate and authoritative report.

To create these analyses, I needed to have top-quality information at my immediate disposal. So I did some digging and began talking with professional information specialists, investigating little-used documents, and developing my own sources. I began to build a bank of information resources. Over the next few years, every time I found a valuable and easy-to-use information source, I added it to the bank. I also developed techniques for quickly finding experts and getting them to share their knowledge, which I also added to the bank.

My friends and family were intrigued when I described this process of finding information and quickly becoming knowledgeable on a subject. Their interest motivated me to create the course "You Can Be an Instant Expert," which I taught at the Learning Annex, an adult education program in New York City, for three years.

The people who took the class had varied backgrounds and reasons for being there. Many were businesspeople who wanted to sharpen their job skills and learn where to find the best information in their field. Some were writers who wanted to unearth new sources of expertise. College students took the class, too, hoping to add unexplored dimensions to their research and to learn to be more creative. Others took the class to learn how to dig up facts about a new field, in the hopes of starting their own business. And, confirming my own experience, students told me that they were amazed to discover that so much good information was available so easily and so cheaply. They were equally surprised at how available experts were, and how easy it could be to talk to them.

Sometimes I heard from people after they had taken the course. Here are some of their success stories: A detective novelist found background information about countries where she set her stories. A director of research at a national television network found the right demographic statistics to back up his report on TV viewing trends. A student found free consumer assistance and resolved a complaint with an automobile manufacturer. A man found inexpensive business advice to assist him in starting a consulting firm in a high-technology field. A woman found out where to apply for a grant to get funding for an art-related project. An international marketing executive discovered how to find free industry forecasts instead of paying hundreds of dollars for them.

You undoubtedly will have your own success stories to tell. Perhaps you'll find the consumer-oriented information you need to help you buy a home, manage your money, or raise your child. Or maybe you'll get important business information, aiding you in finding a new job, making investments, going public, or getting a loan. Some of you will have a need for obscure information that can be answered by offbeat sources—like the Association for Symbolic Logic or the Paint Research Institute!

HOW TO USE THIS BOOK

Here's a brief rundown on how this book works and what the different chapters will provide.

A preliminary section, "Getting Started," will help you define what information you're really after and organize your plan of attack. Part I identifies actual information sources and provides tips on how best to find and use each of them. It contains chapters covering the initial selection of information sources, including how to choose the right library for your needs and discover which print and online sources to check once you get there; how to identify "supersources" on your topic, ranging from associations to museums and much more; how to tap into the huge storehouse of knowledge and data available from the U.S. government—much of it for free; how to locate the best information sources related to business; and, finally, how to perform Internet searches, and quickly find relevant and reliable sources.

Each chapter presents many specific sources, along with suggestions for further avenues to try. You may want to highlight those that sound most interesting to you and appropriate for your needs so you can later locate them quickly. Or scan the "Quickfinder" feature, which begins each resource chapter and lists every information source included in the chapter.

Part II moves into the second component of the information search—talking to the experts. You'll find out how to locate the ten types of experts, and the pros and cons of each type; how to make contact with the experts; and how to get them to open up and share their knowledge. You'll find out that experts *will* talk to you—but it helps to have some strategies to increase their willingness to do so. Part II also has an entire chapter devoted to the topic of evaluating the quality and reliability of the sources of information you find. Finally, you'll get advice on learning how to tell when it's time to wind up your project and some tips on writing up your results.

The book concludes with a "Researcher's Road Map" guide to choosing and understanding information sources, an appendix that lists additional resources, and a comprehensive index that will be helpful in targeting specific sources, techniques, and topics.

Naturally, a book like this cannot include every potential information source, but I believe that I've provided some of the best. The sources selected for this book have been carefully culled from among many. Those included were specifically chosen as being most useful for people who are not professionals in finding information. This means that, to qualify for inclusion, each source had to be easy to obtain and easy to use. Unless otherwise noted, each source is inexpensive or free. I'd greatly appreciate hearing suggestions from readers with suggestions of other sources and information-finding strategies worth including in future editions. Write to me c/o HarperCollins, 10 East 53rd Street, New York, NY 10022.

When you've finished reading this book, keep it handy so you can use it as a ready reference guide. That way, whenever you need a fact, some advice, or information, you can find out where to look to get the answers you need.

Getting Started

Before plunging into your project, take a few minutes to consider your endeavor. Try to define for yourself exactly what kind of information you need, and why. What are your *reasons* for wanting to find this information? What are your overall goals? Try to be as *specific* as possible, even though it may be difficult to do so at this early stage. The more you can narrow your scope and break your task into subprojects, the easier your search will be and the more likely your project will be a success. For example, say your goal is to find information on inexpensive overseas travel. With a little reflection, you can break that topic into its major components: cutting costs on overseas transportation, lodging, meals, car rental, shopping, currency exchange, and so on. Now you have some specific and concrete subtopics to zero in on. If during your research you discover that your subject was too broad to adequately handle within the strictures of your plan, you can decide whether to choose one or more of your subtopics instead. (If you are not familiar enough with your subject at the outset to identify subdivisions, you'll find that you discover them once you begin your research.)

The first step in the information-gathering process is to find the very best *published* information sources in your field (in print or on the Net). Although some of your best results will eventually come from talking to experts, you don't want to begin your project by contacting them. It's much better to first read and learn about your subject, and *then* speak with the experts. This way, when you do eventually talk to the authorities in the field, you'll be knowledgeable enough to ask the right questions and get the most out of your conversation.

Before you actually start your search, you should also come up with a method for recording the information you'll be receiving from your published and expert sources. Your approach to note taking and organization is important because it will affect the course of your entire project. If you need advice on this, see chapter 10. If, however, you feel confident enough to jump right into the information search, continue on to the first chapter.

PART I

Unlocking the Information Vault

1

Libraries

Zeroing in on the Best Resources

QUICKFINDER: LIBRARIES

(continued)

(continued)

WHY DOING RESEARCH AT YOUR LIBRARY IS STILL CRITICAL

You may think that since you have the Internet there's no reason to trudge off to the library. Well, that's flat out incorrect. Although there's unquestionably a truly incredible amount of information on the Internet (described in chapter 5), your library still offers several critical benefits that *can't* be found online. Below are ten reasons why, despite the Internet, any good researcher will treasure libraries and will want to make frequent visits:

1. **Access to Books**
   This may seem obvious, but it can be easy to forget that only at a library are you going to be able to browse thousands of actual books, find the ones you want, and then read them. The Net does many things extremely well—but one thing it does not do is provide the complete text of many books. Yes, you can order books easily, but you can read only a miniscule number of them online. In addition, there are few people who would actually want to read an entire book on their computer screen.

2. Access to Magazines and Newspapers

Although many publishers do put the complete text of their magazine or newspaper online, there are several problems with accessing these on the Web. First, it is still hit or miss as to whether the specific title you seek is available on the Internet, and, even if it does exist online, it can be difficult to find. If you do locate it, you are unlikely to be able to scan the back issues, and almost certainly will not be able to do so for free.

The library is still the best place to go for finding journals and newspapers of interest to you, and for digging up back issues. Interestingly, in many cases the library is also the better choice for finding the current newsstand issue as well: most libraries have a place where the most recent issues are displayed—which makes them easier to find than searching on the Web. Furthermore, it is hard to browse pages on the Internet—but easy to flip through a print copy in your hands.

Also, I find scanning the covers of magazine journals displayed on library shelves to be an interesting exercise. You can discover what issues are hot, see magazines that you previously might not have known about or did not read, and get a sense of how various media are covering some topic you may be researching. This kind of "meta-browsing" is quite difficult to do on the Internet.

3. Access to Directories

As discussed later in this chapter, directories are invaluable tools for researchers, as they pull together related data on a subject and can provide leads for locating further information. Like books, complete directories are not well represented in their full text on the Internet. And when a directory is available, you'll normally have to pay a fee to search it. Many of these directories are quite expensive too—running in the hundreds of dollars—and so the best place to find and use them without having to purchase or pay a search fee, remains your library.

4. Access to Primary Materials

Libraries are also still the place to go when you need to use rare books, maps, manuscripts, letters, photographs, and other primary and special collection documents. While some libraries are scanning in these materials and putting them on the Net (see the discussion of digital libraries in this chapter), these collections, while intriguing and certainly growing, represent a miniscule percentage of the primary documents held in the world's libraries. It is extremely doubtful, given the time and cost of these digital conversion efforts, that a significant number of collections will be digitized anywhere in the near future.

5. Access to the Internet

Most libraries these days let you use their computers to search the Internet. Why use the library to search the Net? While you may have a computer and modem in your home, your library may offer a faster and more reliable connection, since libraries typically use leased lines, not a dial-up connection. Furthermore, when you find the name of a book, magazine, or other print source while at the library, you can check the library's catalog to see if it has the source, and if it does, you can grab it from the shelves right there!

6. Access to Fee-based Databases

As explained in chapter 5, searching a database is different than searching pages on the Internet. Databases provide access to a focused set of *filtered* information (e.g., newspaper articles, company financial data, articles published in sociological journals, etc.) and are set up to allow you to perform sophisticated searching. Unlike the general Internet, fee-based informational databases don't contain advertisements, pornography, or nonsubstantive data—and they are created specifically for researchers.

These databases cost money to subscribe to—sometimes a lot of money—but when a library subscribes, it makes access to these powerful databases free! (Some libraries may restrict this to authorized users and may charge a nominal fee for printing data.) Some of these databases are stored on disks on the library's own computers, and these are called **CD-ROMs**. Other databases are stored remotely on the database vendor's computers and the library connects to them via the telephone;

these are called online databases. In either case, these databases remain some of the most powerful and important tools for any researcher.

7. Organized Information with Expert Finder Tools

As anyone who has ever conducted a search knows, one of the biggest frustrations is trying to pinpoint the information you need from among the millions of Web pages on the Internet. The problem is that nobody has *organized* the information on the Net. Information contained in the library, in contrast, is fully organized around a standardized and consistent cataloguing method. Many libraries also create handy search aids that explicitly describe how to find resources in various disciplines and subject areas. All of which means that searching for what you need at a library is largely without the frustration that accompanies an Internet search and can be quicker, too.

8. Personal Assistance

Not only do the cataloguing and search aids help you find what you need, but the librarians, who are expertly trained in the use and retrieval of information (they have a Master of Library Science degree), are ready and willing to help you. Think about it—for no fee at all, you can enlist the service of a trained expert to help you find what you need and give you suggestions and ideas on other resources and avenues that you probably had not thought of. The antidote for the current malady of information overload is not some pseudo-smart software agent, but a knowledgeable librarian—a human filter and information expert who can efficiently direct you to what you need *and* help you search the Internet more efficiently.

9. The Appropriate Atmosphere

Sure it's convenient and kind of fun to do research on your PC out of your bedroom or on your kitchen table, but is that really the best environment for serious research? Maybe someone's playing the stereo in the next room, or the dog's barking, or the TV is on upstairs, or a member of a religious group is knocking at your front door. Can you truly concentrate in such an environment? Contrast this to a library, the sole purpose of which is to foster quiet study, reading, and information-seeking, where you can sit at comfortable, oversized wooden tables and desks, and are surrounded by books. Not only is the media the message, but so is the environment, and the message of a library is: concentrate, think, reflect.

10. Community Activities

Although the primary function of a public library is to make information freely available, these institutions also serve an important social and community need. If you haven't been to a library recently, go in. Browse its bulletin boards. Look at its handouts. You'll find materials on community activities and programs ranging from free health education classes, career fairs, local transportation alternatives, to upcoming lectures, and much more. Some of these events and activities may be held right at the library, while other postings are to inform you of activities being held elsewhere. You'll also find information that's geared to meeting the needs of the particular population that lives in the neighborhood (e.g., a library located in a largely Italian section should have books on Italian heritage; one located in a high-tech region will focus its collection on computers and other high-tech subjects). A library is a valued part of any neighborhood, and its role is to disseminate information that's going to be of value to members of the community.

Finally, here's another, admittedly subjective, reason to go to the library. Personally, after spending several hours hunched over my computer, typing commands into a search engine, and staring at tiny phosphorescent substances on a cathode-ray-tube monitor, I more than welcome the chance to stretch my legs and walk through my lively urban neighborhood to the library. There I can see actual (not virtual) people, talk to a librarian, and run my hands across the spines of books as they sit in the shelves. It's just more enjoyable. I'm not going to give up going on the Net by any means, but every now and then I need to get into a library and have a nonvirtual, physical experience. This balances my time on the computer and adds a richness that simply can't be found online.

And if your image of a library is of a dusty old place, then it's time to update your image. Today's libraries are sleek, streamlined, and wired, and are often beautifully designed with daring architecture. Some of my favorite modern libraries are the New York Public Library (particularly its Science and Business Library on Madison Avenue), The San Antonio Public Library, and the newly remodeled Rochester, New York Public Library. Paris has built what some think is *the* state-of-the-art library in its National Library—the Bibliothèque Nationale de France. I haven't been there yet, but it's on my definite "must visit" list. I've also been told that the Los Angeles and Cleveland public libraries are stunning buildings.

A very exciting library plan is the project initiated by Egypt, in cooperation with UNESCO, to revive the ancient Great Library of Alexandria on a ten-acre site on the Eastern Harbor in Chatcy, near Alexandria University. At the beginning of the third century B.C., the great library and a later "daughter" library together contained approximately 700,000 volumes. The libraries were destroyed in a fire during a civil war in the third century A.D.

The new library, which was inaugurated in the fall of 1999, will be the eighth largest library in the world, with a collection of 4 to 8 million volumes, 50,000 maps, 100,000 manuscripts, and will contain 13 floors and seating for 3,500 persons. (You can learn more about the project by linking to: www.unesco.org/webworld/alexandria_new.)

Finally, if you really appreciate libraries, you might consider becoming a Friend of a Library. This is a program most libraries run that gives you certain privileges for a small membership fee.

SELECTING A LIBRARY

There are three basic types of library: public libraries, college and university libraries, and special libraries (which include corporate libraries). Let's look at each.

Public Libraries

The best public libraries for information gatherers are large, usually main branches, because these are most likely to contain an extensive reference collection. It's here you'll find some superb information-providing sources. (These sources will be identified and described later in this chapter.) If the only public library in your area is a very small one, you might want to look to one of the other types of libraries described in this section.

College and University Libraries

Academic libraries typically have more information sources than the average town's public library. Many are open to the public. The academic library's collection normally reflects the institution's majors and specialties.

Special Libraries

There are thousands of libraries around the country that specialize in a particular subject—astronomy, baseball, the environment, Asia, minorities, marketing, and countless other topics. Most of these libraries are open to the public, and even those that officially are not may still admit you if you let the librarian know you are working on an important project. Working at one of these special libraries where you are surrounded by resources that pertain to the specific subject you're interested in is like working in a veritable gold mine.

One particularly valuable type of special library is the *corporate library*. Corporate libraries contain a wealth of information on subjects related to a firm's special interests. Exxon's library, for example, has extensive information on energy, while CBS's library contains top-notch information on broadcasting. Unfortunately, many of these libraries allow access only to their company employees. But don't despair—sometimes you can get around the

---

TIP: How to Find an Academic Library
• Contact the Association of College and Research Libraries, American Library Association, 50 Huron Street, Chicago, IL 60611; 312-944-6780. For no charge, the association will help you find college and research libraries that specialize in your subject of interest.

TIPS: Getting the Most Out of Any Library
• If you've located a library that has the information you want, but it is not nearby, you can usually get a certain amount of information and answers by writing or calling with your specific question. You'll find librarians to be very helpful people! Some libraries even take reference questions by e-mail!
• When you get to the library, remember to ask the reference librarian for assistance. That's what these people are there for! By enlisting their help, you can save yourself a lot of research time.
• If the library doesn't have a source you need, don't forget to ask for an interlibrary loan.
• Try calling your town library's reference department on the phone. At no charge, the library will try to find any fact you need. For example, you could ask, "What's the flying time from New York to Istanbul?" or "When was the clock invented?" Answering such questions by mail or phone is a public service that nearly every public library provides.

---

official policy. If you've identified a company library you want to use, call up the librarian, introduce yourself, and politely explain what kind of information you are trying to find, and why. Let the librarian know your project is a serious and important one, and explain that you've heard that the library has the resources you need. Describe specifically what you'll want to do at the library and what kind of materials you'll want to examine.

Once you've identified the right library for your needs, the next step is to find the best information-providing sources kept at the library you select. But don't forget that the library staff is itself a major resource not to be overlooked.

Often—but not always—you'll find that the librarian will allow you to come in and work. Of course, you won't be able to take any-

---

TIPS: Identifying a Special Library
• Contact the Special Libraries Association, 1700 18th Street NW, Washington, DC 20009; 202-234-4700. Ask to speak with one of the information specialists. These people will try to identify a special library in your area of interest. Another way to find a special library is to check a large library's reference department for one of these directories: *Subject Collections*, published by R. R. Bowker, or *Subject Directory of Special Libraries and Information Centers*, published by The Gale Group. Both of these directories list thousands of special libraries.

TIP: Use the *Readers' Guide* to Understand a Technical Subject
• Because the magazines indexed in the *Readers' Guide* are read mainly by the general public, any description of a technical matter will be clearly defined and explained. This makes the guide especially helpful if your subject is technical and you don't quite understand it yet. The term "genetic engineering," for example, would be explained clearly to readers in a magazine like *Newsweek*, but probably would not be in a publication like *Applied Genetic News*.

---

thing out of the library. And when you get to the library, you should work on your own and not use up the corporate librarian's time, which must be dedicated to serving the company's own employees.

If you happen to know someone who works at a company that has a library you want to use, you should be able to gain entrance by using that person as a reference.

Finding a Library on the Internet

Not only can you use the print directories to pinpoint the library you need, you can also find the home pages of libraries by using the Internet. There are several top-notch sites on the Net that serve as directories of libraries, both around the country and around the world. Many of these also describe the library's holdings and collections, so you know the specific subject areas and special collections found in that library.

Remember, too, that if you find a library that has a collection that interests you, you don't necessarily have to actually visit the library in order to tap into it. Most libraries will respond to requests (either by mail, phone, or e-mail), and try to assist you in your research. Some libraries are even digitizing parts of their collections and making them available for viewing over the Internet. More on this exciting development later in the chapter.

Below are the names of sites on the Internet that let you search for and find links to libraries:

• Libweb at Berkeley Digital Library SunSITE lists over 2,500 pages from libraries in over 70 countries. The site can be browsed or searched by keywords. Go to: http://sunsite.berkeley.edu/ Libweb

- Another good collection of links to libraries is maintained by Yahoo. Link to: http://www.yahoo.com/reference/libraries
- For links specifically to academic libraries go to: http://dir.yahoo.com/Reference/Libraries/Academic_Libraries/

"National libraries" are particularly valuable libraries; these are institutions set up by the federal government of a country to serve as a central library. Like the United States' national library, the Library of Congress, national libraries typically collect all publications issued in their respective countries. Below are some good links for finding them over the Internet:

- **National Libraries Catalogs Worldwide**
  http://www.library.uq.edu.au/ssah/jeast

  This site was created by the University of Queensland in Australia, and it identifies and provides links to national libraries around the world.

- **Gabriel (Gateway and Bridge to Europe's National Libraries)**
  http://portico.bl.uk/gabriel

  This one focuses specifically on Europe, as it provides descriptive information and links to 39 of Europe's national libraries.

EASY STARTS:
ALL-PURPOSE RESOURCES

Now we're ready to identify and describe some of the very best library information sources. We'll begin with a few basic—but excellent—sources and then progress to some very valuable lesser-known ones. All of the sources described in this section are typically found in the reference department.

Some of the sources that we will be identifying here are also available in electronic form—either over the Internet or accessible via the library's PCs on a CD-ROM or an online database. However, because this section is devoted primarily to what you can find on hard copy at the library, we will be focusing on print sources here. However, later in this chapter we will discuss in detail how libraries and library resources are intersecting with the Internet. Let's start off simply:

✔ **Source: *New York Times Index***

An index to articles published in *The New York Times*. The user looks up key words, such as a subject or a person's name, and the index provides a brief summary of all pertinent articles published, giving the date of publication and page. Supplements are issued twice every month. You'll find this index in practically every library.

The New York Times is a newspaper of record with historical significance. Checking its index is a quick and easy way to begin an information search. Most likely, the librarian will provide you with the articles on microfilm. Sometimes the short summary of the article provided by the index itself will be all the information you need.

✔ **Source: *Readers' Guide to Periodical Literature*** **(H. W. Wilson Company)**

The *Readers' Guide* indexes articles published in about 250 popular magazines such as *Newsweek, Health, Ms., Sports Illustrated,* and *Popular Science*. Supplements are issued monthly. You can find this guide at nearly every library. As with the *New York Times Index*, the user looks up key words to find articles on subjects he or she is interested in.

These familiar green volumes provide a quick way of finding back issues of popular magazines that have published articles on your subject of interest. You may not always get "inside" information from articles published in these general-interest magazines, but they can still be good information sources. And because these

---

TIP: Why Use a Print Index?

• What would be the value in using a library's print index to journals, rather than searching an online index on the Internet? One important reason is that most Internet-based indexes only let you search back no more than five years. In contrast, if you scan the *Readers' Guide* volumes at the library, you'll find volumes that index articles published back in the 1890s!

TIRANA (Albania). See also Albania, Ap 16
TIRES. See also Astronautics, Ap 20, My 6
Goodyear Tire & Rubber Co expects its US tire plants to run near capacity during 1985 (S), Ap 10,IV,4:5
Tires are again bearing labels indicating how well they wear in comparison to other tires; National Highway Traffic Safety Administration discontinued tread wear grading in 1983, holding tests were unreliable; US Appeals Court ordered practice resumed, acting on suit by Public Citizen and Center for Auto Safety; tires are also graded for traction and temperature resistance (M), My 4,I,52:1
Harvey E Heinbach (Merrill Lynch) comments on strong US sales of imported tires (S), My 12,III,1:1
Dunlop Holdings PLC says it has agreed to sell its United States tire operations to group including management for $118 million, plus repayment of $60 million in loans (S), My 16,IV,4:6
TISCH School of the Arts. See also Dancing, Ap 19
TISDALE, Wayman. See also Basketball, Je 19
TISHMAN, Peggy. See also Jewish Philanthropies, Federation of, Je 30
TISHMAN Realty & Construction Co. See also Building (Construction), Je 1. Disney, Walt, World (Lake Buena Vista, Fla), Ap 30
TISHMAN Speyer Properties. See also Ecumed, Ap 26
TITANIUM
Finland's state-owned chemicals company, Kemira Oy, says it will pay $100 million for American Cyanamid Company's titanium dioxide business, including manufacturing plant at Savannah, Ga (S), My 18,I,36:5
TITCHBOURNE, Julie Christofferson. See also Scientology, Church of, My 18
TITONE, Vito J (Judge). See also Courts, Ap 24, My 29
TITUS, Becky (Judge). See also Roads, Je 6
TLS Co
TLS Company names Larry G Stolte chief financial officer (S), Je 27,IV,2:4
TOBACCO. See also Smoking. Taxation, Je 2
Series of measures designed to reshape Japan's telecommunications, financial and tobacco industries and open them to foreign competition go into effect on April 1; new regulations outlined (M), Ap 1,IV,5:1
Scientists and doctors tell panel of New York State lawmakers that packages of chewing tobacco and snuff should contain labels warning that use of those products may cause oral cancer and other diseases; legislation to require such labeling has been introduced in both houses, and key lawmakers say they expect it to pass (M), My 2, II,4:3
Article by John Crudele in Market Place column discusses conflicting views concerning value of tobacco stocks; graph (M), My 2,IV,8:3
Article on Japan's attempt to open up tobacco market to foreign companies; various factors hindering United States and other foreign tobacco companies from establishing market in Japan discussed; illustration (M), My 13,IV,10:1
Editorial holding that it is possible that teen-agers might believe that chewing tobacco is safer than smoking it, notes that tobacco is just as addictive either way and there is strong link between smokeless products and oral cancer; holds New York should enact legislation requiring package warning on such products, Je 10,I,18:1
Panel of Government scientists, appointed by Surgeon Gen C Everett Koop, is preparing comprehensive report on whether snuff and chewing tobacco are health hazards, decision that is likely to influence whether warning labels should be required on such products (S), Je 13,I,16:5
New York Assembly, 87-53, approves bill that would require packages of smokeless tobacco to contain warning label that use of product is dangerous to health (S), Je 27, II,4:2
TOBEY, Alton. See also Westchester County (NY), My 5
TOBIAS ████████ Taxation, Je 28

TOLLESON, Richard L. See also Oscar Mayer Corp, My 17
TOLLMAN-Hundley Hotels. See also Hotels, A
TOLLS. See also Bridges and Tunnels, Je 2. R█ 24
TOMAHAWK (Missile). See also Eur, Ap 8
TOMB of the Unknown Soldier (Arlington Natio Cemetery)
Article on soldiers who guard Tomb of Unkno Arlington National Cemetery; they are drawn fr US Army's Old Guard, elite ceremonial unit tha at various events in nation's capital; Sgt Larry J comments; photo (M), My 27,I,8:3
TOMKO, Jozef (Bishop). See also RC Ch, My 1
TOMLINSON Junior High School (Fairfield, Conn also Educ, Ap 9, My 17
TOMS, Gerald (Dr). See also Circuses, Ap 11
TOMS River (NJ). See also Amusement Parks, █ Fires, Ap 21
TONAMO Transportation Co. See also Delivery Je 13
TONELSON, Alan. See also Latin America, M█
TONG On (Gang). See also Shootings, My 2█
TONY Awards (Theater Awards). See also T 25, My 3,4,8,13,19, Je 2,3,4,5. Theater—Big Adventures of Huckleberry Finn (Play), Je
TOOL & Engraving Co. See also Explosions,
TOOLE, Ottis. See also Murders, Ap 18
TOOLS. See also Machine Tools and Dies. R█
TOON, Al. See also Football, My 1
TOON, Malcolm. See also Radio, Je 2
TOOTSIE Roll Industries. See also Cella's Confe My 25
TOP Rank Inc. See also Boxing, Je 24
TOPPING, Audrey. See also Archeology, My 1█
TOPPING, David R. See also Gulf Corp, Je 4
TOPPS Chewing Gum Inc. See also Trading Ca
TORADZE, Alexander. See also Music, Ap 14
TORAN, Sylvia. See also Music, Ap 28
TORBORG, Jeff. See also Baseball, My 4
TORELLI, Mario (Prof). See also Archeology, A█
TORES, Pablo Jr. See also Children, Ap 25
TORGAU (East Germany). See also World War
TORIN Machine Division of Clevepak Corp
Workers at Torin Machine Division of Cleve█ Torrington, Conn, weigh making bid to take o█ which employs 90 people; Clevepak has put fa█ sale, and state and local officials fear that if a█ company buys division it may close (M), My
TORNADOES
Four people die as tornadoes and thunderst█ section of US from Illinois to Deep South; tw█ winds strike Ohio, Indiana, Illinois, Tennessee Georgia and Alabama (S), Ap 6,I,5:4
Photo of damage caused by tornado in Doug Ap 7,I,22:3
Texas is struck again by several tornadoes, d█ twister claims lives of three people in state; to█ touch down in Nebraska and Oklahoma in fou█ violent weather across Great Plains (S), Ap 23,
Outburst of violent weather that has caused █ batters parts of Texas again on April 29; rising continues to threaten much of north Texas; at█ tornadoes were reported over Texas during wee April 27 and up to six inches of rain fell in so█ Ap 30,I,16:6
Tornadoes and heavy thunderstorms rip acro█ Midwestern states (S), My 12,I,29:6
Photo of tornado aproaching Agra, Kansas; █ and dozens of tornadoes struck Kansas, Misso South Dakota over weekend, damaging build█ downing trees (S), My 13,I,12:2
Tornadoes and high winds cut five-mile s█

periodicals are so popular, you can usually find back issues of many of them right in the library.

✔ **Source: *Business Periodicals Index* (H. W. Wilson Company)**

The *Business Periodicals Index* is an index to articles published in nearly 350 periodicals oriented toward business. Its scope is broad, ranging from advertising and marketing to real estate, computers, communications, finance, and insurance. Supplements are issued monthly. Almost all libraries have it.

The *Business Periodicals Index* is an extremely valuable index. Its name may mislead some people, because the guide actually indexes periodicals that contain information on topics beyond the scope of what most people consider "business." For example, it indexes articles from publications like the *Journal of Consumer Affairs*, *Human Resource Management*, *Telecommunications*, and *Automotive News*. Trade periodicals like these generally provide more specialized and in-depth information than the popular magazines indexed in the *Readers' Guide*, but at the same time the articles are usually not overly technical or hard to read. This is a nice balance for the information seeker who is not technically oriented or an expert in the field but still wants more than a superficial examination of a subject. I once used this index to find some excellent information about the topic of office ergonomics—how to design and furnish healthy and safe work areas.

✔ **Source: *Subject Guide to Books in Print* (R. R. Bowker Company)**

SGBIP lists all new and old books hardbound, paperback, trade, text, adult, and juvenile that are currently in print, by subject. Virtually all libraries (and bookstores, for that matter) have it.

This is the standard guide for finding books in print on any subject. (Books "in print" are kept in stock by the publisher and can be ordered at a bookstore.) If you look under "Circus," for example, you'll find about 25 books; each entry includes the author's name, book title, date of publication, price, and publisher. There are accompanying volumes that list books by title and by author as well.

TIPS: Finding Out-of-Print Books
• Strand Bookstore in New York City stocks 2.5 million books, and a large percentage of these are out-of-print books. Contact the store to see if it has a book you seek: 828 Broadway, New York, NY 10003; 212-473-1452; e-mail: strand@strandbooks.com
• Book search companies and out-of-print specialty stores often advertise in *The New York Times Book Review* and other literary publications. (A Web site devoted to assisting searchers in finding out-of-print books is called BookFinder.com.)

✔ **Source: *Forthcoming Books* (R. R. Bowker Company)**
This guide lists books that have just been released or are projected to be released within five months. Supplements are issued bimonthly. You'll find this guide in large libraries and most bookstores.

Forthcoming Books is an intriguing source, as it identifies what books are about to be published in a given field. This can be especially useful when you are digging up information on a timely issue and you want to find the very latest books. (Note, however, that because books take a long time to produce, they will probably not be the best source of information on events occurring in the last few months or even year.) This source is good to use in conjunction with the *Subject Guide to Books in Print*.

TIP: Start a Search Narrowly
• If you're gathering information on a topic that combines two subjects (e.g., *marketing* done by *museums* or *new technologies* in *videocassettes*) identify the narrowest approach to take. To find information on marketing by museums, I might look under "museums" in the *Business Periodicals Index*. But it would not be a good idea to use the *Business Periodicals Index* and look under "marketing," because I'd find too much information, and maybe none of it related to museums. If you don't find enough information by taking the narrower path, then you can always try the broader approach.

SPECIAL PERIODICAL INDEXES

✔ **Source: H. W. Wilson Subject Indexes**

The Wilson Subject Indexes are multivolume series that identify articles published within many major subject areas. There are different series for different fields (e.g., humanities, social science, science, art, business, education, agriculture, and law). To use these indexes, you consult the volumes devoted to your field of interest and look up specific subtopics. The index identifies which periodicals have published articles on the topic, and when. You'll find the Wilson indexes at medium-size and large libraries.

Two well-known indexes published by H. W. Wilson have already been described—the *Readers' Guide to Periodical Literature* and the *Business Periodicals Index*—but Wilson also indexes literature published in specific fields. For example, there is the *Education Index,*

TIP: Spotting Hot Periodicals

• Use the periodical indexes described above to identify publications that are worth examining in depth. Take a look at the opening pages, where the magazines and journals that the index scans are listed. Reading this listing is a good way to identify the hottest and most relevant periodicals in your field of interest. Say your subject is the paper industry—you might spot the magazine *Pulp and Paper.* Another way of identifying the best publications is to note whether most of the articles you find when using an index were published in the same magazine or magazines. If so, those publications are also worth looking at in more depth. If you identify such a "hot" publication, try to locate the most recent issues and peruse these for valuable articles not yet indexed, or consider talking to the editors of the publication.

TIP: Newspaper Feature Editors

• One particularly valuable section in the *Gale Directory* is its "newspaper feature editors" listing. This is a compilation of the names and phone numbers of the editors of the most popular newspaper features (e.g., art, automobiles, fashion, movies, real estate, society, sports, and women) appearing in daily newspapers with a circulation of 50,000 or more. It's superb for identifying subject experts and regional publications.

TIP: Identifying the Right Periodical
• If your topic is *very* obscure, look up subjects that are a little broader. For example, while working on an information-finding project on the topic of "rebuilding school buses," I could not find any publications covering just that narrow topic, but I did find a magazine called *School Transportation News*. It seemed logical that such a publication might, at one time or another, have written an article on rebuilding school buses, so I telephoned the magazine and asked for the editorial department. An editor was happy to check the files, and sure enough, the magazine had published three different articles on that topic during the previous two years; the editor mailed me copies. So, if you are having trouble finding a periodical on a very narrow topic, try looking up some broader subjects whose scope may encompass it. You can always try calling a publication to find out if it has published an article on a particular topic during the last year or two.

---

which I've used to locate articles published in education-oriented periodicals on the subject of personal-computer use in schools.

Not only will the articles that you locate be of great assistance, but so will the names of the authors of those articles and the experts cited in the pieces. These are people that you'll want to speak with later on to obtain answers to your own particular questions.

The trick when using these guides is to figure out which subject index to consult. What you need to do is determine into which subject area established by Wilson your topic falls. For example, if you wanted to find out about growing tomatoes, that would be a food science question, and you'd check the *Biological and Agricultural Index*. If your subject were meditation, that would fall

---

TIP: Locating Hard-to-Find Periodicals
• Once you identify the specialized magazine or newsletter you need, how do you obtain it? Because there are so many special-interest and obscure periodicals, it's unlikely that even the largest library will have all the ones you seek. What you need to do is contact the publisher of the periodical you're interested in (the address and phone number are listed in the directory) and request a sample copy or two. Then you can decide whether you want to subscribe or interview the writers and editors for information or find a library that specializes in the subject and contact the librarian to find out if the library subscribes to it (see page 13 for tips on locating special libraries).

---

under psychology, and so you'd look in the *Social Science Index*. (As noted previously, I've found Wilson's *Business Periodicals Index* worth checking for almost any subject.)

Here are some samples of the major subtopics covered in the different Wilson indexes:

If Your Area of Interest Is	The Wilson Guide to Check Is
Fire, mineralogy, oceanology, plastics, transportation, and other applied scientific subjects	*Applied Science and Technology Index*
Architecture, art history, film, industrial design, landscape design, painting, photography	*Art Index*
Animal breeding, food science, nutrition, pesticides	*Biological and Agricultural Index*
Accounting, advertising, banking, economics, finance, investment, labor, management, marketing, public relations, specialized industries	*Business Periodicals Index* (see p. 18)
Curriculums, school administration and supervision, teaching methods	*Education Index*
Astronomy, physics, and broad scientific areas	*General Science Index*
Archaeology, classical studies, folklore, history, language and literature, literary and political criticism, performing arts, philosophy, religion, theology	*Humanities Index*
Legal information, all areas of jurisprudence	*Index to Legal Periodicals*
Anthropology, environmental science, psychology, sociology	*Social Sciences Index*

TIP: Finding Celebrities
• *The Address Book* (Putnam) is a fun book that informs readers where they can reach over 4,000 prominent persons. I used it once to try to find out where I could contact the singer Carly Simon, just to find out if she would be holding another concert. You can find it at many bookstores. (There are also several celebrity-finder sites on the Web.)

TIP: A Fax Directory
• Another useful directory published by The Gale Group is its *National Fax Directory,* which lists the fax numbers of over 170,000 organizations and businesses.

There are two other very useful specialized subject indexes, not published by Wilson, worth mentioning. ***The Engineering Index*** (published by Engineering Information Inc.) covers all aspects of engineering; and the ***Public Affairs Information Service (PAIS) International*** (published by Public Affairs Information Service Inc.) covers politics, legislation, international law, public policy-making, and related topics worldwide. You can find special subject indexes either at a large public library or at an appropriate special library (e.g., the *Index to Legal Periodicals* at a law library).

TIP: Check Periodical Indexes
• Other good library sources of biographical information on well-known individuals are the Wilson Subject Indexes (see page 20). Figure out which of these guides would most likely index periodicals covering the profession in which the person was active. For example, if you want to find information on someone who was well-known in the electronics industry, look up his or her name in the *General Science Index*.

MAGAZINE AND NEWSLETTER DIRECTORIES

✔ **Sources:** *Ulrich's International Periodicals Directory*
   Gale Directory of Publications
   Standard Periodical Directory
   Oxbridge Directory of Newsletters
   Newsletters in Print

There are periodicals and newsletters covering thousands of different subjects. The directories above identify tens of thousands of magazines, newsletters, newspapers, journals, and other periodicals. The most comprehensive of these directories, but the most difficult to use, is *Ulrich's,* which lists 156,000 periodicals in 869 subject areas. Two easier indexes to use are the *Gale Directory* and the *Standard Periodical Directory.* Virtually all libraries have one or more of these directories.

These are all excellent resources for tracking down specific periodicals covering a particular subject. The way these guides work is simple: You look up your subject, and the guide lists the magazines or newsletters published within the field. Entries typically include the name of the periodical, the publisher, address, and circulation.

There are loads of specialized publications being published around the United States. Even if your topic is extremely narrow, there may just be a periodical devoted to that subject alone. Let me give you a few examples. If you looked under "Folklore" in *Ulrich's,* you'd find *Folklore Center News,* and under "Motion Pictures" you'd see magazines like *Amateur Film Maker* and *Motion Picture Investor,* a newsletter that analyzes private and public values of movies and movie stock. Under the category "Nutrition and Dietetics" you'd find loads of publications, including *Jewish Vegetarian,* published by the International Jewish Vegetarian Society of London. Note that there are some sites on the Web that serve a similar look-up purpose as these. See chapter 5 on the Internet for their names, descriptions, and URLs.

✔ **Source: *Magazines for Libraries* (R. R. Bowker Company)**

Another directory of publications. This one covers fewer periodicals (about 7,000) but provides much more in-depth information on each one.

This is an excellent and highly recommended directory for researchers. Although it does not cover the most obscure publications, it provides a superb analysis and review of the coverage and usefulness for those it does include. The directory is actually designed to assist librarians in deciding which magazines to obtain, so it is also an excellent tool for researchers who want to know which publications are considered the best in the field and how their scope compares. The directory is updated every few years. Be sure you are consulting the newest or one of the latest editions.

PEOPLE INFORMATION

✔ **Source: Marquis Who's Who Series**

The Who's Who volumes are the standard and most popular sources of biographical details on people of various accomplishments. The best-known of these books is *Who's Who in America,* which lists facts on prominent Americans. There are scores of more specialized Who's Who volumes, such as *Who's Who in Finance and Industry, Who's Who in the East,* and *Who's Who of American Women.* Virtually all libraries have *Who's Who in America.* Larger and specialized libraries have the other volumes.

Who's Who in America, the most popular of the Who's Who series, lists various information about prominent Americans' place and date of birth, schools attended, degrees awarded, special accomplishments, and current address. A caution in using these books is that the information is often furnished by the biographees themselves, so accuracy will depend on their truthfulness.

✔ **Source: *Current Biography* (H. W. Wilson Company)**

This is a monthly magazine with articles about people prominent in the news in national and international affairs, the sciences, arts, labor, and industry. Obituaries are also included. At the end of each year, the articles are printed in a single volume, and an index at the back helps users find biographies published during the current year and a few years back. Medium-size and large libraries have the set.

Current Biography strives to be "brief, objective, and accurate, with well-documented articles." It may be more reliable than *Who's Who*, since its editors consult many sources of biographical data, rather than rely solely on the biographees' own accounts.

✔ **Source: *Biography Index* (H. W. Wilson Company)**

Biography Index scans more than 3,000 periodicals, many books, and various biographical sources like obituaries, diaries, and memoirs to identify and index sources of information on prominent people. You can find *Biography Index* in large libraries.

Checking *Biography Index* is a fast way to find articles and other sources of information on all sorts of people from comedian Robert Klein to Michelangelo Buonarroti.

✔ **Source: *Biography and Genealogy Master Index*
(The Gale Group)**

Biography and Genealogy Master Index is an index to biographical directories, providing information on more than 8.8 million current and historical figures. Five-hundred-sixty-five publications are indexed, including the various Who's Who volumes. Large libraries have this guide.

This source will tell you whether there is a directory or publication that lists biographical information on a historical or well-known figure. For example, if you looked up Bob Dylan, you'd find that biographical sketches could be found in *Baker's Biographical Dictionary of Musicians*, *Biography Index*, *The New Oxford Companion to Music*, *Who's Who in the World*, and elsewhere. Once you've located a directory, try to find a library that has it. (You might call the Special Libraries Association to help you identify a likely library.) Then write or call the library to find out if the person you need information on is listed in the directory.

✔ **Source: *American Men and Women of Science*
(R. R. Bowker Company)**

Published annually, this directory profiles over 119,000 leading U.S. and Canadian scientists.

If you're looking for information on an accomplished scientist or engineer, this is the source to check. It's very useful for finding quick biographical information on prominent persons involved in the sciences. Each year the publisher adds thousands of new profiles to keep this directory up to date. You'll find it in the larger libraries, or those that have a good scientific and technical collections.

✔ **Source: *New York Times Obituaries Index***

An index to all the obituaries published in *The New York Times* from 1858 to 1978. Most libraries have it.

Obituaries published in the *Times* are a good source of information about well-known people. Usually the obituary will identify organizations and individuals that the person was affiliated with—these are fruitful leads for digging up more information.

(If you seek biographical information on a prominent person who died after 1978, you can find obituary articles published in the *Times* by checking the regular *New York Times Index*. Look under "Deaths" in the volume covering those issues published the year the person died.)

TIP: To find more obscure manufacturers, check trade magazines that publish an annual buyers' guide. These are special issues devoted to listing manufacturers and suppliers.

BUSINESS AND INDUSTRY INFORMATION

Libraries can be particularly valuable to people seeking business information. Specialized periodical indexes, industry directories, and special business guides can provide you with important facts about companies and industries. (Many more business information sources, not found in libraries, are identified in chapter 4.)

The following is a selection of some leading and most broadly useful business library sources.

✔ **Source:** *Wall Street Journal Index*
An index to articles published in the *Wall Street Journal* and *Barron's*. There are two parts: a subject index and a company name index. Supplements are issued monthly. You'll find the *Wall Street Journal Index* in nearly all libraries.

This is one of the quickest and best ways to search for authoritative information on a particular industry, company, or business topic. Articles published in the *Wall Street Journal* are generally not too technical, yet they are in-depth and probing enough to provide very valuable information. Most libraries keep back issues of the *Journal* on microfilm, so you can often read the articles you find right at the library. Like the *New York Times Index*, the *Wall Street*

TIP: The Gale Group is probably the leading publisher of business, statistical, and all-purpose directories in the U.S. Get a catalog of all of its offerings by calling 800-877-GALE.

GAS
(see **Industrial Gases, Natural Gas**)

GASOLINE
Motor gasoline stocks in week ended Nov. 1 totaled 215,796,000 barrels; motor gasoline production totaled 42,532,000 barrels. 11/6-48;6

Motor gasoline stocks in week ended Nov. 8 totaled 215,821,000 barrels; motor gasoline production totaled 43,568,000 barrels. 11/14-53;3

Motor gasoline stocks for week ended Nov. 15 totaled 213,460 barrels; motor gasoline production totaled 45,913,-000 barrels. 11/20-51;3

Motor gasoline stocks in week ended Nov. 22 totaled 214,403,000 barrels; motor gasoline production totaled 45,038,000 barrels. 11/27-38;6

Energy futures prices plunged Nov. 27, with heating oil and gasoline contracts falling by as much as the permissible daily limit amid concern that the past few months' rally may be faltering. (Futures Markets) 11/29-20;3

GASOLINE STATIONS
(see **Service Stations**)

GEKAS, GEORGE
Can staggered filing of returns break up the processing logjam?; Rep. Gekas' bill would let returns claiming refunds be filed early, but would make returns--and taxes owed--due at the later of April 15 or the end of the filer's birth month. (Tax Report) 11/20-1;5

GENEALOGY
Beatrice Bayley Inc. mails postcards offering for $29.85 a 'Family Heritage Book' that promises to trace a family's genealogy; but many buyers have discovered that book contains not their lineage but simply a list of people with the same last names; complaints have led to investigations by the U.S. Postal Inspector and Wisconsin and Pennsylvania state officials. 11/4-27;3

GENERAL ACCOUNTING OFFICE
The SEC, responding to criticism from the General Accounting Office, proposed closing certain loopholes in its program for finding lost or stolen securities; proposal would force 19,000 brokerage firms and banks nationwide to become more active in the program. 11/22-6;4

GENERAL AGREEMENT ON TARIFFS & TRADE
The General Agreement on Tariffs & Trade finds the slowdown in trade is more serious than it expected; GATT estimated that the growth in trade for 1985 will be 2% to 3%, well below the forecasts of other analysts. 11/15-35;2

U.S. trade officials, impatient with opposition from India, Brazil, Egypt, Yugoslavia and Argentina, are prepared to call a vote in an effort to force the beginning of a new round of global trade negotiations under the General Agreement on Tariffs and Trade. 11/20-35;2

U.S. hopes for a new round of global trade talks are expected to get a boost in the upcoming meeting of the General Agreement on Tariffs & Trade; the talks sought by the U.S. are likely to be the most difficult and longest ever. 11/25-32;1

The Mexican government will begin negotiations to enter the General Agreement on Tariffs and Trade, closing another chapter in the country's longstanding debate over external economic policy. 11/26-35;4

Trade officials from 90 countries agreed unanimously to launch a new round of global trade talks next September; at the end of a four-day meeting delegates...

GHANA—Foreign Relations
Justice Department said a cousin of leader has secretly pleaded no contest to c on the U.S.; he was sent back to Ghana about 10 Ghanians 'of interest to the U.S.'

GIFTS
(see also **Illegal Payments**)
New Form 8283 for deducting non-cash c valued at more than $500 should be avai offices by the end of November. (Tax Report

Alexander Calder's widow received 1, from her husband's estate and valued them the $949,750 accepted by the IRS for es reflected 60% discount from retail value; b discounts of 18% to 25%, valued gifts at $2. billed Mrs. Calder for $459,419 more in Report) 11/20-1;5

When Judge Shirley Kram called lawye the pending litigation between Hanson Tr Corp., they were expecting a decision on fight; but judge wanted to know whether sh a complimentary copy of a book written b represents Hanson. (Shop Talk) 11/21-33;3

Colleges find gifts such as racehorses bet; property donations can cost dearly, be lots that slide into the sea. 11/25-1;4

GINNIE MAE
(see **Government National Mortgage Ass**

GIOVANNINI, ALFIO
Yugo Yearning: Editorial page article b nini on how Yugoslavia's latest car import, affect East-West trade. 11/20-30;4

GLICK, ALLEN
A government witness described how application to the Teamsters Central States led him into a partnership with organized Glick's testimony provided substance to a Senate subcommitteee in the late 1970s th fund had served for decades as 'the mob's b

GOING PRIVATE
Beatrice Cos. accepted Kohlberg Kr offer of $50 a share, or $6.2 billion, to after Kohlberg Kravis threatened to with buyout pact ever is set after board spurne a share, or $5.9 billion, from Dart Group 11/15-2;2

GOLD
New methods enable miners to step gold; the more developed process, heap le boost annual U.S. production to 2.3 milli year; second, less-developed technolgy, i thiobacillus ferrooxidans, which eats away s unreachable by cyanide solutions. 11/1-33;1

The U.S. dollar fell against most major f cies after the release of several U.S. economic were more discouraging than the market ha on the Comex, gold fell to $324.70 an ounce.

Foreign-exchange traders are now convi jor nations are serious about lowering the banks' determination was underscored Nov ...reportedly intervened and ...old on the Comex

> **TIP:** Another interesting business source that may come in handy is *Companies and Their Brands* (and *International Companies and Their Brands*), published by The Gale Group. It identifies which companies are behind which trade names (e.g., Band-Aid is the trade name of Johnson & Johnson's adhesive bandages).

Journal Index is itself a source of facts and information, because each entry typically contains a one- or two-line summary of the indexed article. (You can also read *The Wall Street Journal* on the Web at http://www.wsj.com but it is a fee-based, not free, site.)

✔ **Source: *Standard & Poor's Register of Corporations, Directors and Executives***

Standard & Poor's Register, or the *S&P,* is a leading industry directory of company information. The register consists of three volumes. Volume 1, *Corporations,* is a straight alphabetical listing of approximately 75,000 corporations, giving their addresses, phone numbers, names and titles of key officers and directors, subsidiaries, numbers of employees, and certain financial data like gross sales. Volume 2, *Directors and Executives,* is a listing of over 400,000 officers, directors, trustees, partners, and so on. The information provided about them includes date and place of birth, college attended, professional affiliations, and place of residence. Volume 3 is a set of indexes. You'll find the *S&P* volumes in large general libraries and in business libraries.

S&P is a very highly regarded source of information about companies. It and the Dun & Bradstreet volumes described below are considered leading industry directories. Standard & Poor also publishes several other company-, industry-, and investment-oriented guidebooks and reports, such as *Industry Surveys and Corporation Records*, and *Daily News*.

✔ **Source: Dun & Bradstreet *Million Dollar Directory***

The D&B *Million Dollar Directory* is composed of five volumes of information on over 160,000 companies with a net worth in excess of $500,000, with 250 or more employees or with $25 million or more in sales volume. The directory provides an alphabetical listing of company names, subsidiary relationships, headquarters, addresses, phone numbers, officers, numbers of employees, stock exchange numbers, SIC numbers, and annual sales. A cross-reference volume

Purch Agt—Edward Stone
Product Mgr—Fred Deib
Traffic Mgr—Evert Jackson
Mktg & Prod Mgr—Clarence Bowman
Qual Con Mgr—Robert W. Stratton
Accts—Hill, Barth & King, Salem, Ohio
Primary Bank—Farmers National Bank of Canfield
Sales $5.50Mil   Employees: 110
*Also DIRECTORS—Other Directors Are:
John Tonti
PRODUCTS: Tool & die, metal stamping, assembly special machines
S.I.C. 3544; 3469; 3559

QUAKER OATS CO.
221 N. Clark St., Quaker Tower, Chicago, Ill. 60610
Tel. 312-222-7111

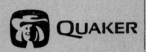

* Chrm & Chief Exec Officer—William D. Smithburg
* Pres & Chief Oper Officer—Frank J. Morgan
Exec V-P (Pres, Grocery Specialties Div)—Philip A. Marineau
Exec V-P (Diversified Grocery Products)—Douglas W. Mills
* Exec V-P (Int'l Grocery Products)—Paul E. Price
Exec V-P (Pres-Fisher-Price Div)—R. Bruce Sampsell
Sr V-P (Human Resources)—Lawrence M. Baytos
Sr V-P (Fin)—Michael J. Callahan
* Sr V-P (Law) & Secy—Luther C. McKinney
Sr V-P (U. S. Grocery Products Serv)—David R. Nogle
V-P & Assoc Gen Cor Coun—John H. Calhoun
V-P (Tax)—Leland R. Chalmers
V-P (Dir-Latin America)—James F. Doyle
V-P & Gen Cor Coun—R. Thomas Howell, Jr
V-P (Bus Devel & Cor Plan)—Terry G. Westbrook
V-P (Pres-Quaker Oats of Canada)—Jon K. Grant
V-P & Treas—Richard D. Jaquith
V-P (Dir-Europe)—Jose A. Rodriguez
V-P (Cor Affairs)—Deborah E. Kelly
V-P (Cor Adm Serv)—Richard E. Kozitka
V-P (New Areas)—William C. Trotter
V-P (Gov't Rel)—Thomas F. Roeser
V-P (Int'l Sys)—Ronald T. Brzezinski
V-P & Cont—Raymond C. Eggleston
V-P (Pres Pet Foods)—George J. Yapp
V-P (Cor Programs)—W. Thomas Phillips
V-P (Pres-Food Service Div)—Russell L. Jones
Accts—Arthur Andersen & Co., Chicago, Ill.
Sales $4.42Bil   Employees: 30,000
Stock Exchange(s): NYS, BST, PAC, MID, TOR, PSE
*Also DIRECTORS—Other Directors Are:
Richard D. Harrison   Weston R. Christopherson
William J. Kennedy, III   Vernon R. Loucks, Jr
Thomas C. MacAvoy   Donald E. Meads
G. G. Michelson (Mrs.)   Walter J. Salmon
William L. Weiss
PRODUCTS: Foods, pet foods & toys
S.I.C. 2032; 2038; 2041; 2043; 2045; 2047; 2051; 2052; 2099; 3942; 3944; 5411; 5621; 5945

QUAKER SALES CORP.
Cooper Ave., Johnstown, Pa. 15907
Tel. 814-536-7541

* Pres—Elvin W. Overdorff, Jr
* V-P—Calvin Q. Overdorff
* Secy & Treas—Donald Overdorff
Accts—Martin, Waltman & Kotzan, Inc., Johnstown, Pa.
Primary Bank—Johnstown Bank & Trust Co.
Primary Law Firm—Kaminsky, Kelly, Wharton & Thomas
Sales Range: $5—8Mil   Employees: 100
*Also DIRECTORS
BUSINESS: Road & paving contractors & supplies
S.I.C. 1611; 5085

QUAKER STATE CORP.-SOUTHEAST REGION
(Subs. Quaker State Corporation)
5500 S. Cobb Dr., Smyrna, Ga. 30080
Tel. 404-799-7212

* Chrm & Chief Exec Officer—Jack W. Corn
* Pres & Chief Oper Officer—Homer M. Ellenburg
* Exec V-P (Admin) & Secy—Maurice G. Erwin
V-P (Coml Sales)—Ennis Mobley
V-P (Sales)—Robert E. Hardesty
V-P (Purch)—Patricia Woodall
Treas—R. Joe Sutton
* Asst Treas—Conrad A. Conrad
Comp—William H. Fields, Jr
Accts—Coopers & Lybrand, Pittsburgh, Pa
Primary Bank—National Bank of Georgia
Primary Law Firm—Smith, Eubanks & Smith, P.C.
Sales $53.60Mil   Employees: 200
*Also DIRECTORS—Other Directors Are:
W. B. Cook
Quentin E. Wood

QUAKER STATE CORPORATION
255 Elm St., Oil City, Pa. 16301
Tel. 814-676-7676

* Chrm—Quentin E. Wood
* Pres & Chief Exec Officer—Jack W. Corn
* Vice-Chrm—Roger A. Markle
Exec V-P—James D. Berry, III
* Exec V-P—Walter B. Cook
V-P, Secy & Coun—Gerald W. Callahan
V-P (Fin) & Chief Fin Officer—Conrad A. Conrad
V-P (Research)—Embert H. DeLong
V-P (Distr)—Homer M. Ellenburg
V-P (Mfg)—William C. Helsley
V-P & Treas—R. Scott Keefer
V-P (Sales)—William E. Marshall
V-P & Cont—John R. Sedlacko
V-P (Mktg)—Earl V. Swift
Public Rel Mgr—Benton H. Faulkner
Purch Mgr—William E. Kingsley
Mktg Dir (Motor Oil)—Richard L. Pennington
Accts—Coopers & Lybrand
Revenue: $847.95Mil   Employees: 4,400
Stock Exchange(s): NYS, BST, MID, PSE
*Also DIRECTORS—Other Directors Are:
Lee R. Forker   Thomas A. Gardner
H. Bryce Jordan   W. Craig McClelland
Kenton E. McElhattan   William J. McFate
Delbert J. McQuaide
PRODUCTS: Lubricants, fuels, other automotive aftermarket products, quick lube serv. centers, ins., truck & auto lights; coal
S.I.C. 5172; 2992; 5013

QUAKER STATE MINIT-LUBE, INC.
(Subs. Quaker State Corporation)
1385 W. 2200 S., Salt Lake City, Utah 84119
Tel. 801-972-6667

* Chrm—Roger A. Markle
* Vice-Chrm—John P Pearson
* Pres & Chief Oper Officer—Jeffrey J. O'Neill
V-P & Cor Coun—David E. Neff
Exec V-P (Mktg)—Paul G. Remund
V-P (Fin) & Cont—Kirk A. Umphrey
V-P (Hallmark Ins)—Wanda M. Hall
V-P & Asst Cont—Kerry A. Scovill
V-P (Oper)—Kay D. Olsen
* Secy & Treas—George D. Morgan
Accts—Coopers & Lybrand, Salt Lake City, Utah
Primary Bank—Key Bank
Primary Law Firm—Jones, Waldo, Holbrook & McDonough
Sales $51Mil   Employees: 1,500
*Also DIRECTORS—Other Directors Are:
Jack W. Corn   Quentin E. Wood
PRODUCTS: Franchisor & operator of fast lube service centers
S.I.C. 5141; 5172; 5812

QUALCORP, INC.
(Affil. Penn Central Federal Systems Co.)
Shelter Rock Rd., Danbury, Conn. 06810
Tel. 203-796-5000

Pres—W. Derek Buckley
Sr V-P (Sys)—Joseph A. Savarese
Sr V-P (Serv)—Adrien R. Schwartz
V-P (Admin)—Phyllis F. Zappala
Chief Fin Officer—D. Joseph Gersuk
Accts—Deloitte Haskins & Sells, New York, N. Y.
Sales $50Mil   Employees: 700
PRODUCTS: Quality assurance service & equip.
S.I.C. 3829; 3825

QUALHEIM, INC.
1225 14th St., Box 368, Racine, Wis. 53401
Tel. 414-634-6671

* Chrm & Pres—Ellen A. Qualheim
* V-P (Mktg)—Robert F. Karls
* Secy & Treas—Julane Nelson
Purch Agt—Garrett Schutz
Accts—Robert G. Berkley, Racine, Wis.
Primary Bank—M&I Bank of Racine
Primary Law Firm—Reinhart, Boerner, Van Deuren, Norris & Rieselbach
Sales $1Mil   Employees: 20
*Also DIRECTORS
PRODUCTS: Electric coml. vegetable cutters, coml. can & bottle crushers, glass washers
S.I.C. 3556; 3565; 3589

QUALITECH MACHINE & ENGINEERING CO.
330 Bond St., Elk Grove Village, Ill. 60007
Tel. 312-439-1311

* Chrm & Pres—Paul Carson, Jr
* V-P—Barbara L. Carson

---

*Also DIRECTORS—Other Directors Ar
Herbert Portes
BUSINESS: Construction, metal work, oil field ser
S.I.C. 1629; 1791; 1799; 3441; 3448; 3449

QUALITAD SALES CORP.
Quality Lane, Rutland, Vt. 05701
Tel. 802-773-9141
* Chrm & Pres—Daniel Bernhardt
* V-P—A. Bernhardt
Sales Range: $2—5Mil   Employees: 50
*Also DIRECTORS
PRODUCTS: Plastic trays & containers
S.I.C. 3089

QUALITEX, INC.
19 Industrial Lane, Providence, R. I. 02919
Tel. 401-751-5727
* V-P & Treas—Mauro Primo
* V-P (Mfg)—David E. Monti
* V-P (Sales)—Nancy Monti
* Secy—Jonathan Cole
* Purch Agt—Joe Riccittelli
Accts—Laventhol & Horwath, Providence, R. I.
Primary Bank—Hospital Trust National Bank
Primary Law Firm—Edwards & Angell
Sales Range: $20—10Mil   Employees: 80
*Also DIRECTORS
PRODUCTS: Extruded rubber thread
S.I.C. 3069; 2241

QUALITONE
(Div. Biscayne Holdings, Inc.)
4931 W. 35th St., Minneapolis, Minn. 55416
Tel. 612-927-7161
Pres—Lane Burger
Exec V-P—Max Harada
V-P (Mktg & Sales)—Joel Wernick
V-P (Fin)—James Anderson
Per Dir—Cleo DeBina
Purch Agt—Thomas McGregor
Sr Engr—Katsumi Tanaka
Mktg Mgr—David Wessell
Audiology—Dawn Galloway
Employees: 170
PRODUCTS: Hearing aids & audiometers
S.I.C. 3842; 3825

QUALITONE INDUSTRIES, INC.
696 Locust St., Mount Vernon, N. Y. 10552
Tel. 914-668-1135
Pres—Robert Karns
Gen Mgr—David Cutler
Sales Range: $2—5Mil   Employees: 10
PRODUCTS: Phonograph needles
S.I.C. 3479

QUALITROL CORP.
(Subs. Danaher Corporation)
1385 Fairport Rd., Fairport, N. Y. 14450
Tel. 716-586-1515
* Pres—John R. Boehm, Jr.
V-P (Mktg & Sales)—Daniel F. McNulty
* Treas—P. W. Allender
* Secy—M. T. Lynch
Cont—David R. Winterton
Accts—Arthur Andersen & Co., New York, N. Y.
Primary Bank—National Westminster Bank USA
Primary Law Firm—Skadden, Arps, Slate, Meagher & Flom
Sales $10Mil   Employees: 150
*Also DIRECTORS—Other Directors Are
Mitchell P. Rales   Steven M. Rales
PRODUCTS: Liquid level gauges controls, thermometers, high temperature alarms, pressure relief devices, pressure electrical switches
S.I.C. 3824; 3492; 3613; 3643

QUALITY ALUMINUM CASTING CO.
1242 Lincoln Ave., Waukesha, Wis. 53186
Tel. 414-542-0731
* Chrm—Gregory E. Pauly, New Holstein, Wis.
* Pres & Chief Exec Officer—C. C. McMullen
V-P (Qual Con & Tech Support)—P. C. Gotgart
V-P (Mfg)—John Nebco
V-P—Paul Thompson
Treas—David J. Rutkowski
Purch Mgr—G. F. Fahl
Mgr Ind Rel—Robert Swanson
Accts—Arthur Young, Milwaukee, Wis.
Primary Bank—M&I Marshall & Ilsley Bank
Sales $11.50Mil   Employees: 200
*Also DIRECTORS—Other Directors Are
J. W. Blakey   James Butler
Gilbert A. Harter   Jeff Pauly
Theodore Pauly
PRODUCTS: Aluminum alloy castings; lost foam molded, permanent molded, cold-set molded, molded & machined
S.I.C. 3365; 3363

QUALITY ARCHITECTURAL PRODUCTS, INC.
16804 S. Gridley Pl., Box 549, Cerritos, Ca.
Tel. 213-402-7864
* Chrm & Pres—Warren R. Olson
* V-P (Fin, Data Proc & Cr) & Treas—John A.
* Secy—Virginia L. Olson
Purch Agt—Da---

enables users to look up companies by geographical location or SIC code. Most large libraries and business libraries have Dun & Bradstreet.

This well-known directory is especially helpful for finding information on smaller firms, because it includes companies that are worth only $500,000. The *Million Dollar Directory* is one of the most popular of Dun & Bradstreet's industry directories.

D&B's other business guides include a directory of international firms, a directory of biographical data about principal officers and directors of 12,000 leading companies, a directory of ranking of company size within industrial categories and states, and a directory that traces the structure and ownership of multinational corporations.

✔ **Source: *Ward's Business Directory* (The Gale Group)**

Ward's Directory is an eight-volume set that provides information on 90,000, U.S. public and private companies. The volumes list companies alphabetically geographically by state, and by their SIC and NAICS code, and then rank them by sales. Data provided include name, address, city, SIC code, sales, number of employees, name of chief executive, year founded, and type of firm (e.g., private, public, subsidiary, or division).

Ward's is a very interesting and useful directory. Unlike other popular company directories, *Ward's* provides various rankings in its listings. For example, *Ward's* lists the largest pharmaceutical firms, and ranks firms geographically and by other categories. *Ward's* also claims that more than 90 percent of the firms in its directory are privately held—data on these companies are harder to find than for public firms.

✔ **Source: *CorpTech Directory of Technology Companies***

Provides key data such as address, phone, number of employees, SIC code, basic business description, and annual sales on over 40,000 companies in the high-tech area.

Like the other company directories listed here, CorpTech is a good source for finding key data on major firms. The difference is that CorpTech focuses exclusively on high-technology companies, which the publisher defines as any firm that operates in these industries: biotechnology, computer hardware or software, energy,

> **TIP:** If you need to find facts on a lesser-known company or one that is in a smaller country, I'd suggest visiting the library of a good university business school and browsing through the business directory reference section. There you will likely find a variety of directories that cover firms operating in *just one specific country*. (By the way, you'll also likely find there many *state directories* as well—compilations of data about firms operating within an individual state. These are often published by chambers of commerce or state economic development offices.)

medical, pharmaceuticals, telecommunications and Internet, transportation, and several others.

✔ **Source: *Hoover's Handbook of American Business* (Hoover's)**

Hoover's Handbook provides one-page profiles of 750 major enterprises in the U.S., arranged alphabetically. For each listing, the directory provides an overview, history, names of top executives, address, phone, fax, major divisions and subsidiaries, rankings, names of competitors, stock price history, and other data.

A relatively new entry to the company directory field, Hoover's has made quite a name for itself by being the first to offer a company directory at a bargain price. While the preceding competitors' books cover many more firms, they cost well into the mid-hundreds of dollars, but you can get your own copy of the *Hoover's Handbook* for much less at many bookstores. Note that Hoover's also publishes several other guides, such as a World Business edition, which covers international firms, a *Handbook of Private Companies*, *Handbook of Emerging Companies*, various regional books (e.g., *Guide to the Top Chicago Companies*, etc.), and industry guides, such as the *Guide to Computer Companies or Guide to Media Companies*. Note that Hoover's has one of the most popular company information sites on the Web (http://www.hoovers.com), where some of this data is made available for free.

✔ **Source: Moody's *Manuals* (Dun & Bradstreet)**

Moody's *Manuals* provide a great deal of background and detail on specific companies. Typical information provided includes company

---

TIP: Getting the Directory You Want

• Many of the directories listed in this guide are cheap or moderately priced, but certain ones are expensive and are best used at a library. To find a library that has a directory you need, contact the Special Libraries Association (see page 13) and find out which libraries specialize in your topic of interest. Then, just call or write the library to see if it has the guide. If it does, you can then ask the librarian there to look up what you need.

For example, let's say you need information on whether a particular food is kosher. Checking the guide, you'll locate a directory called *Kosher Directory: Directory of Kosher Products and Services.* To get this directory, you could write to the address listed and purchase it, or you could contact the Special Libraries Association to find a library devoted to Jewish studies. Such a library may have this directory, and you could ask the librarian there to look up the food and supply you with the answer.

---

history, structure, capital, lines of businesses and products, properties, subsidiaries, names of officers and directors, income statement, balance sheet, financial and operating data, and various stock charts and tables.

Much of the information provided in Moody's comes from documents that public companies are required to file by the Securities and Exchange Commission (SEC). The *Manuals* are a particularly good source for tracing the history of a large company.

✔ **Source: *Business Rankings* (The Gale Group)**

A collection of thousands of citations of ranked lists of companies, for various categories. Also included is a salary list for over 150 occupations.

This directory helps answer the question "Who's number one?" in a certain field. It is actually a compilation of information that the Brooklyn Public Library scans in its daily duties, gleaned from scores of reference sources.

✔ **Source: *Thomas Register of American Manufacturers***

Thomas Register tells you who manufactures what product and where the manufacturer is located. There are three sets of volumes. One set consists of 23 volumes and is organized alphabetically by product. It lists manufacturers' names and addresses in over 62,000

> **TIP:** *Research Centers Directory* is a good source for finding "think tanks"—institutions such as the Center for Democracy and Technology, the Heritage Foundation, the Brookings Institution, and other centers that study public policy–related issues and publish their findings in reports or articles. Think tanks are mainly listed in the section of the directory named "government and public affairs." You can also link to the home page of many think tanks on the World Wide Web.

product headings. A companion three-volume set lists 156,000 U.S. companies in alphabetical order, providing addresses, phone numbers, asset ratings, and other information. These three volumes also include a trademark index at the back. A third set of volumes provides more than 12,000 pages of actual catalog data from about 2,200 companies. Most libraries keep a set of *Thomas Register.*

Thomas Register is a very useful resource. Volume 1 of the first set starts with a listing of abacus manufacturers, and the last volume ends with a listing of manufacturers of Zonolite (a form of insulation). If you look up radiation detectors, you'll find about 25 manufacturers—about the same number of firms that manufacture poultry netting. Although *Thomas Register* does not list every manufacturer of a product, it is still an extraordinarily comprehensive directory. *Thomas Register* is also available for searching on the Web: http://www.thomasregister.com

SUBSIDIARIES AND DIVISIONS DIRECTORIES

One of the most difficult tasks of business researchers is discovering linkages between corporate parents and their subsidiaries and divisions. The following sources will help identify connections.

✔ **Source: *America's Corporate Families* (Dun & Bradstreet)**

A description of 11,000 U.S. parent companies and their 76,000 subsidiaries and divisions. Includes any firm worth more than $500,000, conducting business from two or more locations, with 250+ employees, and having a controlling interest in one or more subsidiaries.

This is a very useful tool for finding out the subsidiaries and divisions a corporation operates and for finding names of division vice presidents and managers. Each listing provides names, addresses, sales, and the industry of each division and subsidiary listed. Volume 2 in this set is titled *International Affiliates,* and provides data about companies with foreign parents and U.S. subsidiaries. These directories are designed to be easy to use.

✔ **Source: *Who Owns Whom* (Dun & Bradstreet)**
Lists connections among companies. Parent firms are listed in alphabetical order.

Not as easy to use as *America's Corporate Families,* but it may still be worth checking to dig up hard-to-find information. Separate directories cover North America; Australia and the Far East; United Kingdom and the Republic of Ireland; and Continental Europe.

✔ **Source: *Directory of Corporate Affiliations* (National Register Publishing)**
Lists data on 4,124 U.S. parent companies and 26,000 divisions, subsidiaries, and affiliates and 12,000 outside the United States.

An easier directory to use than *Who Owns Whom,* but not as simple to use as *America's Corporate Families.*

INTERNATIONAL BUSINESS DIRECTORIES

Today's business world is global, and researchers can no longer confine themselves to finding facts on firms and industries that operate within the boundaries of the United States. The following is a selected listing of some of the most useful directories of information on companies in other parts of the world. If you have trouble finding any of these at your local public library, try visiting a nearby university's business school library.

✔ **Source: *Major Companies of Europe* (Graham & Whiteside, London)**
A four-volume set that provides facts about 24,000 companies in Western Europe, Israel and the United Kingdom. Information provided includes

company name, address, names of top executives, trade names, company activities, subsidiaries, sales, profit, and number of employees.

This is a straightforward directory, broken down into three volumes. Volume 1 contains information on 3,000 firms located in the European Community (EC); volume 2 lists data on 1,300 British firms; and volume 3 lists information about 1,400 firms located in Western Europe that are not part of the EC. A companion directory available from the same publisher is *Major Companies of Central and Eastern Europe and the CIS*.

✔ **Source: *Japan Company Handbook* (Toyo Keizai Inc.)**

Provides financial information on all Japanese companies listed in the first and second sections of the Tokyo, Osaka, and Nagoya stock exchanges. Approximately 2,000 firms are covered.

This directory is considered the leading sourcebook for finding out about Japanese companies. It is filled with loads of useful data, including company descriptions, profit and loss statements, breakdown of sales by categories, methods for raising funds, indepth financial statements, balance sheets, company outlooks, stock price graphs, and more. Amazingly, with so much data provided for each firm, the handbook is still very easy to use and read and is accompanied by clear explanatory material.

TIP: Many European company directories are published or distributed by a U.K.-based firm called Euromonitor. Check them out on the Web at http://www.euromonitor.com

---

✔ **Source: D&B *Principal International Businesses: The World Marketing Directory* (Dun & Bradstreet)**

Lists data on 50,000 firms in 140 countries around the world. Companies are selected for inclusion based on their size and prominence. This directory provides names, addresses, sales, year founded, names of top executives, number of employees, and type of industry.

This is a very useful source if you need to get some basic information on any major company located anywhere around the world. The directory makes it easy to find firms by providing both an alphabetical and industry index.

The authors, Ruth A. Pagell and Michael Halperin, are both well-known experts in the business information world.

Two other directories that you'll sometimes come across in the library that can be helpful for locating information on international business are the *Directory of American Firms Operating in Foreign Countries* and the *Directory of Foreign Firms Operating in the United States.* The former provides key directory data on over 2,000 U.S. firms including the name of a foreign officer (when known) and the names of the foreign countries where it has operations; the latter lists about 4,000 non-U.S. firms that are owned wholly or in part by foreign-based companies. Both are published by Uniworld Business Publications

"INSIDER" DIRECTORIES

✔ **Source: *Directories in Print* (The Gale Group)**

This directory describes over 15,000 different types of specialized directories, covering subjects such as banking, agriculture, law, government, science, engineering, education, information science, biography, arts and entertainment, public affairs, health, religion, hobbies, and sports. You can find this guide, published annually, at most large public libraries.

This excellent source unearths an amazingly diverse range of specialized directories. (A directory is any kind of reference book that tells readers where they can find sources of information within a specific field.) Here are some samples of the directories indexed in this "ultimate" directory: *Special Libraries of Israel, Computer Software Applications in Oceanography, Bicycle Resource Guide, Major Companies of Europe, American Indian Painters, Index of Stolen Art,* and *Free Things for Teachers.* A detailed subject index is provided at the back of the book, so all you need to do is look up the topic of your choice, and *Directories in Print* refers you to a particular directory, giving you its name, publisher and address, phone number, specialties, and other details.

★7622★
AMERICAN COUNCIL ON CONSUMER INTERESTS—MEMBERSHIP LIST
American Council on Consumer Interests
Stanley Hall, Room 240
University of Missouri
Columbia, MO 65211   Phone: (314)882-3817
Number of listings: 2,000. **Frequency:** Biennial, odd years.
Price: Available to members only.

★7623★
AMERICAN GROUP PSYCHOTHERAPY ASSOCIATION—MEMBERSHIP DIRECTORY
American Group Psychotherapy Association
25 E. 21st Street, 6th Floor
New York, NY 10010   Phone: (212)477-2677
Covers: 3,500 physicians, psychologists, clinical social
workers, psychiatric nurses, and other mental health
professionals interested in treatment of emotional problems by
group methods. **Entries include:** Name, office or home
address, highest degree held, affiliate society of which a
member. **Arrangement:** Alphabetical. **Indexes:** Geographical.
Pages (approx.): 160. **Frequency:** Reported as biennial;
previous edition 1984; latest edition summer 1987. **Price:**
$25.00. **Other formats:** Cheshire labels, $65.00 per thousand;
pressure-sensitive labels, $75.00 per thousand.

American Humane Agency Directory *See* **Directory of
Animal Care and Control Agencies (7747)**

★7624★
AMERICAN SOCIETY OF ACCESS PROFESSIONALS—MEMBERSHIP DIRECTORY [Freedom of information]
American Society of Access Professionals
2001 S Street, N. W., Suite 630
Washington, DC 20009   Phone: (202)462-8888
Covers: Over 300 individuals concerned with the methods,
procedures, and techniques of administering statutes
pertaining to the availability of records or information contained
therein, including freedom of information, privacy protection,
open meetings, and fair credit reporting laws. **Entries include:**
Name, address, phone, affiliation. **Arrangement:** Alphabetical.
Indexes: Geographical. **Pages (approx.):** 35. **Frequency:**
Annual, winter. **Editor:** Clifford M. Brownstein. **Price:** Available
to members only.

**American Society of Association Executives—
Convention & Exposition Managers Section Directory**
See **Who's Who in Association Management (8281)**

American Society of Association Executives—Directory
See **Who's Who in Association Management (8281)**

★7625★
AMERICAN SOCIETY OF JOURNALISTS AND AUTHORS—DIRECTORY
American Society of Journalists and Authors
1501 Broadway, Suite 1907
New York, NY 10036   Phone: (212)997-0947
Covers: Over 750 member freelance nonfiction writers.
Entries include: Writer's name, home and office addresses
and phone numbers, specialties, areas of expertise; name,
address, and phone of agent; memberships; books; periodicals
to which contributed; awards; employment history.
Arrangement: Alphabetical. **Indexes:** Subject specialty, type
of material written, geographical. **Pages (approx.):** 90.
Frequency: Biennial, October/November of even years.
Former title(s): Society of Magazine Writers - Directory of
Professional Writers (1975); American Society of Journalists

and Authors - Directory of Professional Writers. **Price:** $50.0
Other formats: Mailing labels.

★7626★
AMERICA'S HIDDEN PHILANTHROPIC WEALTH: TOMORROW'S POTENTIAL FOUNDATION GIANTS
Taft Group
5130 MacArthur Boulevard, N.W.
Washington, DC 20016   Phone: (202)966-708(
Covers: 300 small family foundations with the potential t
become billion dollar philanthropies. Published in four loos
leaf editions covering 75 foundations each. **Entries inclu**
Foundation name, location, analysis of wealth, philanthr(
interests, study of the conditions leading to expansion
future giving interests, biography, giving history, ir
relationship information. **Indexes:** Individuals are alphab
foundations are geographical; grants are by cat
Frequency: Annual; suspended indefinitely. **Price:** :
each edition, postpaid; $197.00 per set.

★7627★
AMERICA'S NEWEST FOUNDATIONS: THE SOURCEBOOK ON RECENTLY CREATED PHILANTHROPIES
Taft Group
5130 MacArthur Boulevard, N. W.
Washington, DC 20016   Phone: (202)966-,
Covers: Over 500 foundations created since 1980 that pro
grants to charitable organizations. **Entries include:** Foundati
name, address, phone, name and title of contact, curre
charitable and geographic preference, previous recipient an
grant types, assets. **Arrangement:** Alphabetical. **Indexes:**
Personal name, type of grant, giving interest, recipient location.
Frequency: Annual, February. **Editor:** Ben Lord. **Price:** $89.95.
Other information: Former publisher, Public Service Materials
Center.

★7628★
ANIMAL ORGANIZATIONS & SERVICES DIRECTORY
Animal Stories
16787 Beach Boulevard
Huntington Beach, CA 92647
Covers: Over 400 national and state organizations involv
animal protection and welfare; also lists veterinary and m(
organizations such as clinics, pet insurance comp
zoological societies, pet transporting and other service
fancier clubs, consultants, and publishers of magazine:
newsletters concerned with animals. **Entries include:** Nar
organization, address, phone, branch offices, year establis
key personnel, membership information, objectives, descrip
of materials available by mail. **Arrangement:** Classified by t
of organization or service. **Indexes:** Alphabetical. **Pag**
(approx.): 230. **Frequency:** Biennial, fall of odd years. **Edito**
Kathleen A. Reece. **Advertising accepted.** Circulation 5,00(
Price: $16.95, plus $1.50 shipping.

**Annotated Directory of Exemplary Family Based
Programs** *See* **Annotated Directory of Selected
Family-Based Service Programs (7629)**

★7629★
ANNOTATED DIRECTORY OF SELECTED FAMILY-BASED SERVICE PROGRAMS
National Resource Center on Family Based Services
Oakdale Hall, Room N240
University of Iowa
Iowa City, IA 52319   Phone: (319)335-4
Covers: 275 social service programs nationwide dealing
family-centered services and operating out of public .
voluntary agencies. **Entries include:** Name, address, pho

✔ **Source: *World Directory of Environmental Organizations*
(California Institute of Public Affairs)**

Covering more than 2,600 organizations in over 200 countries, this
directory provides detailed descriptions and contact information for
key national governmental and nongovernmental organizations. In
addition to the listings, this directory has a number of extra features,
including a timeline, glossary, "who's doing what" analysis, description of UN programs, and more. The book is a cooperative project of
the California Institute of Public Affairs, the Sierra Club, and the
International Union for Conservation of Nature and Natural
Resources.

This source can be helpful to anyone researching environmental issues and needs a place to start looking for data. Other places
to find good environmental reference sources would be *Directories
in Print, The Encyclopedia of Associations,* and *Research Centers
Directory.* Also, the publisher of these three guidebooks (The Gale
Group, Detroit, MI) lists several environmental reference directories in its catalog.

✔ **Source: *Research Centers Directory* (The Gale Group)**

An annual directory of 13,400 university, government, and other
nonprofit research organizations. Major subjects span agriculture,
business, education, government, law, math, social sciences, and
humanities. You'll find this guide in university and other academi-
cally oriented libraries.

The *Research Centers Directory* provides a wealth of information on who's conducting research on what subjects around the
country. You'll find an incredible diversity of studies being conducted. Some examples of the research organizations listed in
this directory: the Alcohol Research Group, the National Bureau
of Economic Research, the International Copper Research
Association, the Birth Defects Institute, the Center for Russian
and East European Studies . . . you get the idea.

I once used this guide when I was researching the topic of
"rebuilding rather than replacing automobiles." By checking the
directory, I found a research institute associated with a university
in Detroit that was conducting a study on just that topic.

The directory is easy to use. You just look up your subject, and
the directory refers you to a particular research center. It provides
the center's name, a contact person, the address, the phone num-

ment grants, and foundations. Staff: 2 research professionals, 8 supporting professionals, 2 technicians, 1 other.

Research Activities and Fields: tress effects on natural ecosystems, integrated pest management, acid rain, solar energy, and behavioral, agricultural, community, and population ecology. Maintains 16 quarter-acre animal enclosures, aviaries, and a database on precipitation chemistry. Offers field ecology courses.

Publications and Services: Research results published in scientific journals. Provides graduate and undergraduate training.

★983★
MIAMI UNIVERSITY
INSECT COLLECTION
Department of Zoology   Phone: (513) 529-5454
Oxford, OH 45056   Founded: 1910
Dr. D.L. Deonier, Curator

Governance: Integral unit of Department of Zoology at Miami University. Supported by parent institution. Staff: 2 research professionals, 2-5 supporting professionals, 1 technician, 1 other.

Research Activities and Fields: Systematics, behavior, and ecology of aquatic insects, primarily Diptera, Ephydridae, and Chironomidae. Maintains an extensive collection of shore flies and rearing facilities for aquatic insects.

Publications and Services: Research results published in professional journals and published symposia. Maintains a library on entomology; Marian Winner, librarian.

★984★
MIAMI UNIVERSITY
INSTITUTE OF ENVIRONMENTAL SCIENCES
Oxford, OH 45056   Phone: (513) 529-5811
Gene E. Willeke, Director   Founded: 1969

Governance: Integral unit of Miami University. Supported by parent institution, U.S. government, and local governmental agencies. Staff: 3 research professionals, 1 supporting professional, 1 other.

Research Activities and Fields: Environmental sciences, including studies on river restoration techniques, hazardous and toxic substances, acid precipitation, environmental history, ecological dynamics, conservation, land use planning, water quality, community environmental planning, and energy. Produces environmental media, especially tape and slide programs. Offers a master's degree in environmental sciences.

Publications and Services: Research results published in scientific and technical journals and project reports. Maintains a library.

★985★
MIAMI UNIVERSITY
RT A. HEFNER ZOOLOGY MU

ber, a description of the activities conducted, and the organization's publications. Gale also publishes a companion volume called International Research Centers Directory.

✔ **Source: *Foundation Directory* (Foundation Center)**

The *Foundation Directory,* published by the Foundation Center, is a guide that can help you find the right foundation to apply to in order to obtain funding and grants. Many libraries have it.

This guide is only one of many directories and publications published by the Foundation Center. The Foundation Center maintains information on over 27,000 active foundations and supports a national network of 170 library reference collections made available for free public use. The biggest collections are located in New York City; Washington, DC; Cleveland; and San Francisco. These libraries provide important reference tools, such as sample application forms and the annual reports, tax information, and publications of foundations.

The center publishes a variety of helpful information sources, including specialized directories that tell you where to get grants for projects that cover subjects like public health, the aged, minorities, museums, and so on. For more information on the Foundation Center's publications and to locate a foundation library collection near you, contact The Foundation Center, 79 Fifth Avenue, New York, NY 10003; 212-620-4230 or 800-424-9836.

Another library directory you may come across to locate similar information is called the *World Guide to Foundations*. This book lists data on over 21,000 foundations in 112 countries. Another related but slightly different one is the *Annual Register of Grant Support*, a guide to over 3,000 grant-giving organizations.

✔ **Source: *National Directory of Nonprofit Organizations* (Taft Group)**

Data on over 260,000 nonprofit organizations. Directory provides addresses, phone numbers, annual income, IRS status, and activities.

Included in this interesting directory are organizations such as hospitals, museums, conservation organizations, alumni organizations, and many other types of nonprofits.

✔ **Source: Congressional Information Service Indexes**

Check university or large public libraries for any of the following comprehensive statistical directories published by the Congressional Information Service: *American Statistics Index,* for sources of government statistics; *Index to International Statistics,* for sources of foreign statistics; *Statistical Research Index,* for sources of U.S. nongovernment statistics.

Together these guides index more than 1,600 sources of statistical information.

✔ **Source: The Yellow Pages**

Don't forget this familiar resource. You can use the Yellow Pages to find manufacturers, dealers, and all types of service firms. It is a great and underestimated source of information! Large libraries have the Yellow Pages of most of the bigger cities, and you can use these listings to supplement what you get out of *Thomas Register* (see page 33). The Manhattan Yellow Pages alone constitute an immense source of information on products and services. (Large libraries usually have the white pages of the major cities, too.) Of course, these days you can easily search a national compilation of yellow and white pages on the Net (see page 254 in chapter 7 for names of specific sites).

THE WIRED LIBRARY

If there's any one place that's at the crossroads of this new information age, it is the library. Does this surprise you? Do you have an image of the library as a place for just finding old books, looking at an encyclopedia or the day's newspaper, and being told to keep your voice down? If so, it's time to update your map!

Libraries and librarians live in the world of information—it's why they exist and information is what they are all about. When information was primarily in print, they collected, organized and made print available; when some of those forms expanded to audio and video, libraries integrated those media as well. They did the same for microfilm and microfiche, and did it again with CD-ROM. Libraries are now reorienting and radically rethinking their modes of operation because of the Internet.

In this age of the Internet, libraries are becoming the public nerve centers for providing access to a wide range of online and electronic information services. This means that when you visit a modern library, you have access to some of the most powerful electronic finding aids and online sources available. It *also* means that in some cases you have access to these library search systems, remotely via the Internet, from your own home!

At today's wired library, when you walk in the door, one of the first things that you may wish to head for is the library's online catalog. Many, if not most libraries, have converted their old card catalog to an electronic system, where you enter keywords into a computer to find book titles, as well as magazines and other resources held within the library.

But even more powerful are the electronic databases that most libraries make available to their patrons. The majority of libraries have a bank of computers available for patrons to do any of the following research:

- Search the Internet.
- Search a collection of CD-ROMs.
- Search fee-based online services.

The first thing, then, you need to be aware of when you sit down at a terminal in the library is on what it is you are searching! Have you selected a terminal that just provides a search of the library's online catalog? Or is it a CD-ROM collection? Or does it access a series of remote online databases?

In some libraries, you can do all of these different tasks on the same computer. In those cases, you need to choose from an initial menu screen that's displayed in front of you which of these tasks you wish to perform. In other libraries, you need to choose a certain computer (or bank of computers) that have been set up to perform just one of these tasks. So, be sure you know what kind of computer you have chosen to work at!

Let's look at these three listed activities, one at a time.

Search the Internet

If you don't have a computer at home, or if you do but don't have a modem or a fast Internet connection, you may be able to surf the Net by going to your library. There's normally no difference in searching the Internet at a library versus searching it at home (though a few libraries have instituted some filtering software to screen out pornographic and other objectionable sites). To learn more about what kind of research and information gathering you can do on the Net, see chapter 5.

Search a Collection of CD-ROMs

Although some libraries are phasing out their CD-ROMs in favor of the Internet and online databases (can you believe that in a few short years CD-ROMs have gone from a cutting edge technology to a nearly outdated one?), many libraries still make them available for searching databases of information.

A CD-ROM, in case you haven't come across one, is a laser disk, much like the CDs you play on your stereo. The difference is that while those disks are encoded with music, the CDs you'll find at a library are encoded with information. A single CD-ROM can store about 250,000 pages of information.

There are thousands of different databases on CD-ROM. Some contain articles from journals and newspapers, others are excerpts from U.S. governmental reports or company financials, and others consist of scholarly literature covering psychology, anthropology, or some other disciplines. The following are the names of some of the more popular CD-ROM databases produced by some of the major vendors.

InfoTrak

- Academic Index: scholarly and general interest journals
- Business Index: business journals and popular newspapers
- General Periodicals Index: indexes and abstracts business and general-interest periodicals
- Government Publications Index: indexes monthly catalog of the Government Printing Office
- Health Index: indexes publications on health, fitness, nutrition, and medicine

- Investext: indexes and provides full text to Wall Street company and industry research reports
- LegalTrac: indexes legal publications
- Magazine Index Plus: indexes general-interest magazines
- National Newspaper Index: indexes several major newspapers

Bell & Howell Learning (previously known as UMI)

- ABI/Inform: articles published in major and leading business periodicals
- Business Dateline: articles from hundreds of regional business journals
- Newspaper Abstracts: indexing and brief abstracts from several major national newspapers
- Newspapers Fulltext: The full text of several major newspapers
- *The New York Times* Ondisc: the full text of articles published in *The New York Times*
- Periodical Abstracts: abstracts of popular magazine articles

H. W. Wilson

- Applied Science and Technology Index
- Biological and Agricultural Index
- Business Periodicals Index
- Index to Legal Periodicals
- Readers' Guide to Periodical Literature
- Social Science Index

Another major vendor of CD-ROMs include SilverPlatter (its products include EconLit, PsychLit, Disclosure). Other specific CD-ROM titles include Books in Print Plus, Historical Abstracts, ERIC (educational literature), NewsBank (recent newspapaer articles), PAIS (public affairs related information), Philosopher's Index, and Religion Index.

One big difference that you'll find among CD-ROMs is that some contain only a summary of the original article or item (usually called an abstract, in some cases it is an actual extract), others have the complete text ("fulltext") but none of the original graphs, charts, photos, etc, while others are faithful reproductions of the originals, and are usually called "full image." Some of Bell & Howell's products are of the "full image" variety.

Search Fee-based Online Services

The other electronic set of information that you can search at a library are the "online" databases—these are the collections of related data that the library pays a subscription fee to connect its computers to for access, and which are available for you to search.

Here are the names of some popular online databases you may come across in your library.

- **InfoTrac Web (formerly SearchBank)**
  Specific databases you'll find here include: General BusinessFile ASAP; European Business ASAP; General Academic ASAP; Expanded Academic ASAP; General Reference Center; Health Reference Center Academic and Computer Database ASAP

- **OCLC**
  OCLC's First Search Electronic Collections Online provides access to about 2,000, primarily academic titles (publishers include various university presses and scholarly societies)

- **SilverPlatter's KnowledgeCite**
  Includes hundreds of databases, ranging from ABI/Inform and Aerospace Database to Water Resource Abstracts and World Textiles). The database can be searched separately or as a group.

- **EBSCO**
  EBSCO Host has dozens of databases, from: AIDSLINE and International Pharmaceutical Abstracts to PsycLit and Vocational Search and many more.

- **Bell & Howell Information and Learning (formerly UMI)**
  Bell & Howell's most popular online service is called PRO-QUEST, and its databases include:

  ABI
  Accounting and Tax Database

Banking Information Source
Canadian Serials
Criminal Justice Periodicals Index
Periodical Abstracts Library
Pharmaceutical News Index
ProQuest Computing
ProQuest Religion
Wilson Databases
Applied Science and Technology Plus Text
Social Sciences Plus Text
Education Plus Text
General Science Plus Text
ProQuest Medical Library
ProQuest Newspaper Library
ProQuest International Academic Research
  Library™
ProQuest Newsstand™ International Newspapers
International Selectable Newspapers
International Newswires
ProQuest Asian Business™
ProQuest European Business™

- **WilsonWeb** databases (both online and CD-ROM) include:

  Applied Science and Technology Fulltext
  Art Fulltext
  Current Biography
  Wilson Business Abstracts
  Education Abstracts
  General Science Abstracts
  Humanities Abstracts Fulltext
  Readers Guide Abstracts Fulltext
  Social Science Abstracts Fulltext
  Wilson Biographies
  World Authors

More powerful databases that are often too expensive for libraries to make available for free to the public are available from online information vendors like Dialog, Lexis-Nexis, and Dow Jones.

Although a full discussion of the art of conducing an online search is covered in chapter 5, here are a few of the most important points you need to know when searching online or CD-ROM databases at a library:

1. Realize that you are not searching the Web, but a database.
2. Select the appropriate database. Be sure that you have selected a database whose scope covers the area you are researching. You can ask your librarian for assistance in making certain the system and databases you've chosen are the best ones available.
3. Realize that most databases let you either "browse" or "search" their contents. You browse when you want to scan what items are in the database under a particular subject heading. You search when you enter a keyword or phrase to instruct the computer to search through all of the items in the database to find those that match your search statement.
4. Realize that not all databases provide the same amount of information. Some just provide bibliographic data (i.e., an article's title, author, date, etc.); others provide a short summary of the piece; others provide the entire text of the original, but not charts, photos, or graphs; and a few provide a replica of the original text with all the graphics intact.
5. Know how to create an effective search statement, which means coming up with effective key words, knowing about Boolean operators, and limiting your search to certain parts of the database. See chapter 5 for more on this.
6. Be sure that the database is up to date. This is particularly important for CD-ROMs, since it is up to the library to have the newest one out loaded into their system (most are issued monthly). You don't want to be searching for news articles for an event that happened three weeks ago on a database that is three months old!

Catalogs and Archives

Finally, one other way that libraries are actively integrating their offerings with the Internet is by making their catalogs available for free browsing and searching on the Internet. Here are the names of a few of the best sources for locating these:

- **Library of Congress**
  http://lcweb.loc.gov/z3950/gateway.html

  This portion of the Library of Congress' web site allows you to search its own as well as other library catalogs.

- **Webcats**
  http://www.lights.com/webcats/libtype.html

  An alphabetical list of library catalogs, broken down by type (e.g., academic, government, law, medical, etc.).

  Not only are many libraries making their catalogs available for searching over the Internet, some are identifying their special collections and archival holdings. So if you want to know where to find, say, where to research the Prague municipal archives or the Albert Einstein archives in Israel, you could find out where the holdings are on the Web. Below is one excellent source for looking these up.

- **Repositories of Primary Sources**
  http://www.uidaho.edu/special-collections/Other.Repositories
  .html

  This very comprehensive site provides a listing of over 3,800 Web sites that describes the holdings of (normally non-digitized) manuscripts, archives, rare books, historical photographs, and other primary sources. Breaks down coverage into: Western United States and Canada; Eastern United States and Canada: States and Provinces A-M; Eastern United States and Canada: States and Provinces N-Z; Latin America and the Caribbean; Europe; Asia and the Pacific; and Africa and the Near East.

Digital Libraries

Some libraries are even going a step further, creating "digital libraries" consisting of digitized versions of various primary sources from the library's collection. These could include documents like personal letters, governmental treaties, original maps, audio interviews, photographs, movies, and other source materials that one would normally have to travel to the library directly in order to gain access. Even the Vatican, which has one of the world's most prominent collections of rare and old precious documents, has digitized some of its materials and made them available on the Web to scholars.

In the U.S., probably the most prominent and best-known digital libraries are the theme libraries that have been created by the U.S. Library of Congress, through its American Memory series. This collection provides Web access to a variety of rare American historical documents that previously could only have been viewed by persons who visited the library in the capital. The American Memory series consisted of several dozen collections with over one million manuscripts, films, sound recordings, and publications in the Library of Congress' collection, and was growing steadily. Specific theme collections in the American Memory Exhibit include, for example:

- Hispano Music and Culture of the Northern Rio Grande
- Music for the Nation, 1870–1885
- Pioneering the Upper Midwest, 1820–1910
- Built in America: Historic American Buildings Survey/Historic American Engineering Record, 1933–present
- An American Time Capsule: Three Centuries of Broadsides
- The Alexander Graham Bell Family Papers
- African American Perspectives
- Washington as It Was: Photographs by Theodore Horydczak 1923–1959
- Civil War Photographs
- Dance Instruction Manuals from 1490–1920
- The Leonard Bernstein Collection ca. 1920–1989
- Voices from the Dust Bowl: The Charles L. Todd and Robert Sonkin Migrant Worker Collection
- Collections of papers and memorabilia from American historical and popular figures ranking from George Washington and Abraham Lincoln to Jackie Robinson

Here, for instance, is an excerpt from the American Memory's Alexander Graham Bell Family Papers site:

The online collection will ultimately represent a portion selected from the original Bell Papers and will comprise approximately 4,700 items, totaling about 38,000 images. The first release contains over 1,000 items consisting of correspondence, scientific notebooks, journals, blueprints, sketches, and photographs documenting Bell's invention of the telephone and his involvement in the first telephone company, his family life, his interest in the education of the deaf, and his aeronautical and other scientific research.

Many other libraries around the country and around the world are making parts of their collection available as a digital library. For example, the University of California, Berkeley, has made its collection of the life of anarchist Emma Goldman, the Emma Goldman Papers, available (http://sunsite.berkeley.edu/goldman).

One caution in using digital libraries: Keep in mind that these are new efforts, and as such, you cannot assume that what a

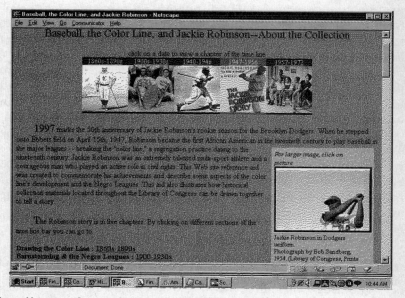

http://memory.loc.gov/ammem/jrhtml/jrabout.html

This exhibit by the Library of Congress on the history of baseball and Jackie Robinson is an example of how some libraries are digitizing their primary materials and making them available on the Web.

library makes available in digital form over the Net anywhere represents its full collection of materials on the topic. In some ways, many of these digital libraries offerings are more akin to museum-like displays and selections rather than exhaustive collections.

THE FUTURE OF LIBRARIES

The Internet has changed everything for libraries, and it's changed nothing. It's changed everything because, as we all know, so much is moving onto the Net—it's where it's all happening. The older, traditional information sources are migrating to the Internet, while at the same time newly created information sources are being "born" fresh on the Net. It's changed everything, then, because libraries, have traditionally been "warehouses" of the now rapidly defunct information "containers"—the pulp-based books, magazines, reports, etc. Libraries have also served as the physical place where the public can go to obtain information, and therefore have been forced to rethink their mission and roles. So the library profession has its work cut out for it, and is facing challenges.

But the Internet has changed nothing as well—because the essential mission of the public library, and its raison d'être remains the same, and that mission is *medium-independent*. The broadest mission of a public library is to better enable all of our participation in our democratic form of government, by making available to all the information that's necessary for self-governance, regardless of economic ability.

In the words of James Madison:

> A popular government without popular information, or the means of acquiring it, is but a prologue to a farce or a tragedy, or perhaps both. Knowledge will forever govern ignorance, and a people who mean to be their own governors must arm themselves with the power which knowledge gives.

Another contemporary of Mr. Madison, Thomas Jefferson, has called information "the currency of democracy."

That higher purpose of the library, then, does not depend on the *form* that information takes—print, microfilm, digital, or however it may evolve in the future. The job of the library professional, and the librarian (whose title may also change to reflect their shifting roles) is to stay true to that overall mission, while making the necessary adjustments given the state of technology, society, and other critical forces. In all cases, the library will collect information based on a specific standard and criteria, filter it, categorize it, organize it, and then make it easily available via whatever finding aids and mechanisms are most appropriate and effective.

But, it's not quite as simple as all of this either. There's no discounting the fact that libraries have been built from the ground up to handle and manage a particular type of information—print-based. As such, a library's mind-set and the form it has taken have been geared toward collecting, archiving, and displaying print-based information. And so a fairly radical shift must be made by libraries to make them not just storage facilities but active and vital cultivators, gatherers, harvesters, sorters, and distributors of information and knowledge.

The success of libraries in making this transition will depend on several factors—the creativity and courage of the librarians themselves, the leadership of those who head the profession, and the level of support shown by the public.

For those readers who are interested in learning more about libraries and their transition to the Internet age, I highly recommend a special issue of the journal *Daedalus*, "Books, Bricks, & Bytes," published by the Journal of the American Academy of Arts and Sciences, Fall 1996, as well as "Buildings, Books, and Bytes: Libraries and Communities in the Digital Age," published by the Benson Foundation in Washington, DC (www.benson.org) 877-2-BENTON. More information is available on the Benson Foundation's Web site, under the "What's Working in Libraries Page" at http://www.benton.org/Practice/Libraries/home.html

The Benson report ends with this summary:

> Americans continue to have a love affair with their libraries, but they have difficulty figuring out where libraries fit in the new digital world. And many Americans would just as soon turn their local libraries into museums and recruit retirees to staff them. Libraries are thus at a crossroads, for they must adjust their traditional values and services to the digital age. But there is good reason for optimism as libraries and their communities take up this challenge.

2

Selected Supersources

The Cream of the Crop

The resources described in this chapter are the cream of the information-source crop. They range from museums to the federal government to bookstores to other storehouses of information, but they all have a few things in common. Each contains information on an enormous scope of subjects. Each can easily be tapped for answers and advice. And each provides answers either for no charge or for dirt cheap.

✔ Source: Associations

Perhaps the single best resource discussed in this book, associations offer a bountiful harvest of information. They are staffed by knowledgeable and helpful people whose job is to provide information about their field to those who need it.

There are thousands of associations, one for nearly every conceivable purpose and field of interest: the Chocolate Manufacturers Association of the U.S.A., the International Barbed Wire Collectors Association, the Laughter Therapy Association, the American Association for Career Education, the Committee to Abolish Legal Sized Files, the Tin Research Institute, even the Flying Funeral Directors of America—for funeral directors who own and operate their own planes. And naturally there is the Star

> **TIP:** Sometimes associations produce reports and studies that are of interest to researchers. However, these can be expensive to purchase, and you may only need a single statistic or data from just a portion of the study. Try contacting either the association's library or, if the association publishes a magazine, the publication's editor. Sometimes the staffers at those departments won't mind finding the report and reading you the significant information you need. (Staff in marketing or publications-ordering departments may only agree to sell you the entire study.)

Trek Welcommittee—an association whose reason for being is to answer fans' questions about the *Star Trek* TV series.

Associations have helped me out more times than I can remember. A couple of occasions stand out: One time I needed to find out the "average life of a flag." Well, naturally a group called the North American Vexillological (a fancy word for the study of flags!) Association had the answer. (Flag life depends on the material and height flown.) Another time, a city agency was seeking advice on how to stop the local water pipes from leaking. To the rescue with an answer was the American Water Works Association, of Denver, Colorado.

Associations can also be a quick source of industry statistics and news. For example, if you want to find out how the sales of potatoes were last year, you need only inquire of the Potato Association of America or, if you prefer, the National Potato Promotion Board.

How to Find:

To find the name of an association that deals with your area of interest, call or write to the American Society of Association Executives (an association of associations!) at 1575 I Street, NW, Washington, DC 20005; 202-626-2723, and it will help identify the right one for you. You can also search the association's Web site of its members at: http://www.asaenet.org. Or look up your subject in the priceless *Encyclopedia of Associations*, published by Gale. Nearly all libraries have it. (Gale publishes companion volumes on international organizations, as well as local and regional associations.)

Often, the *Encyclopedia of Associations* lists more than one association that sounds promising. In such cases, try contacting the largest one first, as it will most likely have the most resources

annual; (3) IFTF Perspectives (newsletter), irregular; also publishes papers and research reports.

★5851★ WORLD FUTURE SOCIETY (WFS)
4916 St. Elmo Ave.   Phone: (301) 656-8274
Bethesda, MD 20814   Edward S. Cornish, Pres.
Founded: 1966. **Members:** 30,000. **Staff:** 20. **Local Groups:** 80. Individuals interested in forecasts and ideas about the future. Formed "to contribute to a reasoned awareness of the future and the importance of its study, without advocating particular ideologies or engaging in political activities; to advance responsible and serious investigation of the future and to promote development of methods for the study of the future; to facilitate communication among groups and individuals interested in studying or planning for the future." Is developing services for professional forecasters and planners, including a register, special studies sections, and professional activities. Offers chapter activities in various U.S. cities as well as in Toronto, ON, Canada and London, England; sponsors book service; maintains library; offers specialized education service. **Publications:** (1) Future Survey, monthly; (2) The Futurist, bimonthly; (3) Futures Research Quarterly; also publishes books and Resource Catalog. **Convention/Meeting:** biennial - 1985 Aug. 8-9, Washington, DC.

★5852★ WORLD FUTURES STUDIES FEDERATION (WFSF)
2424 Maile Way, Office 720
University of Hawaii   Phone: (808) 948-6601
Honolulu, HI 96822   James A. Dator, Sec.Gen.
Founded: 1973. **Members:** 521. Institutions, scholars, policymakers, and individuals involved in futures studies. Promotes futures studies and innovative interdisciplinary analyses. Serves as a forum for the exchange of information and opinions through national and international research projects. Conducts regional colloquia and seminars. Maintains extensive collection of correspondence, monographs, serials, audiovisual materials, and books on social, political, economic, and environmental futures-related topics. **Publications:** (1) Newsletter, quarterly; (2) World Conference Proceedings, biennial; also publishes seminar papers. **Convention/Meeting:** biennial - next 1986.

★5853★ AMERICAN SOCIETY OF GAS ENGINEERS (ASGE)
P.O. Box 936   Phone: (312) 532-5707
Tinley Park, IL 60477   Charles R. Kendall, Exec.Dir.
Founded: 1954. **Members:** 600. **Local Groups:** 10. Professional society of engineers in the field of gas appliances and equipment. **Publications:** (1) Digest, quarterly; (2) Membership Directory, annual. **Formerly:** (1975) Gas Appliance Engineers Society. **Convention/Meeting:** annual technical conference.

INSTITUTE OF GAS TECHNOLOGY
See Index

★5854★ AMERICAN GENETIC ASSOCIATION (Genetics) (AGA)

Urbana, IL.

★5857★ NATIONA
(NCGR)
2855 Telegraph Ave
Berkeley, CA 94705
Founded: 1980. St
and professional or؟
conservation and u؛
resource conservaؤ
information, techni
diversity of geneti
microorganisms reqؤ
the problems, issues
use of genetic resou
continues, the U.S.
quality of life due
pharmaceutical and
including the producti
to initiate statewide
publish newsletter,
Committees: Adviso
Resources; Douglas·
Programs: California

TOMATO GENETICS
See Index

★5858★ U.S. AN
P.O. Box 15426
San Francisco, CA ؟
Founded: 1972. S
the encouragemen
documentation sta
distinctive genetic
and cell samples
nitrogen. Offers
18,000 volume ؛
Review. Publicaؤ
Register, quarterly

GEOCHEMISTRY
See Geoscience

★5859★ AMERIC
156 Fifth Ave., Suiؤ
New York, NY 100ۀ
Founded: 1852.
educators, and otؤ
research in geograؤ
sponsored research

to help you. To compare the size of different associations, examine the published data on the size of the association's staff and the number of members. Many libraries often contain the companion volumes to the *Encyclopedia of Associations—International Associations* and *State and Regional Associations*.

✔ Source: Conventions

Every day, hundreds of conventions and professional conferences are held around the country—the National Accounting Expo, the American Academy of Sports Physicians, the Beekeepers Convention, and the Nuclear Power Expo, to name a few. Conventions are especially good sources of information on fast-changing subjects like computer technology. The seminars and talks presented at these conventions reflect the state of the art in a profession or field. Often brand-new products are displayed and groundbreaking research is presented.

How to Find:

Consult the *Directory of Conventions* (Successful Meetings, New York City) found at large libraries. Or check an "upcoming events" column in a relevant trade publication. (I recently found the convention I needed on computer printers by consulting a popular computer magazine's "events to watch" column.) Another way to find a convention on your subject is to find an association. Nearly all associations hold conventions.

Typically, two major activities take place at such conventions: technical presentations by authorities in the field and product exhibits by vendors who set up booths to try to sell their wares to conference attendees. Although it is often inexpensive or free to visit the exhibition hall, it may run into the hundreds of dollars to sign up for the technical information sessions. However, there is a way you can tap into the information presented there without actually attending.

Here is the secret to tapping into convention information. If you find a convention that interests you, write and request a free "preliminary program." These programs typically describe the technical seminars to be held at the convention and provide the names and affiliations of the speakers or panelists. These speakers are excellent people to speak with to obtain information.

Here's an example of how I utilized this strategy. Once I had to research the subject of asbestos removal from school building insulation. I discovered that a convention of school administrators was being held the following month in Texas. Although I could not attend the convention, I wrote away for the preliminary program. Inside the program, I spotted a description of a planned technical session on asbestos removal. The description included the name of the speaker and the name of his school district. It was then an easy matter to contact that person to set up an information interview. I was then able to obtain his expertise and information for free instead of paying hundreds of dollars to hear him speak.

It's worth noting that programs from past conventions as well as for upcoming ones are often available.

Another way to obtain convention information without actually attending is to request a "conference proceedings," a transcript of the technical sessions published after the conference is over. Conference proceedings vary in cost and occasionally are expensive. Sometimes conference organizers make portions of the proceedings available on a Web site.

If you are interested in actually attending a conference in your area, call your city's convention and visitors bureau or the Chamber of Commerce. They should be able to provide you with a list of upcoming conventions.

✔ Source: Scientific Honor Society (Sigma Xi)

If you have a scientific question for which you need to get a quick answer, the Media Research Service of the Scientific Honor Society may be able to help you. The service can handle just about any scientific inquiry—from toxic wastes to cancer treatments. They've even answered the question as to whether it really is ever hot enough to fry an egg on the sidewalk! (It is possible—depending not only on the temperature but the construction of the sidewalk.) Although the center is designed to serve journalists, the staff will help other researchers as well.

How to Find:
Contact the Scientific Honor Society at P.O. Box 13975, Research Triangle, NC 27709; 800-223-1730.

✔ Source: New York Public Library

The New York Public Library is a tremendous source of all kinds of information. The library's **mid-Manhattan branch** is especially rich in information and regularly answers reference inquiries from around the country. Its collections include the fields of art, business, education, history, literature and language, and science. In addition, it contains an extensive picture collection. Other specialties of the New York Public Library include the Schomburg Center for Research in Black Culture, the Early Childhood Resource and Information Center, and the Job Information Center. There is also the **Performing Arts Research Center**, which answers written or phone inquiries regarding music, dance, and theater at no charge. (Because the New York Public Library handles so many requests, you may have to be patient if you telephone and get a busy signal.)

How to Find:

Contact the mid-Manhattan branch at 455 Fifth Avenue, New York, NY 10016; 212-340-0849. Contact the Performing Arts Research Center at the New York Public Library, 40 Lincoln Plaza, New York, NY 10023; free reference numbers are as follows: dance, 212-870-1657; music, 212-870-1650; theater, 212-870-1639; Rogers & Hammerstein sound, 212-870-1633; Film & Tape, 212-870-1633. For other questions contact the library's public relations office at 8 West 40th Street, New York, NY 10018; 212-221-7676. On the Web: http://www.nypl.org

Pages 61–73 list some of the best and most widely used government information sources. Be sure to read through chapter 3 for details on many more resources available from various federal agencies.

✔ Source: Library of Congress

The U.S. Library of Congress in Washington, DC, is the largest library in the world. Its collection includes 20 million volumes and pamphlets, over a million technical reports, 3.5 million maps, 34 million manuscripts, and 8.5 million photographs, negatives, prints, and slides. The library is also known for its collection of rare books and foreign publications. It sometimes can be tricky to use the Library of Congress' vast resources—not only because there is so much information available, but also because the library's policy discourages phone reference usage by the public when materials are available on a more local level. However, it will assist users when it can help in researching topics unique to the library. Some of these areas include copyright, legislative research, and international law.

One division that may be of help is the library's Telephone Reference Service. If the librarian has time, he or she will try to locate any obscure fact or piece of information that you have been unable to find elsewhere.

If you have an Internet connection, be sure to check out the Library of Congress's Web site, too. There you can conduct an online search of its catalog, learn more about its holdings, view digitized collections in its digital library exhibits, and much more.

How to Find:
You can contact the library's Telephone Reference Service at the Correspondence Section of the Library of Congress, Washington, DC 20540; 202-707-5522. On the Web: http://www.loc.gov

Another excellent resource is the Library of Congress' photo-duplication service. The service will search the library's books, technical reports, maps, manuscripts, and photographic materials to find what you need, and send you photocopies. Turnaround time can run from four to six weeks, but you can't beat the price—you pay only for photocopying, copyright fees, and postage ($10 minimum charge).

How to Find:
Contact the Library of Congress, 101 Independence Ave SE, Photoduplication Service, Washington, DC 20540; 202-707-5640.

A very useful and interesting publication series of the Library of Congress is its *LC Science Tracer Bullets*. These are 12- to 16-page pamphlets covering popular science–oriented topics that identify key information sources, such as introductory textbooks, general books, conference proceedings, government publications, journals, articles, technical books, associations, and more. Subjects have included *Japanese Technology, Inventions and Inventors*; *The History of Technology*; and *Fiber Optics*.

How to Find:

Contact the Library of Congress, Science Reference Section, Science and Technology Division, 10 First Street SE, Washington, DC 20540; 202-707-5522.

Finally, there is the Library of Congress' Performing Arts Library. The Library will try to answer, at no cost, any question regarding the performing arts—dance, music, theater, motion pictures, broadcasting, puppetry, circus, costuming, stage sets, and arts management and administration.

How to Find:

Contact the Performing Arts Reading Room, 101 Independence Ave. SE, Madison Building, Washington, DC 20540; 202-707-5507.

You can keep up with some of the Library of Congress' publishing activities by obtaining a catalog called *New from CDS*, which is the Library of Congress' Cataloging Distribution Service.

How to Find:

Contact the Library of Congress, Cataloging Distribution Service, Washington, DC 20541; 202-707-6100.

TIP: England's equivalent to the Library of Congress is the British Library, with millions of documents ranging from books and maps to worldwide conference proceedings to sheet music from around the globe. The time span of coverage ranges from the first items printed with movable type before 1501 to the present. Much of this invaluable material is available online or through an intercountry lending system. This is truly one of the world's great depositories of information.

Contact the British Library Document Supply Centre, Boston Spa, Wetherby, West Yorkshire, LS23 7BQ, United Kingdom. Phone: 44-1-937-546049; fax: 44-1-937-546333. On the Web: http://www.bl.uk/services/bsds/dsc/delivery.html

---

✔ **Source: Library Home Pages**

As we discuss in chapter 5, which is devoted specifically to the Internet, one of the biggest and ongoing frustrations for searchers is information overload. An excellent cure is to link to a library home page—many have done outstanding jobs of locating, organizing, describing, and making easily available some of the best

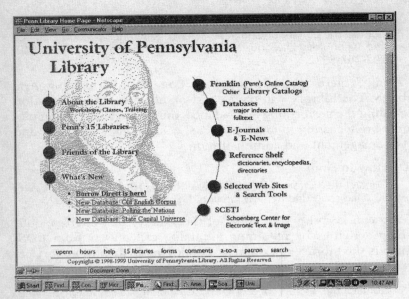

http://www.library.upenn.edu/

This home page from the library at the University of Pennsylvania is an example of the kinds of digital resources that libraries filter and collect for its users.

kinds of sources and sites on the Web. Linking to a top-notch library's Web site can be an excellent first stop on your journey onto the Internet.

How to Find:

There are hundreds, if not thousands, of libraries that have created excellent home pages to collect and sort Web sites. In addition to the Library of Congress, another very well known one is the New York Public Library's site at http://www.nypl.org. You will probably also have good luck by connecting to the home page of any of the major national universities. For example, I've always liked the University of Pennsylvania's home page at http://www.library.upenn.edu/. However, you may find that your nearby local library has a home page that has done a fine job as well. To find links to hundreds of library home pages around the country, see the sites listed in chapter 1, "Libraries."

One caution: if you link to a library site that you are not affiliated with, there will likely be a few restrictions on what you can use.

Subject Bibliography Index

Typically, though all the Web links and access to certain e-journals and texts may be available, you're unlikely to be able to search any fee-based databases.

✔ **Source: Government Printing Office (GPO)**

The U.S. government is the largest publisher in the world. A mind-boggling amount of information pours out of Washington, DC, daily. Tens of thousands of books, pamphlets, and magazines are published each year by federal departments and agencies. Topics span nearly all areas of human endeavor from starting a business to finding a mortgage to getting rid of acne. Documents are typically concise and very readable, and they are specifically aimed at the general, nontechnical public. They are prepared by experts in the various federal departments and agencies whose job is to keep the public informed. Best of all, the information is free or dirt cheap. The only caution in using these documents is to check the issue dates. Although many documents are timely and up to date, sometimes older ones are offered, too.

There are a number of ways to dig out the publications on your subject of interest. One way is to contact a specific department directly. Chapter 3 lists many of the information specialties of the departments and provides addresses and phone numbers.

A typical approach to finding government documents available from the GPO is through consulting *The Monthly Catalog of U.S. Government Publications*. Use the subject index in the back of each volume to identify published literature on your topic of interest. Each listing provides helpful information, such as the office that issued the document, the price, and ordering instructions. You can obtain monthly catalogs directly from the Superintendent of Documents or at a medium-size or large library.

A simpler and quicker way to find publications directly available from the GPO is to order its *Subject Bibliography Index*. The index is a listing of 240 major subject categories for which specific catalogs of bibliographies have been created. The index represents over 15,000 different pamphlets, booklets, guides, and periodicals. You circle which bibliography you'd like to get and send in the form, and the information is then sent to you, along with price information.

TIPS: Government Depository Libraries and Bookstores
• There are 1,400 designated libraries around the United States that are legally required to store government documents and provide the public with free access. Ask the Government Printing Office to send you a free "Government Depository Library" directory, which tells where these libraries are located, what kinds of documents they store, and how to use them.
• You can also ask for a listing of GPO bookstores, which are government bookstores located in most major cities. These carry the most popular of the government's published materials.

How to Find:

Contact the Superintendent of Documents, U.S. Government Printing Office, Washington, DC 20402; 202-512-1800. The GPO takes MasterCard or Visa telephone orders and checks payable to Superintendent of Documents, Government Printing Office. To order a catalog, write to the Superintendent of Documents, Box 371954, Pittsburgh, PA 15250-7954. On the Web: http://www.access.gpo.gov

✔ Source: Bureau of the Census

Do you want to know which neighborhoods have the highest concentration of elderly people? How many men in Latin America own TV sets? Which sections of Wyoming are the wealthiest?

The U.S. Bureau of the Census can supply you with figures on these and countless other data-oriented questions. Major areas covered include agriculture, business, construction, foreign nations, foreign trade, geography, governments, housing, manufacturing, mineral industries, people, retail trade, service industries, and transportation.

You can obtain a listing of the names of subject data experts at the bureau and their phone numbers by ordering an especially

---

TIP: Using census information can be a fairly complex and technical matter, and can be confusing for people who are not used to working with all of the data series, tables, etc., published by the Bureau. If you think you may have a need to go very deep into census data, I highly recommend a book called *Understanding the Census*, by Michael R. Lavin, and published in 1996 by Epoch/Oryx.

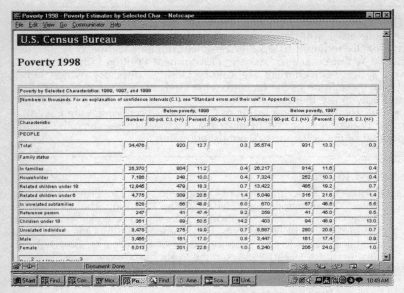

http://www.census.gov/hhes/poverty/poverty98/pv98est1.html

This detailed chart examining the characteristics of persons in poverty in the U.S. is one of countless free tables and data series available from the Bureau of the Census Web site.

useful and free pamphlet, "Telephone Contacts for Data Users." This publication will tell you, for example, who the expert is for statistics on religion or for foreign-owned U.S. firms.

How to Find:

Contact the Customer Services Office, Bureau of the Census, Washington, DC 20233; 301-457-4100. Or call the Public Information Office at 301-457-3030.

Another excellent source is the *Census Catalog & Guide*. This is a clear and comprehensive 400-page book that lists and describes census products, services, and programs, and provides complete ordering information. A useful subject index and table of contents identify sources on topics including agriculture, business, foreign trade, population, transportation, and much more. Remember much of

Assistant Secretary for Public Affairs,* U.S. Dept. of Health and Human Services, Room 647-D, Humphrey Building, 200 Independence Avenue, S.W., Washington, D.C. 20201 Information: 202/245-1850. Locator: 202/245-6296

Administrator for Health Resources and Services, U.S. Dept. of Health and Human Services, 5600 Fishers Lane, Park Lawn Building 14-05, Rockville, MD 20857. Information: 301/443-2216. Publications: 301/443-2086

Alcohol, Drug Abuse, and Mental Health Administration, U.S. Dept. of Health and Human Services, 5600 Fishers Lane, Rm. 12C15, Rockville, MD 20857. Information/Publications: 301/443-3783. Alcohol: 301/443-4733. Drug Abuse: 301/443-6245. Mental Health: 301/443-4536 or 3600. Substance Abuse Prevention: 301/443-0373

Centers for Disease Control, U.S. Dept. of Health and Human Services, 1600 Clifton Road, N.E., Atlanta, GA 30329. Information: 404/639-3311. Public Affairs: 404/639-3286

Food and Drug Administration, U.S. Dept. of Health and Human Services, 5600 Fishers Lane, Rockville, MD 20857. Information: 301/443-2404. Publications: 301/443-3170

Health Care Financing Administration, U.S. Dept. of Health and Human Services, 330 Independence Avenue, S.W., Washington, D.C. 20201. Public Affairs: 202/245-6113. Publications: 301/597-2618

Health Resources and Services Administration, U.S. Dept. of Health and Human Services, 5600 Fishers Lane, Rockville, MD 20857. Public Affairs: 301/443-2086

Indian Health Service, Office of Tribal Affairs, U.S. Dept. of Health and Human Services, 5600 Fishers Lane, Room 6A-07, Rockville, MD 20857. Director's Office: 301/443-1083

National Center for Health Statistics, U.S. Dept. of Health and Human Services, 3700 East-West Highway, Hyattsville, MD 20782. Information: 301/436-8500

National Institutes of Health, U.S. Dept. of Health and Human Services, 9000 Rockville Pike, Bethesda, MD 20892. Information/Publications: 301/496-4000

Office of the Surgeon General, Office of Communications, 725 H, U.S. Dept. of Health and Human Services, 200 Independence Avenue, S.W., Washington, D.C. 20201. Information: 202/245-6867

Public Health Service,* Office of Public Affairs, Office of the Assistant Secretary, U.S. Dept. of Health and Human Services, 200 Independence Avenue, S.W., Washington, D.C. 20201. Public Affairs: 202/245-6867

Social Security Administration, U.S. Dept. of Health and Human Services, Office of Research and Statistics and International Policy, Room 912, Universal North Building, Publications: Room 209, 4301 Connecticut Avenue, N.W., Washington, D.C. 20008. Information/ Publications: 202/282-7138

Housing

Assistant Secretary for Community Planning/ Development, U.S. Dept. of Housing and Urban Development, 451 7th Street, S.W., Washington, D.C. 20410. Information: 202/755-6270

Assistant Secretary for Housing, U.S. Dept. of Housing and Urban Development, 451 7th Street, S.W., Washington, D.C. 20410. Information: 202/755-6600

Immigration

Immigration and Naturalization Service, U.S. Department of Justice, 425 I Street, N.W., Washington, D.C. 20536. Office of Information: 202/633-4316. Statistics Office: 202/633-3053

Income and Taxation

Internal Revenue Service, Statistics of Income Division, U.S. Dept. of Treasury, 1111 Constitution Avenue, N.W., Washington, D.C. 20224. Information/ Publications: 202/376-0216

Office of the Secretary, Public Affairs Office, U.S. Dept. of the Treasury, Room 1500, 15th Street and Pennsylvania N.W., Washington, D.C. 20220. Information: 202/566-2041

Office of Tax Analysis, U.S. Dept. of the Treasury, Room 4217, 15th Street and Pennsylvania Avenue, N.W., Washington, D.C. 20220. Information: 202/566-5374. Publications: 202/566-5282

International

United Nations, D.C. 2 1628, Statistical Office, United Nations, New York, NY 10017. Information: 212/754-4562

Labor and Employment

Bureau of Labor Statistics,* U.S. Dept. of Labor, Washington, D.C. 20212. Information/Publications: 202/523-1221. Locator: 202/523-6666. Latest BLS data: 202/523-9658. CPI detail: 202/523-1239. PPI detail: 202/523-1765

Employment and Training Administration, Office of Public Affairs, U.S. Dept. of Labor, 200 Constitution Avenue, N.W., Room S2322, Washington, D.C. 20210. Information/Publications: 202/523-6871

Miscellaneous

Commission on Civil Rights, 1121 Vermont Avenue, N.W., Washington, D.C. 20425. Locator: 202/376-8177

Executive Office of the President, Office of Management and Budget, Washington, D.C. 20503. Information: 202/395-3000.

Public Affairs: 202/395-3080. Publications: 202/395-7332

National Archives and Records Administration, 7th and Pennsylvania Avenue, N.W., Washington, D.C. 20408. Information/Locator: 202/523-3218

National Technical Information Service, U.S. Dept. of Commerce, 5285 Port Royal Road, Springfield, VA 22161. Information/Orders: 703/487-4650

Science and Technology

National Oceanic and Atmospheric Administration, Office of Public Affairs, U.S. Dept. of Commerce, Room 6013, 14th and Constitution Avenue, N.W., Washington, D.C. 20230. Information/ Publications: 202/377-8090

Energy Information Administration,* Nations Energy Information Center, EI-20, U.S. Dept. of Energy, 1000 Independence Avenue, S.W., Washington, D.C. 20585 General Information: 202/586-8800

Bureau of Mines, U.S. Dept. of the Interior, 4900 LaSalle Road, Avondale, MD 20782. Information: 301/436-7966

Office of Public Information, Bureau of Mines, U.S. Dept. of the Interior, 2401 E Street, N.W., Washington, D.C. 20241. Information: 202/634-1004

U.S. Geological Survey, Public Affairs Office U.S. Dept. of the Interior, 503 Nationa Center, Reston, VA 22092. Information/ Publications: 703/648-6892

National Science Foundation, Office of Legislative and Public Affairs, 1800 G Street, N.W., Washington, D.C. 20550. Information: 202/357-9498

Transportation

Federal Highway Administration, Office of Public Affairs, U.S. Dept. of Transportation, 400 7th Street, S.W., Room 4210, Washington, D.C. 20590. Information/Publications: 202/366-0660

Materials and Transportation Bureau, Information Services Division (BMT-11), Office of Operations/Enforcemen U.S. Dept. of Transportation, 400 7th Street, S.W., Washington, D.C. 20590 Information: 202/426-2301

National Highway Traffic Safety Administration, Office of Public Affair U.S. Dept. of Transportation, 400 7th Street, S.W., Washington, D.C. 20590. Information: 202/366-9550

Urban Mass Transportation Administration, Public Affairs Office, U.S. Dept. of Transportation, 400 7th Street, S.W., Room 9328, Washington, D.C. 20590. Information: 202/366-4040

Veterans

Veterans Administration, 810 Vermont Avenue, N.W., Washington, D.C. 2042u. Information: 202/233-2563

Census Catalog & Guide, "Federal Government Statistical Sources"

the Bureau of the Census' products and services are free or inexpensive. An excerpt from an earlier edition of the catalog's list of sources for statistics within the federal government is on page 69.

How to Find:
Available from the Superintendent of Documents, U.S. Government Printing Office, Washington, DC 20402; 202-512-1800. On the Web: http://www.access.gpo.gov/su_docs

Finally, you should know that during the last few years the Bureau of the Census has been making quite an effort to transfer much of its data onto the Internet. The biggest drive has been to put Census information up on the World Wide Web, virtually all at no cost to the user. You can link to the bureau's home page at http://www.census.gov

Because the bureau has been making such an effort to put most of its data and series onto the Internet, it has established several sites as clearinghouses to assist searchers in quickly locating what they need. Here are the sites to check:

- **The American FactFinder**
  http://factfinder.census.gov

  A single source for broad-based access to virtually all of the bureau's information, including access to the full data from the full census taken every ten years. Also includes tables, maps and "quick reports."

- **Population Publications and Documents**
  http://www.census.gov/prod/www/abs/popula.html

  This site summarizes what's available from the Bureau specifically related to population and demographic data

- **Mapping Information**
  http://www.census.gov/ftp/pub/geo/www/tiger/tigermap.html
  and http://www.census.gov/datamap/www

  The first site is a good starting point to review the various mapping applications available from the bureau, and the latter lets you click on a state to obtain key data on counties in that state.

✔ **Source: Statistical Abstract of the United States**

The bible for statistics of all types is the *Statistical Abstract of the United States*, published annually. The kinds of statistical data you can find in this guide are extremely diverse—the number of eye operations performed, murder victims by weapons used, consumer price indexes, new business failure rates, retail sales of men's fragrances, pottery imports, railroad accidents, consumption of ice cream, and much more.

This book is the standard summary of statistics on the social, political, and economic organization of the United States. Major sections include population; vital statistics; immigration and naturalization; health and nutrition; education; law enforcement; courts and prisons; geography and environment; parks and recreation; elections; state and local government finances and employment; federal government finances and employment; national defense; veterans' affairs; social insurance and human services; labor force, employment, and earnings; income expenditure and wealth; banking, finance, and insurance; business enterprise; communications; energy; science; transportation; agriculture; forests and forest products; fisheries; mining and mineral products; construction and housing; manufacturers; and comparative international statistics.

How to Find:

You can order this guide from the Superintendent of Documents, Box 371954, Pittsburgh, PA 15250-7954; 202-512-1800. Or you can find a copy at GPO bookstores and at nearly all libraries. You can also find at least some summary material from the *Statistical Abstract* on the Web by linking to http://www.census.gov:80/stat_abstract

✔ **Source: United States General Accounting Office (GAO)**

The United States GAO is an independent, nonpolitical agency that serves as the investigative agency for Congress and carries out investigations and makes recommendations. The GAO publishes findings in reports and testimony transcripts that are available to the public for free. These reports cover fields such as education, health, housing, justice, defense, technology, and more. Past reports have included "Air Pollution: Uncertainty Exists in Radon

Measurements," "Hazardous Wastes: Contractors Should Be Accountable for Environmental Performance," "Failed Thrifts: The Resolution Trust Corporation's Working Capital Needs," "Medical Device Recalls: An Overview and Analysis, 1983–1988," "In-Home Services for the Elderly," and "Non-Traditional Organized Crime."

How to Find:

Requests for copies of GAO reports and testimony are available from the U.S. General Accounting Office, Box 37050, Washington DC 20013; 202-512-6000. On the Web: http://www.gao.gov

✔ Source: State Government

Your state government can be an excellent resource for a variety of topics. Subject expertise varies from state to state, but typically you can find information on most of these topics:

Aeronautics	Environment
Aging	Fish and game
Agriculture	Food
Air resources	Handicapped
Alcoholism	Hazardous materials
Archives	Health
Arts	Highways
Banking	Housing
Child labor	Labor
Child welfare	Land
Commerce	Mental health
Consumer affairs	Natural resources
Criminal justice	Occupational safety
Civil rights	Parks and recreation
Community affairs	Taxation
Disabled	Tourism
Disaster preparedness	Transportation
Drug abuse	Veterinary medicine
Economic opportunity	Water resources
Education	Women
Energy	

> **TIP: Consumer and Legal Advice**
> • Your state attorney general's office can answer many questions about your legal rights as a citizen of your state. Typical questions handled by this office relate to subjects like tenant-landlord disputes, buying a car, mail-order fraud, investment fraud, and so forth. The expertise of this office varies from state to state. Check the blue pages in the phone book under "State Government" to locate the address and phone of your state's attorney general.

How to Find:

Consult a library copy of the *State Executive Directory*, published by Carroll Publishing Company. This guide provides a detailed listing of the various offices in each state and a listing of state personnel names, titles, and phone numbers. A subject index makes it easy to locate who in your state can be of assistance to you. (This directory also lists state historic preservation offices and legislative reference numbers.) You'll find the directory at large libraries. Or check the name of the state in your phone book to find the division you need (in many cities, government listings are separated into a special blue-pages section).

You can also find state related information on the Web by linking to the National Association of State Information Resource Executives' "StateSearch" site, which is a topical clearinghouse to state government on the Net. Link to http://www.nasire.org/stateSearch/

✔ Source: College and University Faculty Experts

College and university faculty members can provide information on topics ranging from architecture to international relations as well as other subjects taught at academic institutions. A computer database established in 1993 at the State University of New York (SUNY) in Stony Brook is a network of college public information officers located at over 300 campuses around the country. It was established to serve as a clearinghouse of over 300,000 faculty.

Journalists, writers, those in the media and credentialed researchers can contact ProfNet to pose a question for the faculty experts. For example, not too long ago, a reporter from *The New York Times* used the network to try to locate an expert on computers and children. Another use was by a *Boston Globe* staffer who was looking for someone on the forefront of research in electric vehicles. ProfNet is free for qualified users, but fee based for others.

How to Find:

You can call ProfNet toll-free at 800-PROF-NET. It is also available on the Internet at http://www.profnet.com. Or e-mail to profnet@profnet.com

✔ **Source: Doctoral Dissertations**

An unusual but potentially very valuable source of information is published and unpublished doctoral dissertations. These may provide you with information unavailable elsewhere.

How to Find:

You can locate dissertations on your subject by contacting Bell & Howell Information and Learning in Ann Arbor, Michigan. Through a computerized system called Datrix II, this firm can search more than 500,000 dissertations to find one that covers your subject of interest. If any are located, a copy can be sent to you directly. A modest fee is charged for the service. University Microfilms can also send you a subject index of its dissertations. Contact them at 300 North Zeeb Road, Ann Arbor, MI 48106; 800-521-0600.

Note that there is a movement afoot to have students load their dissertations directly onto the Web in order to provide greater dissemination of their works, to help them possibly earn money from royalties, and to make searching for completed dissertations easier. For more information, see the Networked Digital Library of Theses and Dissertations at http://www.theses.org

✔ **Source: Museums**

There are museums for loads of topics—antiques, whaling, theater, and much more—and many museums have libraries that take written and telephone inquiries on subjects in their specialty areas. For example, the Museum of Radio and Television in New York City, which has a holding of over 40,000 radio and television programs and advertising broadcasts, will tackle any information query relating to a broadcasting matter. Questions it has handled include who produced *The Ed Sullivan Show* and when did the *I Love Lucy* show premiere. You can contact the museum at 25 West 52nd Street, New York, NY 10019; 212-621-6600. The staff takes research questions by fax, Tuesdays–Friday from 10:30–11:30 A.M. and from 4:00–6:00 P.M.

at 212-621-6632. And the museum is open to the public. (P.S. Marlo Lewis coproduced *The Ed Sullivan Show* along with Ed Sullivan himself in the 1950s. *I Love Lucy* premiered October 15, 1951, on CBS.)

TIP:
To find an actual video of a broadcast (and not just a written transcript), contact Vanderbilt University's Television Archives, which contains over 23,000 evening news broadcasts and 8,000 other news-oriented videos. Call 615-322-2927, or search its index on the Web at http://tvnews.vanderbilt.edu

---

How to Find:

To find a museum that matches your subject of interest, take a look at the *Official Museum Directory*, which lists 7,000 institutions. These include art, history, nature, and science museums, as well as more specialized museums—museums of agriculture, antiques, architecture, audiovisual materials and film, the circus, clocks and watches, electricity, fire fighting, forestry, furniture, guns, hobbies, industry, logging and lumber, mining, money and numismatics, musical instruments, philately, religion, scouting, sports, technology, theater, toys and dolls, transportation, typography, whaling, and woodcarving.

The directory provides the museum's name, address, phone number, officers, collections, research fields, facilities, activities, and publications. It's published by the R. R. Bowker Co., New Providence, New Jersey, and can be found at many libraries.

One museum with extensive resources on a number of different subjects is the Smithsonian Institution in Washington, DC. Its specialties include art, history, air and space, zoology, horticulture, and marine life. You can pose a question on any of these or related topics, and the museum will try to answer it. The service is free. Write to the Smithsonian Institution, Washington, DC 20560.

✔ Source: Specialized Bookstores

The Yellow Pages of some of the larger cities group bookstores into specific subject areas. For example, if you get hold of a copy of New York City's Yellow Pages (check any large library), you'll see bookstores devoted solely to art and sculpture, astrology, automobiles, China, cooking, health and nutrition, the occult, philosophy, religion, science fiction, theater, travel, and women.

Remember, too, that the people who work at these bookstores are good sources of information themselves.

✔ Source: Private Companies

One last "everything" source to keep in mind: private companies. Sometimes firms publish free pamphlets and guides related to their industry or products. For example, Prudential-Bache offices offer free advice on money management; Evenflo (Ravenna, Ohio), a maker of products for babies, provides free information and advice to expectant mothers about exercise, nutrition, and child care; and Delsey Luggage (Jessup, Maryland) provides tips on proper packing. Try to identify large firms that sell a product or service related to your subject. You may then want to call the public affairs department of these firms to inquire whether any free materials are available.

Also, individuals who work at companies can naturally be excellent persons to interview on their subjects of expertise. See chapters 6 through 8 on finding and interviewing experts for more information.

✔ Source: Advertisements

Granted, it's an offbeat idea, but one worth considering—especially if other sources don't pan out. Place an advertisement and describe as specifically as possible what kind of information you're looking for and why. (You sometimes see such ads as "author's queries" in popular book review sections.) You may be pleasantly surprised at the response you receive—people do like to help! A friend of mine placed an ad in a large city newspaper requesting input from collectors of "snow dome" paperweights, and she received about 50 responses!

If you've found a trade publication covering your subject, try placing the ad there so that you can reach a specific audience. Otherwise, a daily newspaper is fine, and the bigger the better.

Ads can be an especially good way to find out if anyone has information on a particular person or to find users of a product or customers of a firm.

And if you're hooked to the Internet, you can post your request to a relevant electronic discussion group, which may prove to be even more fruitful—and free! (See chapter 5 for more details.)

3

The U.S. Government
Mining for Information Nuggets

The U.S. government is a gold mine of information. Although many government publications and services have been eliminated during the last few years, an awesome amount of advice, data, and information is still available—and is becoming easier to find, in most cases, because of the Internet, as discussed further. The expertise is all there for the taking—if you know how to find what you need.

Because the government is so huge, it is impossible to describe in a single chapter (or book, for that matter) anywhere near the full amount of information available. However, to give you a feel for what's available, this chapter lists some of the most popular and helpful information sources and provides you with a head start on digging out information from each of the 13 U.S. departments (Department of Justice, Department of Transportation, and so on) and a select number of the government's smaller independent agencies (Federal Communications Commission, Environmental Protection Agency, and so on).

Quick Subject Look-up Reference

For information on	*Check*
Agriculture	Department of Agriculture
Air travel/flight	National Aeronautics and Space Administration
Arts and literature	National Foundation on the Arts/ National Endowment for the Arts

Astronomy	National Aeronautics and Space Administration
Broadcasting	Federal Communications Commission
Business	Small Business Administration; see also chapter 4, "Business Information"
Consumer information	General Services Administration; Consumer Product Safety Commission; Department of Health and Human Services; Federal Trade Commission
Crime	Department of Justice
Education	Department of Education
Energy	Department of Energy
Engineering	Department of Commerce/ National Bureau of Standards
Environment	Environmental Protection Agency; Department of Commerce/National Oceanic and Atmospheric Administration
Food and nutrition	Department of Agriculture
Foreign affairs	Department of State
Health and medicine	Department of Health and Human Services
Housing and real estate	Department of Housing and Urban Development
Humanities	National Endowment for the Humanities
International affairs	Department of State; Department of Defense
Labor and employment	Department of Labor
Minority concerns	Department of Commerce; Department of Education; Department of the Interior; Department of Housing and Urban Development
Natural disasters	Federal Emergency Management Agency
Natural resources	Department of the Interior
Taxes	Department of Justice
Transportation	Department of Transportation
Travel	Department of State

TIP: Guides to Government Information
• If you want to get a much fuller understanding of the structure and offices of the federal government, I'd recommend you check out some of the special publications described at the end of this chapter. These are specifically designed to provide detailed listings of government offices and to examine their organizational structure.

TIP: Government Phone Information

• Because personnel and departments in Washington often change, it's very possible that some of the phone numbers listed below will be outdated by the time you read this. If you dial a number that is no longer accurate, simply call 202-555-1212 and ask the operator to give you the "locator" telephone number for the specific department you are trying to reach.

THE U.S. FEDERAL GOVERNMENT AND THE INTERNET

Until the mid-1990s, the best way to find out what information the U.S. government made available would have been to order one of its print-based subject bibliographies, check one of its regular subscription series, or search a CD-ROM. While these are still options, these days your best bet is to go directly to the Web.

In fact, the U.S. government has been something of a leader in the Internet publishing arena. There are several reasons why the federal government has been doing so much here. A key mandate of governmental agencies is not only to carry out their assigned mission, but also to make their findings, materials, and expertise easily accessible to the public. And what other medium can reach so many people, so easily, and, importantly for the government, so inexpensively—there are no printing or mailing costs on the Web! And, Web sites can be updated in a flash. This is particularly helpful when dealing with time-sensitive data that is released on a regular schedule, such as economic news like the unemployment rate, or newly released census data.

So the federal government has wholeheartedly embraced this new media as the preferred way to carry out its mandate of information dissemination. For this reason, a good part of this chapter focuses specifically on the Web.

We have, in fact, broken this chapter into three sections:

1. Clearinghouses of federal information on the Web
2. Individual department and agency resources—print, phone, and Web
3. Print reference sources for locating federal information

One other important point should be made regarding governmental information and the Internet. While it's true that the U.S. government is rapidly "going Web" it has not—at least not yet—abandoned its traditional methods of disseminating information. So, for those of you who are not online, or do not feel completely comfortable on the Net, you still have other options for locating governmental data. One of the most important and valuable of these are the governmental depository library. There are 1,400 such libraries around the country, which are legally required to store government documents and provide the public with free access.

Note that one of the best government sources of information is the U.S. Bureau of the Census. Its publications and data offerings were covered in chapter 2.

CLEARINGHOUSES OF FEDERAL INFORMATION ON THE WEB

The following sites were established by the government to help researchers find what they need. Because there are several of these, I have added a "Recommended Use" section below to give my view on when its best to choose each particular resource.

✔ **Source: FedStats**

http://www.fedstats.gov

This site provides links to the over 70 agencies in the United States federal government that produce statistics. The site is maintained by the Federal Interagency Council on Statistical Policy. It also includes state, county, and local statistics. You can browse or search by title/keywords or by fulltext. Nice features include advanced search capabilities and a very specific A–Z topic finder that lists topics from "acute conditions" (colds, influenza, etc.) to "weekly earnings."

Recommended Use: This site makes a very good choice when you specifically need statistical data from the government, and, because it allows for advanced searching, when you need to combine keywords to zero in on a specific statistic.

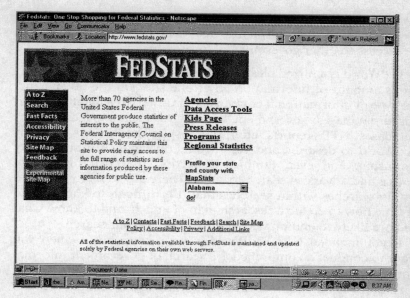

http://www.fedstats.gov

FedStats helps you locate U.S. federal government statistical data.

✔ **Source: FedWorld**

http://www.fedworld.gov

FedWorld is a service of the National Technical Information Service (NTIS) at the U.S. Department of Commerce. In the words of its creators, FedWorld has been designed to be "a comprehensive central access point for searching, locating, ordering, and acquiring government and business information." Included is both information housed within the NTIS repository and information via an electronic gateway to over 100 government-sponsored bulletin boards. On this site you can download chapters from the popular *U.S. Industry and Trade Outlook,* for $10–$25 per chapter, or order the entire book.

On this site, you'll also find:

- Reports from a number of agencies, ranging from army manuals to EPA Superfund studies.
- Access to both free and fee-based searchable databases from a couple dozen agencies.

- Web pages from government agencies.
- Links to the government's own searchable Web sites; and access to other governmental locator sites.

FedWorld is a mixed blessing. On one hand, it provides an enormous amount of information all at one site. On the other hand, the type of information it contains is so varied (free databases, fee-based databases, government Web pages, locator pages, agency databases, NTIS reports, etc.) that despite the obvious effort by FedWorld to describe and organize its offerings, it is still a very confusing, and even jumbled collection that can overwhelm novice and advanced searchers alike. There are so many searches within searches within searches that it is difficult to know ahead of time how to create a research plan of attack, and to know what you are likely to end up with once you begin your search.

Recommended Use: FedWorld is your best choice when you want to conduct a comprehensive search of government information, you have a narrowly defined topic, and you don't mind spending a good chunk of time navigating and searching the site.

✔ **Source: Government Printing Office: Superintendent of Documents Home Page**

http://www.access.gpo.gov (general page)
http://www.access.gpo.gov/su_docs/index.html (searchable page)

The mission of the Government Printing Office (GPO) is to inform the country by producing, procuring, and disseminating both printed and electronic publications of Congress, the executive departments, and agencies of the federal government. GPO sells approximately 12,000 different printed and electronic publications that originate in various government agencies. It also administers the depository library program (a list of depository libraries can be found at www.access.gpo.gov/su_docs/libpro.html).

GPO also provides online access to more than 70 databases of federal government publications, including the Congressional Record and the Federal Register. The most popular items available from the GPO include The Monthly Catalog of U.S. Government Publications, which, according to the GPO, is the most comprehensive listing of government publications issued by federal departments and agencies. Also available are: U.S. Government Books, which lists hundreds of best-selling titles, and New Books, a bimonthly list of all government publications placed on sale in the preceding two months. (These publications can be obtained by calling the Superintendent of Documents at 202-512-1800.)

You have several options on the GPO site: you can search government information databases, use various search tools, locate where to find information in federal depository libraries, and download federal agency files. Among the databases available for free searching are the Federal Register and the Commerce Business Daily.

Recommended Use: Searching for congressional and legislative data and locating popular governmental documents.

✔ **Source: GILS**

http://www.access.gpo.gov/su_docs/gils/gils.html

The Government Information Locator Service (GILS) is part of the Government Printing Office, and offers a method for identifying, locating, and describing publicly available federal information resources, including electronic information resources.

Recommended Use: Good for zeroing in on specific programs (as opposed to actual documents).

✔ **Source: Government Information Exchange**

http://www.info.gov

This General Services Administration site is an electronic equivalent to the traditional Federal Information Center program, which has been the long-time federal government phone program designed to help citizens find the correct government office. On this site you can find the right office by browsing or searching federal phone directories, locator lists, links to major Web pages, and subject lists. In addition to helping you find relevant federal offices, this site also assists the searcher in finding state and local government sites and official sites from countries around the world, as well as links to several major international organizations.

TIP: Four Popular and Free Government Databases
Four databases that are made available for free from the GPO are very popular among information gatherers. These are the Budget of the United States Government, the Commerce Business Daily, the Congressional Record, and the Federal Register.

Recommended Use: Has very useful finder tools that can identify the right person or department within the government.

The sites listed above are not the only places for locating government information on the Web. For example, there are several excellent "locator" sites established by entities other than the federal government. Most notable of these would be The Federal Web Locator, http://www.law.vill.edu/Fed-Agency/fedwebloc.html, another one-stop shopping site that contains links to scores of individual departments and agencies throughout the federal government; and the University of Michigan Documents Center, http://www.lib.umich.edu/libhome/Documents.center. This site not only provides links to the federal government, but to non-U.S. governments, international agencies, and state and local governments.

INDIVIDUAL DEPARTMENTS AND AGENCY RESOURCES—PRINT, PHONE, AND WEB

Departments

✔ **Department of Agriculture**
14th Street and Independence Avenue SW
Washington, DC 20250
Main number: 202-720-8732
Public affairs: 202-720-4623
Web site: http://web.fie.com/fedix/usda.html

Scope Includes

Animal and Plant Health
Consumer Affairs
Family Nutrition
Food Safety and Inspection
Human Nutrition
Veterinary Medicine

Rich Resources

The USDA's Cooperative State Research Education and Extension Service can provide you with information that links research, science, and technology to the needs of the people, where they live and work. There are more than 3,100 county offices located around the country.

Contact: USDA Extension Service, Washington, DC 20250; 202-720-4423 (to find a local office). Or check your phone book's government blue-page listing under "Agriculture."

The USDA's Food and Nutrition Information Center can provide you with information or educational materials on human nutrition and food. The center lends books and audiovisual materials to specified borrowers, makes photocopies of journal articles, and provides comprehensive reference services such as computer searches.

Contact: Food and Nutrition Information Center, National Agricultural Library, 10301 Baltimore Blvd., U.S. Department of Agriculture, Beltsville, MD 20705; 301-504-5755. Reference Desk: 301-504-5479.

The Human Nutrition Information Service will answer your questions about the nutrient composition of food—calories, fat content, vitamins and minerals, food consumption, and dietary levels of the population.

Contact: Human Nutrition Information Service, U.S. Department of Agriculture, Hyattsville, MD 20782; 301-734-8457.

The National Agricultural Library is a great information source. Its specialties include botany, poultry, forestry, veterinary medicine, chemistry, plant pathology, livestock, zoology, and general agriculture topics. The library provides reference service by mail or phone. You can request the "Bibliography Series" that lists topics on which bibliographic citations are available—"Indoor Gardening," "Pesticide Safety," "The U.S. Poultry Industry," and so on.

Contact: The National Agricultural Library, U.S. Department of Agriculture, 10301 Baltimore Blvd., Beltsville, MD 20705; 202-482-2000

✔ **Department of Commerce**
14th Street and Constitution Avenue NW
Washington, DC 20230
Main number: 202-482-2000
Public affairs: 202-482-3263
Free reference: 202-482-2161
Web site: http://www.doc.gov

Scope Includes

Business Outlook Analyses
Economic and Demographic Statistics
Engineering Standards
Imports and Exports
Minority-Owned Business
Patents and Trademarks
Technology
Travel
Weather and Atmosphere

Rich Resources

The Department of Commerce is filled with sources of information about business. Chapter 4, which is devoted to business information, discusses some of the best of these. Here are other offices of the department that provide helpful materials and assistance:

The Minority Business Development Agency provides business management and technical assistance for members of minorities. Personal counseling is available, sometimes for free. The main office will give you a regional location near you.

Contact: Minority Business Development Agency, U.S. Department of Commerce, Washington, DC 20230; 202-482-1936. On the Web: http://www.mbda.gov to find a local office.

The National Computer Systems Laboratory publishes free and inexpensive newsletters that examine computing issues that range from security to networks to buying software. It has a limited capacity for answering technical questions, however.

Contact: National Computer Systems Laboratory, 225-A31 Technology Building, National Bureau of Standards, Gaithersburg, MD 20899; 301-975-3587.

You can order a free guide listing the names of over 150 subject experts in the Department of Commerce. Areas of expertise include, for example, aerospace, biotechnology, economic affairs, environmental research, industry surveys, materials research, patents and trademarks, telecommunication, and much more. Order the list from the department's FlashFax service below.

Contact: Department of Commerce, 202-501-1191 (enter document number 1060).

The National Institute of Standards and Technology is devoted to the science of measurement and develops standards. It has a staff of experts in areas such as manufacturing engineering, chemical engineering, electronics, and electrical engineering. Also covered are radiation, building technology, applied mathematics, chemical physics, analytic chemistry, and computer science and technology. A good publication to get is "Co-operative Research Opportunities at NIST," which includes a directory that identifies the bureau's experts and gives their phone numbers.

Contact: U.S. Department of Commerce, National Institute of Standards and Technology, Research Information Center, Gaithersburg, MD 20899; 301-975-3052. On the Web: http://www.nist.gov

The National Oceanic and Atmospheric Administration will try to answer your questions about climate, earth and ocean sciences, the environment, and marine life. It will also refer you to other agencies and to published information.

Contact: NOAA Central Library, 1315 East-West Highway, Silver Spring, MD 20910; 301-713-2600.

✔ **Department of Defense**
OASD (PA) DPC
1400 Defense Pentagon
Room 1E757
Washington, DC 20301-1400
The Pentagon
Washington, DC 20301
Main number: 703-545-6700
Press/Public affairs: 703-697-5131
Web site: http://www.defenselink.mil

Scope Includes

Atomic Energy
Foreign Country Security
Mapping
Military History
Nuclear Operations and Technology
Tactical Warfare

Rich Resources

The Department of Defense publishes about 150 "foreign area studies," which are in-depth studies of a particular country's social, economic, political, and military organization and are revised every three to five years. These are clothbound books, usually a few hundred pages long and very detailed. They are designed for the nonspecialist. Prices are very reasonable.

Contact: Superintendent of Documents, Box 371954, Pittsburgh, PA 15250-7954; 202-512-1800.

The U.S. Army Military History Institute answers thousands of inquiries per year on military history. The institute has an extensive collection of unofficial documents, such as personal papers. You can call or write with your question.

Contact: Historical Reference Branch, U.S. Army Military History Institute, Carlisle Barracks, PA 17013-5008; 717-245-3611.

✔ **Department of Education**
400 Maryland Avenue SW
Washington, DC 20202
Main office: 202-401-2000
Public affairs: 202-401-1576
Web site: http://www.ed.gov

Scope Includes

Adult Education
Bilingual Education
Civil Rights
Educational Statistics
Elementary and Secondary Education
Handicapped
Higher Education
Libraries
Special Education

Rich Resources

The Office of Educational Research and Improvement (OERI), Education Information Branch, disseminates statistics and other data related to education in the United States and other nations. OERI conducts studies and publishes reports regarding all kinds of educational data. Past publications include "The Condition of Education," "Hispanic Students in American High Schools," and "Faculty Salaries."

Contact: OERI, U.S. Department of Education, 400 Maryland Ave SW, Washington, DC 20202; 202-219-1692. On the Web: http://www.ed. gov/tollfree.html

Education Resource Information Center (ERIC) provides users with ready access to literature dealing with education through abstracting journals, computer searches, document reproductions, and other means. There are 16 subject-specialized clearinghouses: adult, career, and vocational; counseling and personnel; educational management; elementary and early childhood; handicapped and gifted children; higher education; information resources; junior colleges; languages and linguistics; reading and communication skills; rural education and small schools; science, mathematics, and environmental; social studies/social science; teacher education; tests, measurement, and evaluation; and urban education. These clearinghouses answer more than 100,000 written and telephone inquiries per year.

Contact: ERIC, U.S. Department of Education, 2277 Research Blvd, Rockville MD 20850; 202-219-2289 or 800-872-5327

✔ **Department of Energy**

Forrestal Building
1000 Independence Avenue SW
Washington, DC 20585
Main number: 202-586-5000
Public information: 202-586-5575
Web site: http://www.em.doe.gov
DOE Reports Bibliographic Database Web site:
    http://www.doe.gov/html/dra/dra.html

Scope Includes

Coal Liquids, Gas, Shale, Oil
Conservation
Energy Emergencies
Fusion Energy
Inventions
Nuclear Energy
Nuclear Physics
Radioactive Waste

Rich Resources

DOE's Office of Scientific and Technical Information has information on nearly any energy-related topic. The scientists on the staff may be able to help you with a question, or even run a free computer search on the "EDB"—Energy Data Base—the world's largest database on energy.

Contact: Office of Scientific and Technical Information, Box 62, Oak Ridge, TN 37831; 423-576-1188

The Energy Information Administration (EIA) provides energy information and referral assistance to the public. The best publication to ask for is "The Energy Information Directory," which is a list of government offices and experts. Topics in its subject index include appliances, buildings, coal, dams, diesel fuel, fusion power, ocean energy, safety, solar energy, and vehicles. The directory refers the user to a specific government office, describes the function of that office, and provides the name of a contact person. The publication is free and published semiannually. The EIA also publishes a free newsletter.

Contact: National Energy Information Center, Energy Information Administration, U.S. Department of Energy, EI-231 Forrestal Building, Washington, DC 20585; 202-586-8800

The Energy Efficiency and Renewable Energy Clearinghouse is an information clearinghouse on energy conservation and renewable energy (e.g., solar, wind, and ocean). The service will answer questions or refer you to an expert. Various free pamphlets and books are available.

Contact: Energy Efficiency and Renewable Energy Clearinghouse, Box 3048, Merrifield, VA 22116; 800-363-3732

✔ **Department of Health and Human Services**
200 Independence Avenue SW
Washington, DC 20201
Main number: 202-619-0527
Locator service: 202-619-0257
Web site: http://www.hhs.gov

TIP: If your research requires investigation of federal courts, you should get hold of a book called *The Sourcebook of Public Record Information*, which provides contact information and search advice for each of the 295 U.S. District, 184 U.S. Bankruptcy, and 13 Federal Records Center courts. The directory also provides data on county and state records. It can be ordered from BRB Publications, P.O. Box 27869, Tempe AZ 85285-7869.

Scope Includes

The department's Public Health Service division has key offices devoted to the following medical and health-related subjects:

AIDS
Alcohol Abuse
Diseases
Drug Abuse
Drug Research
Family Planning
Food Safety
Minority Health
Occupational Safety
Smoking
Statistical Data
Toxic Substances
Veterinary Medicine

The department's National Institutes of Health (NIH) include:

National Cancer Institute
National Eye Institute
National Heart, Lung, and Blood Institute
National Institute of Arthritis and Musculoskeletal and Skin Diseases
National Institute of Child Health and Human Development
National Institute of Diabetes and Digestive and Kidney Diseases
National Institute of Dental and Craniofacial Research
National Institute of Environmental Health Sciences
National Institute of Neurological and Communicative Disorders and Stroke

NIH has its own Web site: http://nih.gov/icd

In the Office of Human Development Services, you can find these offices:

Administration on Aging
Administration for Children, Youth, and Families
Administration on Developmental Disabilities

Administration for Native Americans
President's Committee on Mental Retardation

Other major divisions of HHS include:

Family Support Administration
Health Care Financing Administration
Social Security Administration

Rich Resources

The Office of Disease Prevention and Health Promotion's (ODPHP) National Health Information Center provides information on virtually all health-oriented questions ranging from weight control to rare disorders. Up-to-date expertise and literature are available on most health problems, including alcoholism, allergies, arthritis, birth defects, cancer, child diseases, dental problems, depression, drug addiction, genetic diseases, high blood pressure, poisoning, and sexually transmitted diseases.

Contact: Telephone the Information Center at its toll-free number: 800-336-4797. To request information in writing: Box 1133, Washington, DC 20013-1133. On the Web: http://nhic-nt.health.org; e-mail: nhicinfo@health.org

The National Center for Health Statistics provides expert advice and statistical data relating to health matters, including illness, disabilities, and hospital and health care utilization and financing. You can call to talk to an expert or write to receive a publication—many are free. This center can also help you track down vital statistics: records on births, deaths, marriages, and divorce. You will be provided with the vital statistics office to contact in the proper state.

Contact: National Center for Health Statistics, U.S. Department of Health and Human Services, 6525 Belcrest Road, Hyattsville, MD 20782; 301-436-8500

The department maintains clearinghouses of information on special health concerns, including:

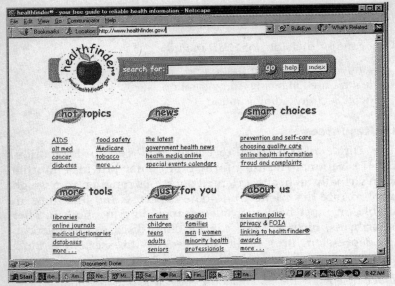

http://www.healthfinder.gov

Healthfinder is a consumer service of the Department of Health and Human Services that assists the public in quickly finding health and medical information.

Aging

Contact: Office of Program Development, Administration on Aging, U.S. Department of Health and Human Services, 330 Independence Avenue SW, Room 4661 Cohen Building, Washington, DC 20201; 202-619-7501. On the Web: http://www.aoa.dhhs.gov

Family Planning

Contact: Population Affairs, Office of Family Planning, U.S. Department of Health and Human Services, Box 30686, Bethesda, MD 20814; 301-654-6190

Mental Health

Contact: National Institute of Mental Health, Public Inquiry Branch, 5600 Fishers Lane, Room 7C02, Rockville, MD 20857; 301-443-4513

The National Institute for Occupational Safety and Health (NIOSH) publishes a variety of free reports and publications. You can talk to a staff expert who specializes in a particular hazard (e.g., asbestos, formaldehyde).

Contact: NIOSH Publications, 4676 Columbia Parkway, Cincinnati, OH 45226; 513-533-8328

The National Library of Medicine is the world's largest medical library, with over 4 million items. Specialties include the health sciences and, to a lesser degree, chemistry, physics, botany, and zoology. The library will assist you by checking its resources or by referring you to another organization.

Contact: U.S. Department of Health and Human Services, National Institutes of Health, National Library of Medicine, Bethesda, MD 20894; Reference Desk: 800-346-3656

The U.S. Office of Consumer Affairs, located in HHS, will try to tell you who can help you with a consumer complaint. The Office maintains clearinghouses of health information at http://www.healthfinder.gov. You can also find a subject directory and a referral list on topics from adoption to youth crisis hotlines by linking to http://hhs.gov/about/referlist.html

Contact: U.S. Office of Consumer Affairs, HHS 1009 Premier Building, Washington, DC 20201; 202-727-7000

✔ Department of Housing and Urban Development
451 7th Street SW
Washington, DC 20410
Main number: 202-708-1422
Public affairs: 202-708-0980
Web site: http://www.hud.gov

Scope Includes

Block Grants
Elderly Housing
Energy Conservation
Fair Housing
Indian/Public Housing
Urban Studies

Rich Resources

HUD's Library and Information Services will answer housing-related questions or will refer people with housing questions to the correct department.

Contact: HUD Library and Information Services, U.S. Department of Housing and Urban Development, Room 8141, 451 7th Street SW, Washington, DC 20410; 202-708-2370

HUD User is a service that will try to locate research reports sponsored by the department and help you get them. Many of these reports are inexpensive.

Contact: HUD User, Box 6091, Rockville, MD 20850; 301-251-5154 or 800-245-2691. On the Web: http://www.huduser.org

The Housing Information and Statistics Division can provide various housing statistics free, as well as answer inquiries. Topics on which statistics are generated include mortgages, neighborhoods, construction, and prices.

Contact: Statistical and Actuarial Staff, U.S. Department of Housing and Urban Development, 451 7th Street SW, Washington, DC 20410; 202-755-7510

Finally, the Department of Housing and Urban Development has a hotline for discrimination complaints: 800-669-9777.

✔ **Department of the Interior**
   18th and C Streets NW
   Washington, DC 20240
   Main number: 202-208-3100
   Communications: 202-208-6416
   Web site: http://www.doi.gov

Scope Includes

   Archaeology
   Fish and Wildlife
   Geology
   Mapping
   Minerals

Native Americans
Natural Resources
Water

Rich Resources

Do you want to know how to place reservations to go to Yosemite? When the Cherry Blossom Festival is being held? The best time to visit Shenandoah National Park to see the peak foliage? The National Park Service's public inquiries office answers such questions and provides information on national parks. Written or telephone inquiries are accepted.

Contact: National Park Service, Public Inquiries Office, Box 37127, Washington, DC 20013-7127; 202-208-4747

The Department of the Interior's Natural Resource Library will try to answer phone or mail inquiries on matters related to natural resources, including conservation, public lands, Native Americans, the environment, and fish and wildlife. The library also publishes bibliographies on topics of current interest ranging from the survival of the Florida panther to pollution problems in wildlife areas.

Contact: Natural Resources Library, U.S. Department of the Interior, 18th and C Streets NW, Washington, DC 20240; 202-208-5815

The Bureau of Indian Affairs will help you obtain information about Native Americans, their culture, and their relationship with the federal government.

Contact: Bureau of Indian Affairs, Public Affairs Office, U.S. Department of the Interior, MS 4542, 18th and C Streets NW, Washington, DC 20245; 202-208-3710. For inquiries, call 202-219-4150

✔ **Department of Justice**
950 Pennsylvania Ave NW
Washington, DC 20530-0001
Main number: 202-514-2000
Public affairs: 202-514-2008
Web site: http://www.usdoj.gov

Scope Includes

Antitrust
Civil Rights
Drug Enforcement
Immigration
Justice Statistics
Juvenile Justice
Prisons

Rich Resources

A special division of the Bureau's National Institute of Justice is its National Criminal Justice Reference Service (NCJRS). NCJRS provides the latest criminal justice findings via databases, reference and referral sources, publications, audiovisual materials, and more. Membership in NCJRS is free.

Contact: National Institute of Justice, NCJRS, Box 6000, Department F, Rockville, MD 20849-6000; 800-851-3420 (in Washington, DC: 301-519-5500). On the Web, it's the "Justice Information Center": http://ncjrs.org

A relatively new program from the department is the Justice Statistics Clearinghouse. Among the services offered by the clearinghouse are responding to statistical requests (e.g., how many burglaries occurred in the past year), providing information about JSC services, suggesting referrals to other sources, and conducting custom literature searches of the NCJRS database.

Contact: Telephone the Justice Statistics Clearinghouse at its toll-free number: 800-732-3277 (in Washington, DC: 301-251-5500)

The bureau also publishes its free *Bureau of Justice Statistics Bulletin*. The bulletin identifies key individuals within the department and their area of expertise, and lists various free studies and reports.

Contact: Bureau of Justice Statistics, U.S. Department of Justice, Box 6000, 633 Indiana Avenue NW, Washington, DC 20521; 800-732-3277 (in Washington, DC: 301-251-5500)

The FBI's "Uniform Crime Reports" is a reliable set of criminal statistics used in law enforcement operations and management. It covers such areas as crime trends in the United States by state, city, and county; number of types of crime; statistics on officers; and so forth. The division will answer inquiries from the public on these statistics. It also publishes the annual *Crime in the United States*, available from the U.S. Government Printing Office.

Contact: Uniform Crime Reports, Federal Bureau of Investigation, Washington, DC 20535; 202-324-3000. On the Web: http://www.fbi.gov/ucr/ucreports.htm

✔ **Department of Labor**
200 Constitution Avenue NW
Washington, DC 20210
Main number: 202-219-6666
Public affairs: 202-693-4650
Web site: http://www.dol.gov

Scope Includes

Employment Training
Labor-Management Relations
Labor Statistics
Occupational Safety and Health
Pension and Welfare Benefits
Productivity and Technology
Veterans' Employment
Women

Rich Resources

The Bureau of Labor Statistics publishes statistical data on employment, prices, wages, living conditions, and productivity. Other specialties include state economic statistics, industry statistics, consumer expenditures, economic growth projections, and occupational outlooks. A special free directory, "Telephone Contacts for Data Users," identifies the bureau's experts and specialties. Also available free is a periodical titled *Bureau of Labor Statistics News*.

Contact: U.S. Department of Labor, Bureau of Labor Statistics, Postal Square Building, 2 Massachusetts Ave NE, Room 4110, Washington, DC 20212; 202-606-5900

The Occupational Safety and Health Administration will answer general inquiries regarding health and safety in the workplace. It also publishes various pamphlets and materials. A helpful guide is "All about OSHA," which lists its regional offices.

Contact: OSHA Publications, OSHA Publications Distribution Office, U.S. Department of Labor, 200 Constitution Ave. NW, Room N-3101, Washington, DC 20210; 202-219-3649

✔ **Department of State**
2201 C Street NW
Washington, DC 20520
Main number: 202-647-4000
Public affairs: 202-647-6575
Web site: http://www.state.gov/index.html

Scope Includes

African Affairs
Arms Control
Canadian and European Affairs
East Asian and Pacific Affairs
Human Rights
Inter-American Affairs
International Environmental Affairs
International Narcotics
Near Eastern and South Asian Affairs
Nuclear and Space Arms Negotiations
Passport Inquiries
Prisoners of War/Missing in Action
Refugees
Visa Inquiries

Rich Resources

The department publishes short "background note" booklets that contain information on approximately 170 countries' social, economic, political, and military organization. These booklets are designed for the nonspecialist. They are inexpensive and provide both a cultural and historical overview.

Contact: Superintendent of Documents, Box 371954, Pittsburgh, PA 15250-7954; 202-512-1800

The State Department publishes many free short periodicals, too. To get a list of what is available, order the document "Selected State Department Publications."

Contact: Public Information Service, Room 6808, U.S. Department of State, Washington, DC 20520; 202-647-6575

An especially useful publication, reasonably priced, is the "Diplomatic List," a listing of foreign diplomatic representatives in Washington, DC, and their addresses.

Contact: Superintendent of Documents, Box 371954, Pittsburgh, PA 15250-7954; 202-512-1800.

The State Department publishes "Foreign Consular Offices in the U.S.," which lists country consulates, their addresses, phone numbers, and personnel. You can obtain help on questions you have about a particular country by contacting its consulate. The British consulate, for example, reports that it receives questions such as: Where is the county of Middlesex, England, located? How can I trace my relatives? How can I find information about what the British law says regarding divorce? How can I get information on the fashion industry in your country?

Contact: Superintendent of Documents, U.S. Government Printing Office, Washington, DC 20402. Or check the white pages of a major city phone book to find the consulate you seek.

✔ **Department of Transportation**
400 7th Street SW
Washington, DC 20590
Main number: 202-366-5580
Public affairs: 202-366-4570
Web site: http://www.dot.gov

Scope Includes

Automobile Safety
Aviation Safety
Aviation Standards

Boating
Hazardous Materials Transportation
Highway Safety
Mass Transit
National Highway Traffic Safety Administration
Railroad Safety
Shipbuilding
Vehicle Accident Statistics
Vehicle Crashworthiness

Rich Resources

The department's library will try to answer your questions related to transportation. Topics it covers include accident prevention, automobile safety, boating information, bus technology, driver education, energy, environmental research, highway research, mass transit, pollution, railroad information, traffic safety, and transportation for the handicapped.

Contact: U.S. Department of Transportation Library, Room 2200, SVC-122.20, 400 7th Street SW, Washington, DC 20590; 202-366-0746. On the Web: http://www.bts.gov/ntl

A separate branch of the library can assist you with reference inquiries.

Contact: U.S. Department of Transportation Library, FOB-10A, SVC-122.40, 800 Independence Avenue SW, Room 931, Washington, DC 20591; 202-267-3117

✔ **Department of the Treasury**
15th Street and Pennsylvania Avenue NW
Washington, DC 20220
Main number: 202—622-2000
Public affairs: 202-622-2960
Web site: http://www.ustreas.gov/

Scope Includes

Coin and Medal Production
Currency Production
Currency Research and Development

Customs
Savings Bonds
Secret Service Protection
Taxpayer Assistance
Tax Return Investigation

Rich Resources

The U.S. Customs Service publishes various free leaflets and newsletters. For example, "Customs Hints—Know Before You Go" explains customs privileges for returning U.S. residents and lists prohibited and restricted imports. Other publications cover importing pets and wildlife, cars, and alcoholic beverages.

Contact: U.S. Customs Service, 1300 Pennsylvania Avenue NW, Washington, DC 20229; 202-927-1770. On the Web: http://www.customs.treas.gov

If you have questions about your taxes, you'll likely find the answer you need in the Internal Revenue Service's publication number 910. Inside you'll find out about all of the services and publications available to help you prepare a tax return. The IRS also makes all of its forms and publications available over its Web site: http://www.irs.gov

Contact: Telephone IRS Information at its toll-free number: 800-829-1040

Selected Administrative Agencies

✔ **Consumer Product Safety Commission**
Washington, DC 20207
Main number: 800-638-2772
Public affairs: 301-504-0580
Web site: http://www.cpsc.gov

Scope Includes

Fire and thermal burn hazards, product safety assessment, mechanical hazards, injury information, electrical shock hazards, safety packaging, chemical hazards.

Rich Resources

The Consumer Product Safety Commission publishes a number of free pamphlets and reports on product safety, mostly devoted to specific products, such as wood stoves or toys. It also has a toll-free number that you can call if you have a complaint about a hazardous product or if you want to report an injury resulting from a consumer product.

Contact: Consumer Product Safety Commission, Washington, DC 20207; 800-638-2772

✔ **Environmental Protection Agency**
  401 M Street SW
  Washington, DC 20460
  Main number: 202-260-2090
  Public affairs: 202-260-7963
  Publications: 800-490-9198
  Web site: http://www.epa.gov

Scope Includes

Air and radiation, pesticides and toxic substances, acid deposition, environmental monitoring and quality assurance, solid waste and emergency response, water, noise control.

Rich Resources

The EPA supports a staff of experts who specialize in subjects such as air quality, drinking water, noise, radiation, and toxic substances. A $39 headquarters telephone directory will identify exactly the person you need. In this directory you can look up the name and telephone number of the Director of the Office of Solid Waste, the Director of Acid Deposition, and so on.

Contact: Superintendent of Documents, Box 371954, Pittsburgh, PA 15250-7954; 202-512-2250

✔ **Federal Communications Commission**
  445 12th Street NW
  Washington, DC 20554
  Main number: 202-418-6190
  Public affairs: 888-CALL-FCC

Web site: http://fcc.gov
E-mail: fccinfo@fcc.gov

Scope Includes

Cable television, broadcast stations, radio regulation.

Rich Resources

The FCC publishes some helpful documents, among them "The Information Seekers Guide," issued by the Consumer Assistance and Small Business Division. That division provides personal assistance and publishes free bulletins regarding communication issues (including cable television and other broadcasting matters).

Contact: Federal Communications Division, Public Services Division, 445 12th Street SW, Washington, DC 20554; 202-418-0190. On the Web: http://fcc.gov/consumers

The FCC Library is a good source of information on various telecommunications issues.

Contact: FCC Library, 1919 M Street NW, Washington, DC 20554; 202-418-0450

✔ **Federal Emergency Management Agency**
Federal Center Plaza
500 C Street SW
Washington, DC 20472
Main number: 202-646-2500
Public affairs: 202-646-4600
Web site: http://www.fema.gov

Scope Includes

Arson information, flood insurance, fire education, fire statistics, terrorism, radioactive hazards, earthquake research.

Rich Resources

FEMA publishes a catalog of free publications covering various issues related to emergency preparedness. Subjects range from shelter design to earthquakes, winter storm safety tips, and so forth.

TIP: The Freedom of Information Act of 1966 requires federal agencies to provide the public with any identifiable records on request, unless the information falls into a special exempted category, such as classified national defense secrets or internal personnel data. If your request for some information is denied, you may seek assistance from the Freedom of Information Clearinghouse, Box 19367, Washington, DC 20036; 202-588-1000.

Contact: FEMA, 500 C Street SW, Washington, DC 20472; 202-646-3484 or 800-480-2520 to order publications. On the Web: http://fema.gov/library/publicat.htm

✔ **Federal Trade Commission**
Pennsylvania Avenue and 6th Street NW
Washington, DC 20580
Main number: 202-326-2000
Public affairs: 202-326-2180
Web site: http://www.ftc.gov

Scope Includes

Advertising practices, competition and antitrust matters, consumer protection, financial statistics.

Rich Resources

The Federal Trade Commission (FTC) can provide information and advice regarding consumer problems and complaints, especially in areas such as deceptive advertising and unordered merchandise.

Contact: FTC, Correspondence Branch, Room 692, Pennsylvania Avenue and 6th Street NW, Washington, DC 20580; 202-326-3768

✔ **General Services Administration**
7th and D Streets SW
Washington, DC 20407
Main number: 202-708-5082
Public affairs: 202-501-0705
Web site: http://www.gsa.gov

Scope Includes

Consumer information, government audits and investigations, fraud hotline, federal property, purchasing of equipment

HEALTH

FDA Consumer. Interesting articles for consumers based on recent developments in the regulation of foods, drugs, and cosmetics by the Food and Drug Administration. **Annual subscription—10 issues.** (FDA) **252W. $12.00.**

Fitness Fundamentals. A "must" for anyone starting to exercise. Discusses how to set up a program and monitor your progress. 7 pp. (1987. PCPFS) **129W. $1.00.**

How to Take Weight Off Without Getting Ripped Off. Discusses weight reduction and products, fad diets, and other diet aids; and provides tips on a sensible weight loss program. 4 pp. (1985. FDA) **529W. Free.**

Indoor Tanning. How tanning devices work, and why they can be as hazardous to your health as tanning outdoors. 4 pp. (1988. FTC) **422W. 50¢.**

Quackery—The Billion Dollar "Miracle" Business. How to protect yourself from health fraud. Discusses how bogus remedies for cancer, arthritis, and the "battle of the bulge" can hurt you much more than help. 4 pp. (1985. FDA) **530W. Free.**

Who Donates Better Blood For You Than You? Discusses the advantages of donating blood to yourself before undergoing planned surgery. 3 pp. (1988. FDA) **531W. Free.**

Drugs & Health Aids

Anabolic Steroids: Losing at Winning. Discusses the dangerous side-effects and reactions of these popular muscle-building drugs. 5 pp. (1988. FDA) **532W. Free.**

Comparing Contraceptives. Discusses effectiveness and possible side effects of nine types of birth control with a comparison chart and statistics on use. 8 pp. (1985. FDA) **533W. Free.**

A Doctor's Advice on Self-Care. There are more over-the-counter drugs available now than ever before which can cure, prevent and diagnose illnesses. The U.S. Commissioner of Food and Drugs tells how to use them safely and effectively. 7 pp. (1989. FDA) **534W. Free.**

Do-It-Yourself Medical Testing. Medical self-tests are available today for everything from eyesight to pregnancy to high blood pressure. Explains how some tests are used, how they work and their accuracy. 7 pp. (1986. FD)

Food and Drug Interactions. How some commonly used drugs affect nutritional needs. How some foods affect drug actions; and how to avoid ill effects. 4 pp. (1988. FDA) **549W. Free.**

Myths and Facts of Generic Drugs. What they are and how they may save you money. Also corrects some common misconceptions about generic prescriptions. 3 pp. (1988. FDA) **536W. Free.**

Some Things You Should Know About Prescription Drugs. Even prescription drugs can be dangerous. Here's tips for safe use. 4 pp. (1983. FDA) **537W. Free.**

X-Ray Record Card. Wallet-sized card for recording X-ray examinations. (1980. FDA) **538W. Free.**

Medical Problems

AIDS. How AIDS is spread, how to prevent it, and what to do if you think you've been infected. 2 pp. (1988. FDA) **539W. Free.**

Breast Exams: What You Should Know. Eighty percent of breast lumps are not cancer. How to check for lumps, how doctors examine them, and treatments available. 17 pp. (1986. NIH) **540W. Free.**

Chew Or Snuff is Real Bad Stuff. Poster/booklet for teenagers describing dangers from smokeless tobacco including cancer, gum disease, stained teeth, and more. (1988. NIH) **542W. Free.**

Clearing the Air: A Guide to Quitting Smoking. No-nonsense tips on kicking the habit. 32 pp. (1985. NIH) **543W. Free.**

The Colon. While this part of the body is not generally discussed, it performs important functions and is the site of many problems, such as colitis, diverticulitis, and cancer. 6 pp. (1985. FDA) **544W. Free.**

Dizziness. Explains the various causes, diagnostic tests, and treatments for people suffering from dizzy spells. 27 pp. (1986. NIH) **130W. $1.00.**

Facing Surgery? Why Not Get a Second Opinion? Answers these and other questions of the prospective patient. Includes a toll-free number for locating specialists.

and supplies, information management, public buildings management.

Rich Resources

The GSA's Consumer Information Center publishes an extremely useful free quarterly catalog that describes more than 100 free and inexpensive consumer pamphlets and guides available from the government.

These pamphlets are very practical and helpful. "Ideas into Dollars," for example, provides advice on patenting, financing, and marketing a new invention or product. It lists various sources of assistance, such as universities, government offices, inventors, and associations. "Occupational Outlook Quarterly" provides descriptions of new occupations, salary figures, job trends, and a lot of helpful advice.

Contact: Consumer Information Center, Box 100, Pueblo, CO 81009

The *Consumer Resource Handbook* describes how and where to go to get help in resolving complaints and problems with companies. The handbook provides a complaint contact person at more than 1,000 well-known companies and gives advice on how to get help from a wide variety of sources, such as third-party resolution organizations, Better Business Bureaus, media programs, municipal consumer offices, licensing boards, and federal agencies. The handbook is free.

Contact: Consumer Information Center, Pueblo, CO 81009; 719-948-3334 or 800-878-3256

The Washington headquarters of the Consumer Information Center may be able to help you further.

Contact: Consumer Information Center, General Services Administration, 18th and F Streets NW, Room G-142, Washington, DC 20405; 202-501-1794

✔ **National Aeronautics and Space Administration**
300 East Street SW
Washington, DC 20546
Main number: 202-358-0000
Public affairs: 202-358-1750
Web site: http://www.nasa.gov/

Center for Aerospace Information Technical Report Server: http://www.sti.nasa.gov/RECONselect.html

Scope Includes

Aeronautics and space technology, life sciences, astrophysics, earth sciences, solar system exploration, space shuttle payload, Mars observer program, microgravity science, upper atmosphere research, solar flares.

Rich Resources

NASA's Industrial Application Centers are designed to provide assistance in solving technical problems or meeting information needs. The centers offer online computer retrieval to 2 million technical reports in the NASA database and to more than 100 million reports and articles in 250 other computer databases. Topics

http://www.nasa.gov

NASA, like all U.S. federal agencies, has a Web page that describes its mission, provides recent news, and offers various information services to the public.

covered include aerospace, energy, engineering, chemicals, food technology, textile technology, metallurgy, medicine, electronics, surface coatings, oceanography, and more. The centers operate on a cost-recovery basis.

Contact: To find the center closest to you, write or phone NASA, Technology Programs and Commercialization Office at 407-867-6226. http://technology.ksc.nasa.gov

Do you want to know how work is progressing toward development of a plane that can fly to Japan in two hours? Curious about the atmosphere on Venus? The NASA headquarters library will try to answer questions you have on flight and space. It can also send you documents from its collection or tell you where to obtain them.

Contact: NASA Headquarters Library, 300 East Street SW, Washington, DC 20546; 202-358-0168

You can obtain an overview and a full description of several useful reports and information services available from NASA by getting a very valuable catalog called *NASA STI Products and Services at a Glance.*

Contact: NASA Access Help Desk, NASA Center for Aerospace Information, Box 8757, Baltimore, MD 21240; 301-621-0390. E-mail help is available at help@sti.nasa.gov

NASA also makes its inventions available to the public for licensing. For more details, see page 158.

✔ **National Archives and Records Administration**
NARA, Washington DC 20408
Main number: 202-501-5400
Public affairs: 301-713-6800
Web site: http://www.nara.gov/

Scope Includes

Naturalization records, census data, military records, land records, passenger lists, passport applications, selected vital statistics, presidential documents and audio tapes.

Rich Resources

One popular use (among many others) of the National Archives is researching genealogy records. Although major projects need to be performed in person in Washington, DC, a reference services department will answer phone questions about holdings and furnish copies of documents for a modest fee. A useful bibliography is the agency's *Select List of Publications*.

Contact: Reference Services Branch, National Archives and Records Administration, Washington DC 20408; 202-501-5400

✔ **National Endowment for the Arts and the Humanities**
Arts: 1100 Pennsylvania Avenue NW
Washington, DC 20506
Main number: 202-682-5400
Public affairs: 202-682-5400
Humanities: 1100 Pennsylvania Avenue NW, Room 406
Washington, DC 20506
Main number: 202-606-8438
Public affairs: 202-606-8438

Scope Includes

Literature, museums, folk arts, visual arts, dance arts, music arts, theater arts and musical theater, opera, media arts (film, radio, TV), history, language, and so on.

Rich Resources

Program specialists at the National Endowment for the Arts may be able to help you with questions on design arts, expansion arts, folk arts, interarts, literature, media arts, museums, and visual arts.

Contact: National Endowment for the Arts, Old Post Office Building, Nancy Hanks Center, 1100 Pennsylvania Avenue, Washington, DC 20506; 202-682-5400

The Division of Research Programs of the National Endowment for the Humanities will refer you to a division that can help you track down an answer to a humanities-related question, including inquiries related to history, philosophy, languages, linguistics, literature, archaeology, jurisprudence, the arts, ethics, and comparative religion. You can call the division directly or send for a booklet that will help you identify the expert you need.

Contact: Division of Research Programs, Room 318, National Endowment for the Humanities, 1100 Pennsylvania Avenue NW, Washington, DC 20506; 202-606-8200

✔ **National Science Foundation**
4201 Wilson Blvd.
Arlington VA 22230
Main number: 703-306-1234
Public affairs: 703-306-1234
Web site: http://www.nsf.gov
E-mail: pubs@nsf.gov

Scope Includes

Atmospheric/astronomical and earth-ocean sciences, mathematical and physical sciences, arctic and antarctic research, anthropology, engineering, biology, genetic biology, chemistry, computer science, earthquakes, economics, ethics in science, meteorology, galactic and extragalactic astronomy, geography, geology, history and philosophy of science, nutrition, linguistics, marine chemistry, metallurgy, minority research, nuclear physics, science and technology to aid the handicapped, small-business research and development, sociology.

Rich Resources

The National Science Foundation funds research in all fields of science and engineering, except for clinical research, by issuing grants and contracts. If you'd like information on how to apply for a grant, you can obtain the publication "Grants for Scientific and Engineering Research," which describes the guidelines for preparation of proposals, proposal processing and evaluation, and all other steps related to applying for NSF grants.

Contact: Public Affairs, National Science Foundation, Washington, DC 20550; 703-306-1234

✔ **National Transportation Safety Board**
490 L'Enfant Plaza East
Washington, DC 20594

Main number: 202-314-6000
Public affairs: 202-314-6000
Web site: http://www.ntsb.gov

Scope Includes

Accident investigations involving aviation, railroads, highways, and hazardous materials.

Rich Resources

The National Transportation Safety Board (NTSB) conducts independent accident investigations and formulates safety improvement recommendations. The public can find out about these investigations by obtaining the board's "Accident Briefs" and "Accident Reports," which identify the circumstances and probable cause of the accident investigated. The reports are reasonably priced. To find out more, send for the board's publication "NTSB Documents and Information."

Contact: National Transportation Safety Board, Public Inquiries Section, 490 L'Enfant Plaza East, Washington, DC 20594; 202-382-6735

NTSB's Safety Studies and Analysis Division will provide you with data regarding air accidents. For example, you can ask how many accidents occurred that involved a particular type of aircraft, or airline, during a specific year. There is no cost for the information.

Contact: National Transportation Safety Board, Safety Studies and Analysis Division, 490 L'Enfant Plaza East, Washington, DC 20594; 202-382-6536

✔ Small Business Administration
409 Third Street SW
Washington, DC 20416
Main number: 202-606-4000
Public affairs: 202-205-6744
Toll-free help: 800-827-5722
Web site: http://www.sba.gov

Scope Includes

Women's businesses, veteran affairs, disaster assistance, financial assistance, management assistance, minority small businesses, statistical data, export advice.

Rich Resources

See chapter 4, "Business Information," for a description of the various kinds of business help available.

✔ **U.S. International Trade Commission**
500 E Street SW
Washington, DC 20436
Main number: 202-205-1819
Public affairs: 202-205-1819
Web site: http://usitc.gov

Scope Includes

Agriculture, fisheries and forests, textiles, leather products and apparel, energy and chemicals, machinery and equipment, minerals and metals, instruments and precision manufacturers, automotive statistics.

Rich Resources

For a description of ITC's research reports, see chapter 4, "Business Information."

PRINT REFERENCE SOURCES FOR LOCATING FEDERAL INFORMATION

There are a number of excellent resources available to help you track down the precise bureau, division, or even person that can provide you with the information you need. These guides are published by both the government itself and commercial publishers. Here's the best of the bunch:

✔ **Source:** *United States Government Manual*

This comprehensive guide to the agencies and offices that make up the federal government is published by the office of the Federal Register, United States General Services Administration. All the departments are broken down into their various bureaus and offices, and key personnel within those offices are identified. The guide also includes information on quasi-governmental organizations like the Smithsonian Institution and multilateral organizations such as the Pan American Health Organization. Regional offices and Federal Information Centers—a specialized source of help described below—are also identified. Many libraries have this reasonably priced book, or you can order it from the Superintendent of Documents, Box 371954, Pittsburgh, PA 15250-7954; 202-512-1800.

✔ **Source: *Washington Information Directory***

Published by Congressional Quarterly, this is an excellent guide to information resources in Washington, DC. The directory breaks down the various departments and agencies into their particular divisions, and it provides a one-paragraph description of the divi-

---

TIP: I've found this guide—and Washington sources in general—especially helpful for answering consumer-oriented questions. For example, once I had to find out whether a certain energy-saving device really worked as claimed. The product was a device that fit on top of a furnace's flue, and the vendor claimed it recirculated the hot air and thereby cut heating bills. I figured that the U.S. Department of Energy might have some kind of expert who could handle a question like this. The *Washington Information Directory* listed a Department of Energy division called Building Technologies, whose purpose is to keep up to date on technologies that may reduce building energy costs. Upon contacting the division, I discovered that, sure enough, there was a technical person in the division who was able to help. (Final verdict on the device: It can save some energy on older, inefficient furnaces, but not very much on newer ones.)

---

sion's specialties and scope. A contact person and phone number for each division are also provided. This directory identifies sources of information within not only federal agencies but also virtually any important organization—private or public—that operates out of Washington, DC. These organizations deal with topics that range from health to the environment, labor, minorities, and much more. A subject index at the back of the book makes it easy to track down the particular information source that can best help you. The directory also lists the current top-level government personnel, such as members of the cabinet, Senate, and House of Representatives. You'll find the Washington Information Directory in many libraries.

Finally, the best print source for finding government information is *Government Information on the Web*, 2nd edition, written by the search expert Greg Notess and published by Bernan Press (1998).

4

Business Information

A Sampling of Sources

(continued)

121

Of all types of research, it is business research that the Internet has probably impacted the most. Indeed, it would be fair to say that the Internet has revolutionized business research.

There are a few reasons why this has occurred. First, in today's global, high-tech–dominated economy, a critical competitive factor for business is speed and flexibility. Being the first to grasp a new market opportunity, the first out the door with a new product, the first to size up competitors and competitive forces, is vital for success. And the main currency the Internet deals in is speed. Speed, in fact, is one of, if not *the* core characteristic of the Net, and is its "message," à la McLuhan. Those who perform business-related research need information fast—extremely fast—and here the Internet certainly delivers.

Another reason why the Internet has revolutionized business research is that serious business researchers have already been accustomed to doing much of their information gathering online. They've been doing this for years by searching high-powered fee-based databases on services like Dialog, Lexis-Nexis, and Dow Jones. But now those online services are migrating to the Internet, and newer ones are "born" on the Web. In addition, many businesses allocate many thousands of dollars for a research budget, making the business market a potentially lucrative one for the new dot.com vendors, and spurring the creation of new web-based business information services.

This is not to say, though, that *all* business research is being conducted on the Internet—though that percentage increases all the time. There are still resources available only in print—certain key company and industry directories for example, textbooks, and many trade journals are not fully available on the Web. Furthermore, although a great deal of the business-related information produced by the U.S. government is moving quickly to the Web, much of it remains available in print, on CD-ROM, or available through telephone inquiries directly to a federal agency.

This chapter, which lists and describes key sources for business research, is broken down into seven parts, each representing a common business research activity. Those seven activities are:

1. Industry research
2. Company research (which is further segmented into large firms, small firms, and IPOs)
3. Market research
4. Economic research
5. Investment-related research
6. Start-up/Entrepreneurial research
7. International-business research and reaching overseas markets

Within each of those sections, I will identify and describe key sources available from libraries, the U.S. government, the Internet, and a miscellaneous category. (Not all categories will apply to every section.)

Note: You should also see the broader information sources identified earlier in this book that include business information within their scope (e.g., *Subject Guide to Books in Print*, periodical directories, trade associations, and so on). In addition, you should read about basic business sources found in the library, which are identified in chapter 1.

INDUSTRY RESEARCH

Do you want to find out all about the jewelry industry? Need to dig up some business growth projections on the restaurant business? Here are the places to turn to for information about industries:

At the Library

First See: Basic business directory sources listed in chapter 1 under "Business and Industry Information"

✔ Source: *Ward's Manufacturing USA*

This directory is packed with data and charts and provides a massive amount of statistical data. You'll find pre-analyzed statistics on industry performance and company participation. There are graphs of shipments, employment, general statistics (number of establishments, production figures), indices of change, and selected ratios (e.g., employees per establishment, wages per hour, etc.). You'll also see the names of leading companies within an industry, including address, name of CEO, sales and employment figures, materials consumed, product shares details, and more.

✔ Source: *Nelson's Directory of Investment Research*

Let's say you need to find out the latest developments in the hotel industry, or discover what the experts think the chances are of a takeover of a television network. An excellent place to get information is a brokerage house, often found on Wall Street. A stock analyst is one of the very best sources for obtaining inside information about industries and about companies within an industry. Often, you'll see these analysts quoted in newspapers like *The Wall Street Journal*, giving an expert opinion about some industry development.

TIP: You can search for and download brokerage reports from multiple brokerage houses by linking to either Multex (www.multexinvestor.com) or Investext's Research Bank at (www.investext.com). Both are fee-based databases.

TIP: Often, excerpts of these research reports are published in relevant trade publications. See page 22 for advice on identifying publications in your field of interest. Alternatively, you might identify a relevant trade association and check to see if its library will make a copy available. Some market research providers also make some of the aggregate or top-level data from their studies available for free on their Web site. If you have the name of a market research firm that you want to check but not its Web site, use one of the search engines to try to find it (see chapter 5) or try guessing the site by entering the firm's name. For example, to see if the market research firm Dataquest has any of its findings up on the Web, you might try entering http://www.dataquest. com (and you'd get to that company's home page).

How do you find these analysts? The bible is probably a guide called Nelson's Directory of Investment Research, which provides the names, phone numbers, and areas of expertise of 14,000 security analysts whose expertise ranges from aerospace to waste disposal. If you find an analyst whom you'd like to contact and interview, see chapters 6–8 for strategies on finding and interviewing experts.

From the U.S. Government

✔ Source: *U.S. Industry and Trade Outlook*

Provides key facts on major industries in manufacturing, services, construction, and natural resources. Each chapter includes "Facts at a glance" charts showing historical industry performance and one- and five-year forecasts based on most current industry and trade data. Reference lists include useful contact information for further research. The *Outlook* is written by authors from the Department of Commerce, other government agencies, McGraw-Hill Inc., and by independent analysts.

✔ Source: Congressional Committee Hearings

Before final action is taken on a proposed piece of legislation, the Congress holds hearings. As part of these hearings, Congress often obtains testimony from various industry experts and notable persons. Transcripts of these hearings are ultimately created, and they are available to the public.

The following sample of standing committees and subcommittees in the House of Representatives should give you a feel for the scope of subject areas and industries that these hearings may cover.

- **Agriculture:**
  Subcommittees include cotton, rice, and sugar; forests, family farms, and energy; livestock, dairy, and poultry; tobacco and peanuts; and wheat, soybeans, and feed grains.

- **Energy and Commerce:**
  Subcommittees include commerce, transportation, and tourism; energy conservation and power; fossil and synthetic fuels; health and the environment; and telecommunications, consumer protection, and finance.

- **Public Works and Transportation:**
  Subcommittees include aviation, public buildings and grounds, and surface transportation.

- **Veterans Affairs:**
  Subcommittees include hospitals and health care, housing, and memorial affairs.

- **Select Committees:**
  These include aging; children, youth, and families; hunger; and narcotics abuse and control.

How to Find:

Here's how to track down transcripts of past hearings as well as find out what is currently happening in Congress. First, to find out if there are any *current* bills pending in the House or Senate on your subject of interest, call **Washington Legislative Information** at 202-225-1772. The person at that number will be able to tell you if there is such a bill and which committee is sponsoring it. The office can provide information as timely as one-day old and as far back as 1979. The office will also perform free keyword searches on its own database to locate legislative information and provide printouts from its legislative database for ten cents per page.

To get the best results from this office you should try to be as specific as possible in your request; rather than asking for anything on "child care," narrow the topic down further to prevent being swamped with data. You can call the committee and ask to speak with an aide to the congressperson sponsoring the bill. He or she will be able to give you more details on the bill and tell you how to obtain copies of transcript hearings.

✔ Source: Federal Trade Commission

The Federal Trade Commission issues reports concerning industries. These are related to its activities in protecting consumers from deceptive advertising and marketing.

How to Find:

Contact the Federal Trade Commission, Public Reference, Room 130, Washington, DC 20580; 202-326-2222 or 1-800-FTC-HELP. On the Web: http://www.ftc.org. Complaints and requests should be sent to: Freedom of Information Act Request, c/o FTC, 600 Pennsylvania Ave NW, Washington, DC 20580

On the Net

✔ Source: Industry Look-up Sites

There are several sites on the Web that pull together various data, statistics, news, and links on specified industries. These "vertical portals" are sometimes called "vertals." Here are a few good ones:

- **VerticalNet.com**
  http://www.verticalnet.com

  Geared specifically for providing news, links, and data on industries related to engineering, science, and manufacturing around the world. VerticalNet's goal is to create communities by bringing persons with similar interests together on its site.

- **Dow Jones Business Directory**
  http://www.businessdirectory.dowjones.com

  This is a highly recommended site. Dow Jones editors select important business-related Web sites, which can be viewed

---

TIPS: Locating a Committee/Finding Transcripts

For a list of all the House's standing and select committees, contact Office of the Clerk, Legislative Resource Center, B106 Canon House Office Building, Washington, DC 20515; 202-226-5200. For Senate committees, contact: The Office of Printing & Document Services, The Senate Document Room, Hart Building, 2nd & Constitution Avenue, Washington, DC 20510; 202-224-7701. The Legislative Resource Center at 202-226-5200 (on the Web: http://clerkweb.house.gov/lrc/lrc.htm).

To find transcripts of past hearings, get hold of the Congressional Information Services *CIS Index* or its *Index to Congressional Committee Hearings*. Both list index hearings held prior to 1970, and the *CIS Index* also lists other committee reports and documents. These sources can be found in university libraries or large public libraries. The actual transcripts themselves may be kept on microfilm at the library.

TIP: Magazine Archives on the Web

As discussed in chapter 5, many trade magazines have put a searchable archive of their back issues on the Web, and, of course, journal articles are a top source for industry (and company) information. Be warned that this is a spotty area, and that many of those magazines that put their archives up charge a fee. Your best bet may still be to check your library for the most comprehensive archive. A few top-notch business magazines that have put up free searchable archives include *American Demographics* (www.demographics.com), *Inc.* (www.inc.com), and *FastCompany* (www.fastcompany.com).

---

broken down by industry. Each review summarizes and rates the site's content. Dow Jones Business Directory serves as an excellent antidote for information overload.

- **Yahoo**

http://dir.yahoo.com/Business_and_Economy/Companies/

Yahoo is also an excellent source of industry-related sites in one grouping. You view a list of dozens of specific industries, from aerospace to weather, and click on relevant sites for the industry of interest to you.

COMPANY RESEARCH/LARGE FIRMS

If you're trying to get information on a particular company, there are several avenues to try, ranging from the company itself to a directory or the Internet.

At the Library

See the basic company directory guidebooks listed in chapter 1 on pages 27–33.

From the U.S. Government

✔ **Source: Securities and Exchange Commission**

The SEC keeps information on corporations with publicly traded stock. All publicly held corporations and investment companies must file certain documents with the SEC, which are then made available to the public at no charge.

The following types of documents are among those filed and available from the SEC:

- **Annual Report:**
  See page 133 for a description.

- **Prospectus:**
  This is the basic business and financial information on the issuer. Investors use it to help appraise the merits of the offering.

- **10K Report:**
  This important document identifies the company's principal products and services, tells where properties are located, describes any legal proceedings pending, identifies owners of 10 percent or more of the stock, provides data on the background and salaries of the officers, and gives extensive financial information.

TIP: If you do not know how to read financial tables, send for Merrill Lynch's excellent free publication How to Read a Financial Report. Contact Merrill Lynch, Market Communications, Box 9019, Princeton, NJ 08543; 800-MERRILL. Another superb guide, which concentrates on how to analyze business rations, is Dun & Bradstreet's *Understanding Financial Statements: A Guide for Non-Financial Professionals.* Contact Dun & Bradstreet, One Diamond Hill Road, Murray Hill, NJ 07974; 800-234-3867. Or, on the Web, check out IBM's "Guide to Understanding Financials" at http://www.prars.com/ibm/ibmframe.html

TIP: An alternative to the SEC's own EDGAR is EDGAR ONLINE at http://www.edgar-online.com. This private sector version offers extra benefits to registered users, not available on SEC's own EDGAR system. These include real-time SEC filings, 144 insider transaction filings, the ability to view presentation-quality SEC filings in word processor formats, and special search tools. You can also find non-EDGAR filings (older material, paper reports, due diligence, etc.) from a firm called Disclosure, a division of Primark of Waltham, MA; on the Web at: http://www.primark.com/pfid/content/disclosure.shtml

- **8Q Report:**
  This is a quarterly report that provides more timely data than the 10K.

- **8K Report:**
  The 8K Report must be filed within fifteen days of certain specified significant developments; these include filing for bankruptcy, a major acquisition, or a change in control.

How to Find:

For filings from the last three to five years, you can go directly to the SEC's Web to search and download the documents for free. Link to: http://www.sec.gov/edgarhp.htm

For older reports, you can obtain the documents you need by visiting, writing, or e-mailing the SEC offices. Public reference rooms are maintained in New York, Chicago, and the Washington DC, headquarters. During normal business hours, individuals are permitted to review and photocopy all public findings. Or you can ask for request forms; contact SEC Public Reference Branch, Stop 1-2, 450

5th Street NW, Washington, DC 20549; 202-942-8088; e-mail: publicinfo@sec.gov. Turnaround time is seven to ten days.

A free booklet, *A User's Guide to the Facilities of the Public Reference Room*, explains all the information and services available and how to make the best use of them.

On the Net

The Internet is a wealth of facts and data on companies—the kind of data that up until the late 1990s was hard to find, pricey, or both. Now, much of this information is easy to find and free. There are literally thousands of good sources; the following are some of those I've found to be most helpful:

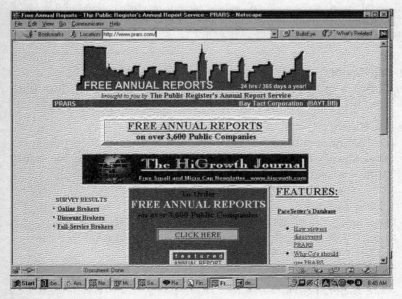

http://www.prars.com

The Public Register Annual Reports Service (PRARS) lets you search for and order public company annual reports—at no charge!

- **Free Annual Reports**
  http://www.prars.com
  Order free annual reports of over 3,600 public companies from the Public Register's Annual Report Service (PRARS).

- **Look-Up Directories.** Link to these sites to find basic facts on companies such as their address, sales, number of employees, SIC code, etc.

  ### Hoovers
  http://www.hoovers.com

  Perhaps the best known of the company information sites, Hoovers has a wealth of useful company information—its bread and butter is the directory data, but it also has narrative profiles, basic financial information, related links, and much more.

  ### Companiesonline.com
  http://www.companiesonline.com.

  You can search for information on over 100,000 public and private companies on this site operated by Dun & Bradstreet and Lycos. (Another Dun & Bradstreet site that's also free and contains more extensive information is available at http://www.dnb.imarketinc.com/)

  ### Corptech
  http://www.corptech.com

  This database specializes in providing data on firms in high-technology industries.

  ### Forbes Searchable 800
  http://www.forbes.com/tool/toolbox/int500

  Search Forbes' top firms by name, company, industry, or rank.

Tip: Find Company Information through Press Releases

Before the Internet, it wasn't easy to get a press release unless you were with the media, but now, they have become a free commodity. Press releases can be one of the best and most accessible sources on the Internet for getting news and facts about a company. While the information presented will naturally be slanted to the interests of the company, press releases can still be an excellent intelligence tool for getting data on new products, the latest financial news, personnel changes and more. The best way to find a firm's press releases, if you know the name and URL of the firm itself, is to link to the company's home page. Most firms have a "recent news" section where they post an archive of current press releases. You can also do a search for press releases on one of the major press wire sites, such as PR Newswire (www.prnewswire.com) or Businesswire (www.businesswire.com), or via a news aggregator site like Newsalert (www.newsalert.com).

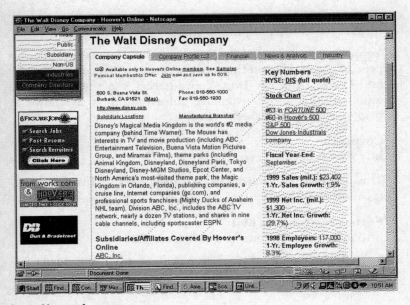

http://www.hoovers.com

Company profiles like this one on the Disney Corporation can be found for free on many parts of the Web, such as the popular Hoovers.com site.

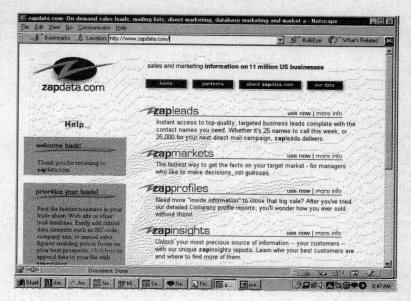

http://www.zapdata.com

You can obtain free company profiles from this site, which is a joint venture between Dun & Bradstreet and iMarket.

VaultReports
http://www.vaultreports.com

Designed for job seekers (and employers), VaultReports is a comprehensive employer-information bank that includes insider reviews of companies for prospective employees, facts on hiring firms, and gossipy message boards. An offbeat, but interesting alternative source for company information. (You can get similarly gossipy—though often of iffy credibility—comments about companies at various message boards, such as the Yahoo Message Board: http://messages.yahoo.com/index.html)

Tip: Finding a Company's Home Page

What do you do when you want to get to a firm's home page, but don't have its correct Web address (URL)? Sure, you can enter the firm's name in a search engine, but this will likely just bring you back scores of irrelevant sites that happen to mention the name of the company somewhere on the page.

You have other, preferable options. You can check one of these directory sites listed above, most of these include the company's URL. If that doesn't work, you can always try guessing the URL by entering the company's name into your browser (e.g., if you were trying to find General Motors' home page, you'd guess www.generalmotors.com). Another approach would be to use the AltaVista search engine, which integrates a third-party search service called realnames.com. If a company has registered its sites with Realnames, its page will be retrieved and set off from the regular search-engine listing when you search on the firm's name (or product, or trademark or whatever else the firm registered with Realnames).

Finally, you might want to use a search engine like Google (www.google.com) that returns hits based on the number of pages linking to a site. This may increase the odds that the company's own home page will come up toward the top.

- **Aggregator Sites.** These are sites that bring together a wide range of information on companies—news, stock reports, directory data, research reports, SEC filings, charts and graphs, and other business data. There are dozens of these, but two we like in particular are:

  - **Wall Street Research Net.** http://www.wsrn.com
  - **NewsAlert.** http://www.newsalert.com

Miscellaneous

Don't forget that you can contact the company you are researching directly. Call the public affairs or public relations office and ask for a copy of the company's *annual report*, a document issued by any publicly held corporation. The annual report will give you a broad overview of the company's goals and operations, including an opening letter from the chief executive, results of continuing operations, market segment information, new prod-

> **TIP:** Brokerage houses, discussed previously with regard to finding information on industries, can also provide information about large companies that operate in industries they follow.

uct plans, subsidiary activities, research and development activities, information on the highest officers, an evaluation of performance over the last year, and a detailed financial statement. If the firm is not publicly held and does not issue an annual report, it may produce a *company fact book* that serves a similar purpose. You can ask for it from the public affairs or public relations office.

COMPANY RESEARCH/SMALL AND PRIVATELY HELD FIRMS

It can be hard to find information about smaller companies. If they are public, they normally only have to file with the SEC if they have $10 million or more in assets and 500 or more shareholders, or list their securities on an exchange or Nasdaq. If they are private, they don't have to file anything with the SEC at all.

At the Library

Some of the basic business directories identified in chapter 1, such as *Ward's Business Directory* and *Standard and Poor's Register*, cover private firms, though even these usually don't include data on the *very* smallest.

> **TIP:** If you need to find information on a nonprofit organization—a charity, religious organization, professional association, and so on—you are legally permitted to examine a copy of that organization's tax return (Form 990), for a fee. Contact the IRS at Freedom of Information Reading Room, Internal Revenue Service, U.S. Department of the Treasury, Box 388, Ben Franklin Station, Washington, DC 20044; 202-622-5000. Include the full name of the organization, the year of the tax return requested, and the city/state or tax ID number of the organization.

If you are lucky, your library may have a directory published by Washington Researchers called *How to Find Information on Private Companies*. It's filled with sources and strategies for digging out facts on private firms.

On the Net

There are several strategies you might follow in using the Internet to obtain information on the smaller, privately held firms. You can run the name of the company—or its CEO—through a search engine, to see if it has a home page, or if another Web site mentions it in some context. You can also search Internet discussion groups to see if anyone is talking about the company (see pages 214–221 in chapter 5 for more on discussion groups). Or you might try one of the message boards discussed later in this chapter under "Investment-Related Research," or one of the job-related message boards such as VaultReports (http://www.vaultreports.com).

A search of one of the Net's telephone directory look-up sites (such as www.infospace.com) can at least provide you with a company's address and phone number.

You can also search for press releases issued by the firm, or search newspapers and journals that are local to where the firm is located. An excellent site for searching journal back issues is the free American City Business Journal site, providing searchable fulltext for about 40 business journals. Link to http://www.bizjournals.com

Finally some of the sites mentioned in the large-company section, such as Hoovers (http://www.hoovers.com) and CorpTech (http://www.corptech.com), also include smaller, private firms as well.

Miscellaneous

✔ **Source: Chambers of Commerce**

Local Chambers of Commerce keep certain information on companies operating within their town or city: for example, the

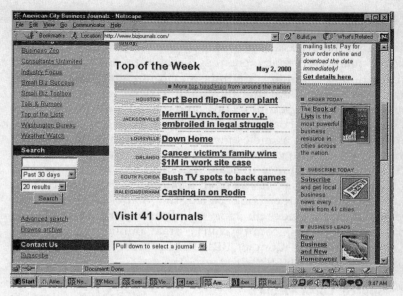

http://www.bizjournals.com

Unlike most newspapers on the Web, the American City Business Journals allows searchers free access to its archives of past published articles

number of years a firm has been conducting business and whether any problems, such as customer complaints, have been reported.

✔ Source: Better Business Bureaus

BBBs keep reports on the performance records of companies based on their files and investigations. To find a local BBB office, check your phone book's white pages. (Also note that the Council of Better Business Bureaus, 4200 Wilson Boulevard, Suite 800, Arlington, VA 22203; 703-276-0100, publishes inexpensive consumer advisory materials, such as *Tips on Buying a Home Computer* and *Tips on Car Repair*.)

✔ Source: Local Government

According to Washington Researcher's *How to Find Information About Companies,* city hall may have certain records on file that you could find useful. For example, the county or city clerk could tell you the buyer and seller and description of a parcel of land; the tax assessor could tell you the property value and tax; the planning department may be able to provide you with information on building permits, environmental impact statements, and other data; and the building department could give you information on permit records and the building itself, such as its size and type of construction. Similarly, state and county economic-development agencies may have information on tax break arrangements, zoning variances and planning paperwork.

If you need assistance in searching local government records, you should request a catalog from a publisher called BRB. That firm has published a book called the *Sourcebook of Public Records*, which provides directory information for finding records from federal courts, county courts, state public agencies, and asset/lien searching. Contact BRB Publications, P.O. Box 27869, Tempe, AZ 85385; 800-929-3811.

✔ Source: Local Media

Editors of local business journals and business editors of the local dailies can be excellent sources of information on firms operating within their community. These people are generally very easy to speak with and may not mind spending a few minutes telling you what they know.

✔ Source: Credit Bureaus

Large credit reporting agencies like Dun & Bradstreet and Experian collect payment and certain financial information on millions of firms. You'll have to pay to order these reports, though. Experian can be reached at 888-EXPERIAN; on the Web at http://www.experian.com. Dun and Bradstreet can be contacted at 800-234-3867 and on the Web at http://www.dnb.com

✔ Source: Detective Work

You may need to do some detective work to unearth the information you need. Here are some hints on how to do the digging:

- Call the company itself. You might be surprised how much help you receive.

- Talk to customers. To find customers, send for company literature, which often provides names, or just call the company and ask for references. Once you've contacted the customers, ask them if they know of other customer; this way you'll get to speak to people who were not directly named by the company. Another way to find customers is to post a request on a relevant Internet discussion group.
- Talk to competitors. Check the Yellow Pages to find them.
- Talk to businesses that operate in the same building or are nearby neighbors.
- Talk to suppliers.
- Talk to employees.
- Attend trade shows where the company exhibits.

Digging up information on companies is a recognized discipline called *competitive intelligence*. See page 275 for ethical guidelines and considerations when undertaking this type of research.

COMPANY RESEARCH/IPOS

With all the new dot.com initial public offering (IPO) start-ups, an increasingly popular kind of business research relates to finding out about new IPOs. Naturally, an excellent place to find information about Internet firms turns out to be the Internet itself. Here are some top choices (thanks to the business librarians list-serv BUSLIB for recommendations):

- **Edgar Online**
  http://www.edgar-online.com/bin/esearch/fullsearch.asp

  Search for company filings on Edgar Online (for full description see page 131).

- **IPO Data Systems Inc.**
  http://www.ipodata.com

  See headlines for up-to-the-minute IPO filings and offerings.

- **IPO Central**
  http://www.ipocentral.hoovers.com

  This section of the popular Hoovers site provides a "market buzz" on the latest IPO news as well as a free tracking service, among other offerings.

- **Alert-IPO**
  http://www.ostman.com

  Provides a database of thousands of filings and underwriters. Can conduct searches by several types of criteria.

- **Venture One**
  http://www.ventureone.com

  According to the site, this is geared to be "an all-in-one resource that would enable venture capital professionals to quickly access timely, accurate, and comprehensive information on private venture-backed companies." Its database can be used to find leads, evaluate private companies, and find co-investors.

- **Article: "A Quick Tour Around Value-Added IPO Web Sites," Bruce Liebman, Houlihan Lokey Howard & Zukin.**
  http://www.onlineinc.com/database/DB1998/liebman10.html

  A guide to the premier IPO information sites on the Web.

- **Renaissance Capital's IPO Investing Guide**
  http://www.ipo-fund.com/intro.htm

  Very helpful how-to piece geared to those interested in finding and investing in IPOs.

MARKET RESEARCH

While there are many definitions of market research, typically the term signifies gathering data on buyers in a specific market, on the industry, regional demand, and key products found in that market.

Also sometimes included are company research and research on the regulatory environment. Market research is often conducted when a firm is entering a new area and when start-up firms research the market for the first time. Because there is overlap between conducting market research and some other business-research activities, be sure to read the other sections in this chapter as well as the "Business and Industry" section of chapter 1.

At the Library

✔ **Source: *Gale's Market Share Reporter***

This very useful directory, organized by SIC code, provides market share data on over 2,000 products. Among the types of market share data provided are: corporate market share, institutional shares, and brand market shares. Consulting this directory will tell you, for example, who the top compact refrigerator makers are, or the leading pet-supply stores, or the leading candy vending-machine suppliers.

From the U.S. Government

The previously mentioned *U.S. Industry and Trade Outlook* on page 126 is an excellent source for some basic market data. Much of the market research data provided by the government relates to international markets, and can be found in that section of this chapter.

✔ **Source: Stat-USA**

Although Stat-USA is a fee-based site, it represents the most powerful and extensive market-data offerings from the federal government. Here you can search the enormous National Trade Data Bank (NTDB), "Market and Country Research" reports, "Industry Sector Analysis Reports," "International Marketing Insight Reports" and much more.

Although this is a fee-based service, the fees are not very steep, and are *much* less than what you would pay from a traditional market research publisher.

How to Find:

Call 800-USA-TRADE or link to http://www.stat-usa.gov

✔ **Source: International Trade Commission**

The International Trade Commission publishes free reports that cover various industries. Past reports include the monthly report on the steel industry, the world market for fresh-cut roses, generic pharmaceuticals from Canada, an annual report on selected economic indicators for rum, and studies of natural-bristle paint brushes from the People's Republic of China and cellular mobile telephones from Japan. These are the kinds of reports that, if prepared by a private research firm, could cost well into the hundreds, or even thousands, of dollars.

How to Find:

Contact the International Trade Commission, Attention: Publications, 500 E Street SW, Washington, DC 20436; 202-205-1806. Ask for *Selected Publications of the United States International Trade Commission* (on the Web: http://www.usitc.gov/reports.htm

On the Net

Conducting serious market research on the Internet is something of a mixed blessing—no doubt that there's an enormous amount of information waiting for you out there, and a lot of it will be valuable. The down side, though, is that most of what you

---

TIP: Doing Market Research with a Search Engine

Although I've cautioned against doing market research on a search engine, you can still give it a try. If you do, I'd recommend, as a strategy for focusing your search, you include in your search statement at least one, if not more, of the following words and phrases. These often appear on pages that contain market research–related data:

"units shipped" forecast projected "market share" shipments

Avoid the word "sales" as it is too broad and will pull up too many irrelevant pages.

---

turn up probably won't be of use to you. It's generally not advisable to use a general search engine to conduct intensive market research because you can get so many irrelevant hits, which can be time consuming. It's better to link to sites that are geared to providing market research information.

Market Research Report Directories

One of the best ways to get market research information is to purchase an "off the shelf" prepackaged market research study. These studies, (which have titles like "The Personal Care Product Market" or "The Online Healthcare Information Market," etc.) are filled with market research facts, statistics, and analysis. The following are sites on the Web that will let you search and find one that fits your needs:

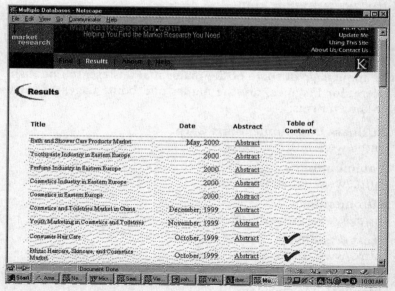

http://www.informationcatalog.com

The Information Catalog, published by Kalorama LLC, lists and describes market research reports on a wide range of consumer, business, and industrial categories.

✔ **Source: The Information Catalog**

http://www.marketresearch.com

You can conduct a free search of thousands of market research studies published in "The Information Catalog" on this site. There is also a more extensive, fee-based search available on a database called Findex.

✔ **Source: MarketSearch**

http://www.marketsearch-dir.com

Search thousands of market research reports on this U.K.-based site. There is a convenient numerical code for browsing by subject and by industry.

✔ **Source: Publications Resource Group, Inc. (PRG)**

http://www.prguide.com

This database also includes newsletters and directories.

Market Research Vendor Home Pages

Another way to find market research reports is to link directly to the home page of some of the major market research publishers. Here, for instance, are the names and home pages of some better-known firms:

- **Business Communications Corp.**
  http://www.buscom.com

- **Datamonitor**
  http://www.datamonitor.com

- **Euromonitor**
  http://www.euromonitor.com

- **Frost & Sullivan**
  http://www.frost.com

- **The Gartner Group**
  http://www.gartner.com

- **Kalorama Information**
  http://www.marketresearch.com

There is also an Internet "mall" that brings together reports from dozens of the largest market research report publishers all under one roof, so to speak. Its called the IMR Mall and you can link to it at http://www.imrmall.com

Eveluating Market Research Reports

When reading a study that purports to measure the size of a market, or forecast an industry's or product's growth, it is wise to be a bit skeptical. Here are some guidelines for analyzing these types of reports:

- Where did the data come from? A seemingly obvious question, but Portia Isaacson, Ph.D., chairman of DREAM IT of Boulder, Colorado, says published market numbers are derived from all manner of sources: complex and statistically valid measurement studies, informal questionnaires, someone's educated guess, or even a remark overheard at a trade show. You need to pin down specifically where the data came from.
- How were the data collected? Was it via personal interviews, phone calls, mail surveys, or a combination of the three? If you can, get a copy of the actual questionnaire and examine it closely.
- Who provided the data? Isaacson notes that data that are "demand driven"—derived from *users* rather than manufacturers—are the most reliable. Reliability of data obtained from distributors or dealers sits between the two.
- Does the study provide text? Raw data alone is not enough. You need to be able to find out what the assumptions, reasoning, and logic were behind those numbers. Then you can determine for yourself whether the numbers derived from those assumptions are legitimate.
- Can you speak with the researcher? This is important if you are to get your specific questions answered.
- Does the firm have experience and credibility? Is the subject of the report a field in which the firm has credibility? If not, be sure to find out what the analysts' competencies are in this field. Recent MBAs, says Isaacson, may some day be experts, but they will not be right away. Sometimes you can find out a firm's track record by obtaining copies of their previous market reports and checking to see how accurate they were.
- If the study is a forecast, it should try to take into account the

various social, economic, and political events that may affect the phenomena being measured. Be wary of forecasts whose projections increase or decrease in a strict linear manner, because these calculations are not taking into account real-world events that alter neat progressions.

- How is the report marketed? Beware of published data that appears to be sensational. In those cases, the need to market and sell the information can take precedence over the truth. Also be careful of slickly packaged market studies that scream of exploding markets and industries without providing convincing evidence. Some firms tend to be extremely optimistic in their projections because a soaring new market will mean more buyers of their reports and consulting services. Similarly, beware of very positive projections when the issuer has something to gain. For example, city chamber of commerce studies nearly always show growth and positive trends for their region.

Experts in this field advise users of market studies not to rely on a single study, but to try to find as many studies as possible and compare the findings. Plot low and high points, and look for consensus. When in doubt, go with the most conservative numbers and assume that even those numbers may be optimistic. Even more to the point, never use published market data alone as the basis for making a major decision. Instead, get input from many different sources—talking to vendors, attending trade shows, talking to customers, and doing your own research.

Keep in mind, too, that for fast-moving industries, such as high technology, health care, and finance, some reports (just like books) may go out of date very quickly and be too tied to conventional ways of defining the market and competition to be able to provide much of an edge.

Miscellaneous

✔ Source: Mailing-list Brokers

Here's a good way of finding the type of person or organization that might be most interested in buying your product or using your service. Mailing-list brokers can provide you with thousands of names and addresses of people in specific professions (say, rabbis or biologists) and types of business and organizations (pet shops, funeral homes, and so on). You can order the names and addresses on pressure-sensitive labels, so you can stick them on envelopes and mail your promotional flyer or other information. Prices for the names are less than what you may think—typically running about $45 to $100 per thousand labels.

How to Find:
Look in the Yellow Pages under "Mailing Lists" to find a firm.

✔ Source: Associations

Professional associations often poll their members and conduct surveys and studies related to their particular industry. To find a relevant association, check the *Encyclopedia of Associations* (see page 57), or search for associations on the Net at http://info. asaenet.org/Gateway/OnlineAssocslist.html

ECONOMIC RESEARCH

From the U.S. Government

In addition to the STAT-USA database highlighted on page 143, here are some other key sources for finding the latest economic news and statistics:

✔ Source: Bureau of Economic Analysis

This bureau within the Department of Commerce measures and analyzes U.S. economic activity and provides information on issues such as economic growth, inflation, regional development, and the nation's role in the world economy. An excellent periodical issued by the bureau is the *Survey of Current Business,* which provides estimates and analyses of U.S. economic activity and includes a review of current economic developments and quarterly national-income and product-account tables. The bureau also publishes various economic papers, such as *Selected Data on U.S. Direct Investment Abroad 1950–1976* and *New Foreign Securities Offered in the United States 1952–1964*.

How to Find:

Contact the Bureau of Economic Analysis, U.S. Department of Commerce, 1441 L Street NW, Washington, DC 20230; 202-606-9900; on the Web: http://www.bea.doc.gov. A helpful document is *Catalog of Products*, which can be ordered by calling 800-704-0415.

✔ Source: Bureau of Labor Statistics

The Department of Labor publishes statistical data on employment, prices, wages, living conditions, and productivity. Other specialties include state economic statistics, industry statistics, consumer expenditures, economic growth projections, and occupational outlooks. The BLS publishes a directory called the *Customer Service Guide*, which identifies the bureau's experts and specialists and gives their phone numbers.

How to Find:

Contact the U.S. Department of Labor, Bureau of Labor Statistics, Division of Information Services, 2 Massachusetts Avenue NE, Washington, DC 20212; 202-606-5886.

✔ Source: Federal Reserve Board Publications

The Federal Reserve Board publishes statistical data on banking and monetary interest rates, subjects like flow of funds and savings, business conditions, wages, prices, and productivity.

How to Find:

Contact the publications service of the Board of Governors of the Federal Reserve System, Publications Services, MS 127, Washington, DC 20551; 202-452-3245. Ask for the guide *Federal Reserve Board Publications*.

You can also see the latest economic news releases and search for historical data on the Federal Reserve Board's Web site at http://www.federalreserve.gov/releases/

✔ Source: Bureau of the Census

The Census Bureau makes available data about employment, unemployment, housing starts, wholesale and retail trade, manufacturers' shipments, inventories and orders, and exports and imports, as well as other business and economic statistics.

Two helpful guides published by the Bureau are designed specifically to assist businesspersons who want to understand various economic reports and series. *Introduction to the Economic Censuses* is a short pamphlet that identifies the different economic censuses and advises businesses how to use data appropriately; *Census ABCs* explains more broadly how the census collects its data, and how to choose the right type of data depending on a business' particular needs.

How to Find:

Contact the Bureau of the Census, Customer Services Office, Washington, DC 20233; 301-457-4100.

One particularly useful series is *County Business Patterns*. These are employment and payroll statistics in each county in the United States, broken down by SIC code. For each SIC classification, information is provided on number of people employed, payroll figures, and other data. (Be careful in using this source—sometimes the information is old.)

How to Find:

Contact the Superintendent of Documents, Box 371954, Pittsburgh, PA 15250-7954; 202-512-1800. For more details on census information sources, see page 67.

✔ Source: IRS Statistics of Income Division

This division can provide you with various financial statistics drawn from past tax returns. Statistics are broken down into various filing categories—corporation income tax returns, industry statistics, investment tax credit statistics, estate tax returns, foreign income and taxes, partnership returns, the underground economy, and so forth. The statistics are published in the *Statistics of Income Bulletin*, which includes both statistics and summaries that explain and interpret the data. Many statistics are not published in the bulletin but are available if you write to the division directly.

How to Find:

The bulletin is available from the U.S. Government Printing Office. To contact the division itself, write Internal Revenue Service, Statistics of Income Division, 500 North Capitol Street NW, Washington, DC 20224; 202-874-0410. (Or fax your request to 202-874-0964.)

✔ **Source: United Nations**

Annual publications issued by the United Nations are a good source of facts and statistics on international business. Samples include *Agricultural Trends in Europe*, *International Trade Statistics: Concepts and Definitions*, *Statistics of World Trade in Steel*, and *World Economic Survey*. Some UN publications are expensive, but many are reasonably priced.

How to Find:

Contact United Nations Publications, Room DC2-0853, United Nations, New York, NY 10017; 212-963-8325/8302. On the Web: http://www.un.org/publications

On the Net

✔ **Source: National Bureau of Economic Research**

http://www.nber.org

A private, nonprofit, nonpartisan organization that engages in economic research, the NBER makes available scores of papers and reports on its Web sites. Sample titles include: "The Future of Health Economics," "Occupational Gender Composition and Wages in Canada," and "The Effect of Marginal Tax Rates on Income."

✔ **Source: FRED**

http://www.stls.frb.org/fred/abotfred.html

A free service from the Federal Reserve Bank of St. Louis, FRED provides an easy-to-use system to search for historical U.S. economic and financial data, including daily U.S. interest rates, monetary and business indicators, exchange rates, balance of payments, and regional economic data.

✔ **Source: Resources for Economists on the Internet**
   http://www.rfe.org
Sponsored by the American Economic Association, this site lists more than 1,000 screened resources on the Internet of interest to academic and practicing economists, and those interested in economics.

INVESTMENT-RELATED RESEARCH

Although this book is not geared for providing investment information and advice, there are several general-purpose sites that I can recommend as starting points for the beginning investor.

At the Library

✔ **Source: Standard & Poor's *The Outlook* (McGraw-Hill)**
This is a leading source designed to provide some general investment information for nonexperts. *The Outlook* is a weekly bulletin that analyzes and projects business and market trends. It analyzes changes in the stock market, discusses firms currently in the limelight, and evaluates the worthiness of buying or selling particular stocks. The graphics are pleasing, and it is easy to use and read. It can be found in most large public libraries or in nearly all business libraries.

From the U.S. Government

✔ **Source: Securities and Exchange Commission (SEC)**
The SEC publishes free advice on investing. Their booklet is titled *What Every Investor Should Know*. Call 202-942-8088 for more details. The SEC's consumer information line is 800-SEC-0330.

On the Net

✔ **Source: New York Stock Exchange (NYSE)**

The NYSE publishes free and inexpensive guides on how to invest.

How to Find:

Contact the New York Stock Exchange, Inc., Publications Division, 11 Wall Street, New York, NY 10005; 212-656-2089. On the Web: http://www.nyse.com

✔ **Source: National Association of Securities Dealers**

This is the self-regulating organization of the securities industry. Its members represent virtually all the broker-dealers in the nation doing a securities business with the public. The association publishes two useful guides that are free: *Guide to Information and Services*, which lists various specialists within the association, and the *NASDAQ Fact Book*, which provides various data and summaries of stock prices and volume of the NASDAQ (National Association of Securities Dealers Automated Quotation System) securities. The association can also help you if you have a complaint against a broker or are looking for market statistics.

How to Find:

Contact the National Association of Securities Dealers Inc., 1735 K Street NW, Washington, DC 20006; 202-728-6900. On the Web: http://www.nasd.com

✔ **Source: Investment News and Information Sites**

Some very popular and comprehensive sites for the online investor are:

- **CBS MarketWatch**
  http://marketwatch.com

- **CNNfn**
  http://www.cnnfn.com

- **Stockmaster**
  http://www.stockmaster.com

- ***Wall Street Journal* Interactive (fee-based)**
  http://www.wsj.com

- **Motley Fool**
  http://www.fool.com

- **BigCharts**
  http://www.bigcharts.com

✔ **Source: Message Boards**

While you need to be careful in evaluating the accuracy and credibility of what you find on these unfiltered discussion groups, they represent an intriguing and alternative source of information on the prospects for investing in various public firms. Three of the best known are:

- **Yahoo Message Boards**
  http://mess ages.yahoo.com/index.html

- **Raging Bull Message Boards**
  http://www.ragingbull.com

- **SiliconInvestor**
  http://www.siliconinvestor.com

✔ **Source: Online Brokerage Sites**

There is a mountain of online investing information available from the brokers themselves, both full service and discount. Here, for example, are the names and URLs of some of the most popular:

- **Ameritrade**
  http://www.ameritrade.com

- **E* Trade**
  http://www.etrade.com

- **Fidelity**
  http://www.fidelity.com

- **Charles Schwab**
  http://www.eschwab.com

COMPANY START-UP/ ENTREPRENEURIAL RESEARCH

Looking to start your own business? Try these excellent sources for quick assistance:

At the Library

✔ **Source: *Small Business Sourcebook* (Gale Research)**

An extremely comprehensive yet easy-to-use directory for finding all sorts of sources of information and assistance for the small business. The book not only identifies where to find general business help but also includes special sections covering 250 specific types of small business and where to find advice and assistance. Some of those industries include antique shops, art galleries, bed and breakfasts, bookstores, gourmet food stores, consumer electronic stores, day-care centers, ice cream shops, magazine publishing, pet shops, pizzerias, software publishing, and videocassette stores. Overall, the guide is an excellent place to begin digging out information on starting a new business.

✔ **Source: *The Best Home Businesses for the 21st Century: The Inside Information You Need to Know to Select a Home-Based Business That's Right for You*, Paul and Sarah Edwards, (Jeremy P. Tarcher).**

This book provides a wealth of data for budding entrepreneurs, such as the skills and knowledge needed to start up a business; the start-up costs, pricing, and earning potential of different businesses; the best ways to find new clients; the advantages and disadvantages of various businesses; and the hands-on advice of those already in the field.

Also try to get hold of the following books at the library:

- *Business Plan Handbook* (Gale Group) or *Anatomy of a Business Plan: A Step-by-Step Guide to Starting Smart, Building the Business, and Securing Your Company's Future*, Linda Pinson and Jerry Jinnett (Dearborn Trade)
- *Pratt's Guide to Venture Capital Sources* (Venture Economics)

Cheese/Wine/Gourmet Food Shop

Start-up Information

2681
"Cheese and Wine Shop" in *Small Businesses That Grow and Grow and Grow (pp. 206-207)*
Betterway Publications, Inc.
White Hall, VA 22987   Phone: (804)823-5661

Woy, Patricia A. 1984. $7.95 (paper). A chapter about establishing a cheese and wine shop.

2682
Gourmet Wine and Cheese Shop Start-up Manual
American Entrepreneurs Association (AEA)
2311 Pontius Ave.
Los Angeles, CA 90064   Phone: (800)421-2300

$59.50 ($54.50 for AEA members). Contains step-by-step instructions on how to start a cheese, wine, and gourmet food store. Includes information on profits and costs, location, market potential, financing, advertising and promotion, customers, and related data. **Toll-free/Additional Phone Number:** 800-352-7449 (in California).

Primary Associations

2683
American Cheese Society (ACS)
Main St.
P.O. Box 97
Ashfield, MA 01330   Phone: (201)236-2990

Purpose: To provide a network for members who seek solutions to problems regarding cheesemaking processes or related regulations. Activities include cheese tastings, gourmet cooking demonstrations, and cheese making demonstrations. **Membership:** Primarily small-scale cheese producers; also includes retailers and wholesalers.

2684
International Dairy-Deli Association (IDDA)
313 Price Pl., Suite 202
P.O. Box 5528
Madison, WI 53705   Phone: (608)238-7908

Purpose: Promotes professional development and the exchange of information and ideas among members. Bestows awards for outstanding achievement. Holds annual seminar and exposition. **Membership:** Companies and organizations engaged in the production, processing, packaging, marketing, promotion, and/or selling of cheese, bakery, or delicatessen-related products. **Publications:** 1) *Dairy-Deli Digest* (monthly); 2) *Dairy-Deli Wrap-Up* (quarterly); 3) *Who's Who in Deli*Dairy*Bakery* (semiannual); 4) *Annual Seminar Proceedings.* Also publishes research reports and produces educational slide-tape programs.

2685
National Association for the Specialty Food Trade (NASFT)
215 Park Ave., S., Suite 1606
New York, NY 10003   Phone: (212)505-177

Purpose: To promote the specialty food industry. Sponsors competitions; bestows awards. Holds annual trade show. **Membership:** Manufacturers, processors, importers, and brokers of specialty and gourmet foods. **Publications:** 1) *NASFT Showcase* (semimonthly); 2) *RD Trends* (bimonthly).

Other Organizations of Interest

2686
International Federation of Wine and Spirits (IFWS)
103 Blvd. Haussmann
F-75008 Paris, France   Phone: 1 265

Purpose: To protect the industry at all levels of comm **Membership:** Industrialists and wholesalers of wine, spirits, br and liqueurs. **Publications:** 1) *Bulletin* (5/year); 2) *Newsletter* (5/...

2687
National Association of Specialty Food and Confection Broker (NASFCB)
Burgess, Bradstreet, and Associates
14229 Bessemer St.
Van Nuys, CA 91401   Phone: (818)997-056

Membership: Professional food brokers who supply department stores, gourmet shops, grocery chains, health food trades, and other companies with quality products for retail purposes. **Publications:** 1) *Newsletter* (quarterly); 2) *Directory of Members* (annual).

Educational Programs

2688
International Dairy-Deli Association (IDDA)
313 Price Pl., Suite 202
P.O. Box 5528
Madison, WI 53705   Phone: (608)238-79

Provides slide-tape programs on merchandising, sales, emplo motivation and training, customer satisfaction, and research in cheese and deli industry. Offers home-study courses, cosponsore the Cornell University Food Industry Management Program.

Reference Works

2689
The Cheese Handbook: A Guide to the World's Best Cheeses
Dover Publications, Inc.
31 E. Second St.
Mineola, NY 11501   Phone: (516)294-7000

Layton, T. A. Revised edition. 1973. $3.50 (paper).

253

From the U.S. Government

✔ Source: Small Business Administration

Among the services and resources offered by the SBA are business loans; assisting small high-technology firms; special programs for veteran-, minority-, and women-owned small businesses; encouraging international trade by educational, outreach, and trade programs; assistance in procuring federal contracts; counseling and training in developing new business; and other programs.

Various books and pamphlets to help people in business are published by the SBA. Materials include general advisory publications that would be of interest to all beginning businesspersons, like *Going into Business*, *Business Plan for Home-Based Businesses*, *Researching Your Market*, and *Outwitting Bad-Check Passers*, as well as publications about starting a business in one particular field, such as *Starting Out in Cosmetology*. The booklets are all free or very inexpensive.

How to Find:

A useful free brochure outlining the various programs available is titled *Programs & Services*. Write Office of Public Communications, Small Business Administration, 409 Third Street SW, Washington, DC 20416. For a free catalog of publications, contact SBA Publications, 800-827-5722.

✔ Source: Patent and Trademark Office

If you want to find out whether your idea for a new product has already been registered for a patent, or find out about the use of a trademark, contact the U.S. Patent Office. The office registers and grants patents and trademarks, and it provides information on them to the public. You can obtain an index of patents and order printed copies of patents for $3 each. There are also many depository libraries around the United States where you can inspect copies of patents.

How to Find:

Contact the Patent and Trademark Office, Washington, DC 20231; 800-786-9199 (General Information). On the Web: http://uspto.gov

On the Net

✔ **Source: National Small Business Development Center Research Network**

http://www.smallbiz.suny.edu

The National Small Business Development Center Research Network provides a wide range of information and assistance to smaller businesses, entrepreneurs, and so on.

TIP: You can find out about patent depository libraries located nearer to you; request a copy of "Basic Facts about Patents," available from the Patent and Trademark Office. You can also search a free database of patent filings on IBM's Intellectual Property Network on the Web. Link to: http://patent.womplex.ibm.com

---

✔ **Source: Derwent Patent Reference Center**

http://www.derwent.com/resource/frameset.html

Derwent is a leading supplier of (fee-based) patent search-and-retrieval technologies. Its site includes very helpful advice on understanding and using patents and patent search technologies.

✔ **Source: American Express Small Business Exchange**

http://www6.americanexpress.com/smallbusiness/resources/expanding/global/

A variety of useful advice and information for the small business, from buying and selling a business, to hiring, marketing, taxes and more.

Miscellaneous

✔ **Source: *Business Planning for Scientists and Engineers***

A combined textbook and workbook that serves as a how-to guide to commercializing a product or technology. Focuses on creating the business plan, including finding funding, sizing markets, choosing a commercialization strategy and more. Integrates a creative method for developing the business plan through mind

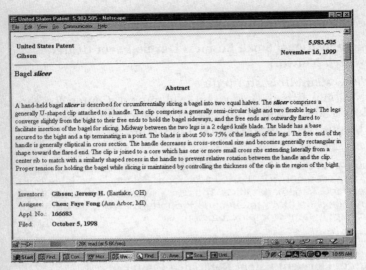

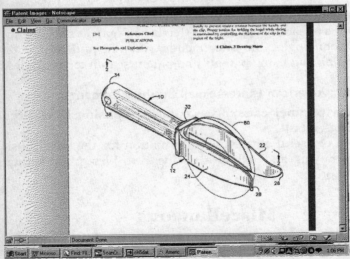

Source: www.uspto.gov

The U.S. Patent and Trademark Office lets you search for patent filings and then view them at no charge—including all of the accompanying illustrations and images.

mapping, strategic planning, and much more. A great combination planning, reference, and idea generation manual for anyone who needs to know how to introduce a new product or technology to the market.

How to Find:
To inquire about pricing and to place an order, contact: Dawnbreaker Press, Suite 193, 2117 Buffalo Road, Rochester, NY 14624; 716-264-0510.

✔ **Source: *Deciding to Go Public***

A free 140-page booklet, *Deciding to Go Public: Understanding the Process and Alternatives*, is offered by the national accounting firm Ernst & Young. Among the subjects discussed in the book are the benefits and drawbacks of going public, selecting an underwriter, use of an accountant, and alternatives to going public.

How to Find:
Contact Customer Service at Ernst & Young, 1559 Superior Ave, Cleveland, OH 44114; 216-861-5000, or call a local branch office.

TIP: Marketing Information
• The previously mentioned *County Business Patterns* (page 153), published by the Bureau of the Census, can be used as a marketing tool to find out what kinds of establishments exist in a particular region of the country. For example, according to the Census Bureau, an East Coast department store chain considered opening a new store in an established shopping mall when store planners used census data to find the numbers and types of retail outlets in the area. From this information, they established business growth in the area and potential sales in the new store.

INTERNATIONAL BUSINESS RESEARCH/REACHING OVERSEAS MARKETS

In the global economy, it's critical to be able to extend your research beyond your own country's borders. Here are some recommended information sources for conducting international business research. Also listed here are sources and sites that will help businesses export and sell to overseas markets.

At the Library

First See: The section in chapter 1 on "International Business Directories" to find the names of the basic look-up sources. Two other very helpful sources you'll find are:

✔ **Source: *World Business Directory* (Gale Research)**

Provides data on 140,000 businesses involved in international trade, importing, and exporting.

TIP: Consumer Demographic and Opinion Sources
Here are three handy sources for finding out about characteristics, opinions, and other data on potential customers.

• *Population Reference Bureau* is a private, scientific, and educational organization established to gather, interpret, and disseminate facts and implications of population trends. It covers almost all areas in the field, such as income statistics, the elderly in America, the world labor market, international demographics, and much more. Most of the Bureau's reports and publications are very inexpensive. Contact Population Reference Bureau, 1875 Connecticut Ave NW, Suite 520, Washington DC 20009; 202-483-1100.

• *The Roper Center for Public Opinion Research,* located at the University of Connecticut in Storrs, has a database of over 7,000 "opinions" of the public on subjects ranging from views on AIDS to supermarket buying habits. You can find out answers to questions such as how many people own home computers or whether consumers are willing to pay more for a brand name. Contact the Roper Center at 860-486-4440.

• *The Insider's Guide to Demographic Know-How* (American Demographics, Ithaca, New York) provides a do-it-yourself approach to analyzing demographic data (e.g., analyzing characteristics of certain targeted populations by key variables such as sex, age, and income) and lists 600 federal, state, local, and private sources of demographic information. This site, established by the publishers of *American Demographics* magazine, is a trove of useful resources for demographic and consumer-marketing oriented research. Link to http://www.demographics.com

---

✔ **Source: *International Business Information: How to Find It, How to Use It* (Oryx)**

An excellent and comprehensive guide to finding international company information, marketing data, and economic reports. Appendices include a glossary, a comparison chart of accounting standards in 48 countries, sample balance sheets, and more. The authors, Ruth A. Pagell and Michael Halperin, are well-known experts in the information industry.

From the U.S. Government

One of the primary missions of several agencies in the federal government is to help U.S. businesses penetrate and succeed in selling goods and services to overseas markets. As such, there are several top-notch programs and services—mostly free—geared just to those who want information and contacts for exporting and learning about new international markets.

The ITA's Office of Trade and Economic Analysis supports trade promotion by analyzing and disseminating international trade data. Among the trade information offered are links to global data sources; downloadable tables of goods and service data by country and region; statistics for U.S. industry sectors; export data by state and cities; and more.

How to Find:

Contact the OTEA by linking to its Web site: www.ita.gov/itd/industry/otea/index.html

✔ **Source: International Trade Administration, Office of Trade and Economic Development**

The ITA's Office of Trade and Economic Analysis supports trade promotion by analyzing and disseminating international trade data. Among the trade informaion offered are links to global data sources; downloadable tables of goods and service data by country and region; statistics for U.S. industry sectors; export data by state and cities; and more.

How to Find:
Contact the OTEA by linking to its Web site:
www.ita.gov/td/industry/otea/index.html

✔ **Source: International Trade Administration,
Trade Development Office**

The Trade Development Office promites U.S. exports by providing industry expertise on a wide range of U.S. business sectors. you can link to an "Industries page" to obtain links and data for industries from aerospace to telecommunications, and get a list of "industry specialists" e-mail and phone numbers on areas of expertise ranging from adhesives to zinc.

How to Find:
Link to: www.ita.doc.gov/ita_home/itacnreg.html

✔ **Source: International Trade Administration,
Countries and Regions**

This section of the ITA provides access to ITA Web sites, which provide information on the "Big Emerging Markets" (BEMs) and other leading markets of the world.

How to Find:
Link to: www.ita.doc.gov/ita_home/itacnreg.htm

✔ **Source: USA Trade.Gov**

USA Trade is operated by the U.S. Commercial Services, whose mission is to promote exports; support U.S. international commercial interests in the U.S. and abroad; and assist the U.S. business community in the identifying new markets and expanding sales and market share around the globe. Among it's offerings are: Customized Market Analysis for specific products in specific countries (fee-based); Country COmmercial Guides (economic trends; political environment; marketing U.S. products, leading sectors; trade regulations/sanctions; investment climate travel and more) guides to exporting

How to Find:
Link to: www.usatrade.gov

✔ Source: USA Trade Center

USA Trade Center is a major clearinghouse of information, created by the U.S. Department of Commerce. Among its services are export counseling, country-specific commercial information, and trade opportunities. The USA Trade Center includes the "Trade Information Center" and the "Trade Reference Information Service" (see separate listings below).

How to Find:

Contact the USA Trade Center at 800-USA-TRADE or link to its Web site at: http://usatc.doc.gov

✔ Source: Trade Information Center

A part of the Commerce Department's USA Trade Center, the Trade Information Center is billed as a "first stop" for export assistance. Included is industry-specific information; publications such as *A Business Guide to Federal Export Assistance*; latest export news and current events; country and regional market information; international trade offices nationwide; foreign tariff, taxes, and customs information; trade promotion events; trade lead information; financing information; links to related sites; and more.

How to Find:

Contact the Trade Information Center at 800-USA-TRADE or link to its Web site at: http://tradeinfo.doc.gov

✔ Source: Trade Reference Information Service

Another division of USA Trade Center, this service provides international business directories (e.g., *The Polish Yellow Pages*) and country and regional market information such as customs, services and product information, laws and procedures, U.S. governmental regulations and embargoes, financing regulations and contacts, general economic information, and business travel and etiquette.

How to Find:

Contact the Trade Reference Information Service at 202-482-3433. On the Web: http://www.ita.doc.gov/trac/

✔ **Source: Market Access and Compliance (MAC)**

The goal of the Department of Commerce's newly formed Market Access and Compliance division is to "level the playing field for U.S. exporters" by helping U.S. businesses overcome barriers to trade and investment. Geared particulary for small and midsized businesses, MAC provides information on rights and benefits under existing trade agreements, advises on strategies, and assists businesses in resolving trade issues with foreign governments.

There are individual subdivisions that deal particularly with issues related to NAFTA and to Japan. NAFTA & Inter-American Affairs helps firms facing trade barriers in Canada or Mexico and offers counsling by trade specialists. It also has an automated fax-on-demand information service called "NAFTA Facts" that provides various trade statistics, demographics, and other data on doing business in Canada and Mexico.

The Office of Japan provides news, and market-opening initiatives by specific industry: automotive, building materials and housing, computers, construction, medical, pharmaceutical, photographic, telecommunications, and more. Also available are *Fact Sheets on Japan*, trade data, investment statistics, regulations, certification systems, a guide to Japan's patent system and other useful reports.

How to Find:

You can learn all you need by linking to MAC's Web page at: http://www.mac.doc.gov. Or you can call a desk officer for assistance. Desk officers are experts that keep track of markets and they are divided into regions as follows:

- Western Hemisphere: 202-482-5324
- Europe: 202-482-5638
- Africa and the Near East: 202-482-4925
- Asia and the Pacific: 202-482-5251
- Japan: 202-482-4527

✔ **Source: Central & Eastern Europe Business Information Center (CEEBIC)**

The CEEBIC is designed to be a first-stop clearinghouse for companies interested in doing business in Eastern Europe.

One of the specialties of the CEEBIC is assisting businesses in analyzing a country's overall climate for doing business. For example, the center will advise whether a country's phone systems are workable. Also available is the Eastern Europe Looks for Partners service, whereby Eastern European firms send in requests for U.S. partners, and the *Bulletin*, a monthly newsletter profiling countries, industry sectors, and trade opportunities.

How to Find:

Contact the CEEBIC at 1401 Constitution Ave NW, Department of Commerce, R-CEEBIC Washington, DC 20230; 202-482-2645; e-mail: ceebic@ita.doc.gov; on the Web: http://www.mac.doc.gov/eebic/eebic.html

✔ Source: Export Counseling Center

If you've decided you'd like to give selling overseas a try, you can obtain free help from the International Trade Administration's Export Counseling Center, a one-stop shopping location set up by the government to assist exporters. The center publishes a variety of helpful publications, such as *How to Get the Most from Overseas Exhibitions*, *A Guide to Financing Exports*, and a weekly bulletin on export opportunities for U.S. firms. The bulletin includes direct sales leads from overseas buyers, foreign government bid invitations, notification of foreign buyer visits to the United States, and more. Lots of other help is available, too, including a mailing list of foreign business contacts, agents, distributors, retailers, wholesalers, manufacturers, and exporters for virtually any industry in 116 countries.

How to Find:

Contact the Trade Information Center, U.S. Department of Commerce, USA Trade Center, 1401 Constitution Ave NW R-TIC, Washington DC 20230; 800-872-8723. A particularly useful guide to ask for is called *Export Programs: A Business Directory of U.S. Government Resources*. The guide is also available on the Web at http://tradeinfo.doc.gov

✔ Source: U.S. Bureau of the Census

The U.S. Bureau of Census' International Database provides demographic, economic, and social data for 227 countries. For information contact: Pat Dickerson or Peter Johnson, International Programs Center, U.S. Bureau of the Census, Washington, DC 20233-8860; 301-457-1403; e-mail: idb@census.gov; on the Web at: http://www.census.gov/ftp/pub/ipc/www/idbnew.html

✔ **Source: *CIA World Factbook***

This book has become one of the standard geographic references, especially for Internet users. Click on a country to see a full official profile, including a map, and scores of facts on geography, people and demographics, form of government, economy, communications, transportation, military and transnational issues. You can purchase a hard copy or browse information for free on the Internet at: http://www.odci.gov/cia/publications/factbook/

On the Net

✔ **Source: The Electronic Embassy**
http://www.embassy.org
A country's embassy is an excellent source of information for facts on that particular country. This useful site provides complete contact information, including an e-mail address and home page (where it exists) for every country's embassy.

✔ **Source: CorporateInformation**
http://www.corporateinformation.com
Excellent and comprehensive site for researching facts on companies around the world. Contains profiles, research studies, links, and virtually anything else you'll need to find information on international firms and businesses.

✔ **Source: International Business Resources on the WWW**
http://ciber.bus.msu.edu/busres.htm
A service of Michigan State University's Center for International Business Education and Research, this site is a wealth of sources and links for performing international business research.

✔ **Source: InfoNation**
**http://www.un.org/Pubs/CyberSchoolBus/infonation/
e_infonation.htm**
A service of the United Nations, InfoNation is a database that allows you to view and compare the latest statistical data for the member states of the United Nations.

✔ **Source: Strategis Canada**
   http://strategis.ic.gc.ca/engdoc/main.html
A comprehensive business information site geared primarily
for Canadian businesses who wish to export and those interested
in Canadian business. The site lets one identify new markets, find
business partners, form alliances, locate emerging technologies or
processes, and assess various risk factors. Sections include
Company Directories; Trade and Investment; Business
Information by Sector; Economic Analysis and Statistics;
Research, Technology and Innovation; Business Support and
Financing Licences; Legislation and Regulations; and more.

✔ **Source: British Trade International Export Market**
   Information Centre
   http://www.brittrade.com/emic/international.html
Provides links to international sites providing market and
export information. Geared to the British exporter, but potentially
useful for anyone wishing to reach foreign markets, especially
those in Europe.

Miscellaneous

✔ **Source: The United Nations**

The UN has, as you might expect, several sources of interest to
those conducting international business research. Its *Statistical
Yearbook* is a wealth of data with over 1 million entries on the member
states of the UN, including comparative information. Other publications
include: *World Investment Report*, *Trade and Development
Report*, *World Economic and Social Survey*, and many more.

For information contact the UN's Publications department at
publications@un.org or 800-253-9646. On the Web link to:
http://www.un.org/Pubs/sales.htm

The United Nations also publishes a list called *UN Services and
Embassies*. This is a listing of the addresses and phone numbers
of consulate and embassy locations. Contact the UN Public
Inquiries Unit General Building, UN Headquarters, New York, NY
10017; 212-963-4475.

> **TIP:** If you need to gather facts, statistics, and analyses of European countries and markets, request a catalog from a United Kingdom firm called Euromonitor. This company produces some of the most comprehensive and detailed reference directories on European business issues. Note, though, that most are quite expensive, so your best bet may be looking for these guides in a university business library and/or one whose scope includes international trade. You can reach the firm at Euromonitor, 60-61 Britton St., London EC1M 5UX, UK. Phone (from the U.S.): 44-171-251-8024. On the Web: http://www.euromonitor.com

A distributor for many of the UN's and other international organizations' publications is a company called Bernan. Not only is the firm a distributor for the United Nations, but it also sells for the European Communities, the Food & Agriculture Organization (FAO), the World Bank, International Monetary Fund (IMF), General Agreement on Tariffs and Trade (GATT), the official British government publisher HMSO, Organization for Economic Cooperation and Development (OECD), the International Labor Organization (ILO), and other well-known international and non-U.S. institutions.

How to Find:

Contact Bernan, 4611-F Assembly Drive, Lanham, MD 20706-4391; 800-274-4888. On the Web: www.bernan.com

✔ Source: Association for Asian Studies

The Association for Asian Studies is a scholarly, nonpolitical, nonprofit professional association that facilitates contact and exchange of information among scholars, students, businesspersons, journalists, and others for an increased understanding of Asia. On the Web: http://www.aasianst.org

How to Find:

Contact Association for Asian Studies, 1021 E. Huron St., University of Michigan, Ann Arbor, MI 48104; 734-665-2490

✔ Source: Country Consulates and Embassies

You can obtain help on questions you have about a particular market in a country by contacting its consulate office. Check the white pages of a major city phone book to find the consulate you seek. Or you can try the country's embassy in Washington, DC. The State Department publishes a *Diplomatic List*, which gives the names and addresses of embassy personnel.

How to Find:

You can obtain this list from the Superintendent of Documents, Box 371954, Pittsburgh, PA 15250-7954; 202-512-1800; or check a library for a copy.

✔ **Source: NAFTA and Doing Business in Mexico**

Chambers of commerce are some of the best places to turn for information on NAFTA and trade with Mexico. The following two can be of assistance:

American Chamber of Commerce of Mexico. Among its publications are *Business Mexico, Directory of American Company Operations in Mexico, The Guide to Mexico for Business,* and *Markets in Mexico: Location and Logistics.*

How to Find:

Contact the American Chamber of Commerce of Mexico, Lucerna 78, Co. Juarez, 06600 Mexico City, Mexico; fax 011-525-703-3908; e-mail: dp@amchammex.com.mx; on the Web: http://www.amcham. com.mx/

U.S. Mexico Chamber of Commerce. Promotes private-sector trade, conducts seminars, and publishes a newsletter, bulletin, and various booklets.

How to Find:

Contact the U.S. Mexico Chamber of Commerce, 1300 Pennsylvania Ave NW, Suite 270, Washington, DC 20004; 202-296-5198.

BUSINESS SUPERSOURCES

The following are the names of several comprehensive business information sources, of all types and of different media, that provide such comprehensive information that they cannot be fit into a single business-information category.

✔ Source: Brooklyn, New York Business Library

Whether you need industry statistics, company financial data, or stock information, or have an inquiry on virtually any other business-related subject, the Brooklyn, New York Business Library may be able to help you. It's one of the leading, if not *the* leading business library in the country. It takes phone inquiries and tries to answer any financial, economic, or industry-oriented question that can be answered with a fact or referral.

How to Find:
Call the library's reference desk at 718-623-7000.

✔ Source: State Government

Lots of buried business-related information is available from state governments. The best department to contact is the state's "corporations division." Among the documents available there are annual reports, articles of incorporation, and sometimes balance sheet and sales information. These offices may also be called the state's department of commerce. Another useful office is the department of economic development. The trigger for determining whether or not a company needs to file within a state is whether or not it maintains an office in the state—it need not be headquartered there. The documents themselves provide finances for the entire company (not just for locations within the state), unless a separate company has been created just to do business in that state.

As an example, here is what I uncovered by contacting the Arizona Department of Commerce:

Arizona's business and trade division of its department of commerce publishes a number of free guides packed with business-related information. For example, it collects state export statistics and publishes an international trade directory that lists companies in Arizona that do exporting, and it publishes a guide to establishing a business in Arizona—licenses required, regulations, and so forth. The office prepares an economic profile of the state that gives data on areas like population, labor, and financing programs. Special research reports are issued, too. Past subjects have included a review of high-tech companies in Arizona and a study of the aerospace industry and its suppliers. The directory of high-tech companies listed the firms' names, addresses, current products, SIC codes, numbers of employees, and other data. All of these are made available free to the public.

Another division of the Arizona Department of Commerce is devoted to policy and research. That division publishes a book, *Arizona's Changing Economy: Trends and Projections*, that lists data on trends in land, population, and different manufacturing and service economies.

Other departments that looked promising were the Arizona Department of Economic Security, for free employment and job search information; the Department of Revenue, for licensing information; and the Department of Tourism, for information on expenditures made by out-of-state visitors.

How to Find:

Check your phone book for a listing, or consult the *State Executive Directory* in a library (p. 73). Or you can simply call directory assistance in your state capital. Many states have also set up home pages on the Web where you can at least find out how to place an order, if you can't actually view documents themselves.

✔ Source: Databases

Be sure to read the information in chapter 5 on databases and Internet searching. As explained in that chapter, a database is simply a collection of related information, and online databases are those made available over a computer. Here's a tiny sample of the kind of business information you can tap into by using this technology:

- Summaries of articles from top business and management journals
- Company directory listings from Dun & Bradstreet
- Indexes to articles from economic journals and books
- Text of the *Harvard Business Review*
- The full text of *The Wall Street Journal*
- Summaries of published industry forecasts and historical data
- Late-breaking financial news on U.S. public corporations from Standard & Poor's
- Management summaries from Arthur D. Little's market research reports
- Detailed financial report listings from the SEC

- A nationwide electronic Yellow Pages, with over 9 million listings
- Descriptions of sources of financial and marketing data in major industries worldwide
- Highlights of business and management topics from business journals and proceedings
- Information on product introductions, market shares, strategic planning
- Trade opportunity information based on purchase requests by the international market for U.S. goods and services

Again, this list doesn't even scratch the surface. For much more information on the subject, see chapter 5.

Although there are thousands of databases, and the proper selection of a database is not always a simple task, I have a few specific favorites. There is a fee to search all of the following business databases, but they offer some of the most powerful and comprehensive sets of information available and are highly recommended:

- **Intelliscope (Thomson Financial).**
  http://www.intelliscope.com
  Wall Street brokerage and market research reports.

- **Insite (The Gale Group).**
  http://www.iac-insite.com/
  Thousands of trade journal articles and other valuable information sources.

- **Dow Jones Interactive (Dow Jones).**
  http://askdowjones.com
  The Wall Street Journal, thousands of trade journals, market research, brokerage studies and much more.

There are also free databases, such as Powerize.Com (http://www.powerize.com) for searching and reading trade magazine articles. If you want to find other free databases, I suggest browsing a very helpful site called Bighub (http://www.Bighub.com) that identifies and categorizes many hundreds of databases spanning a wide range of disciplines. The site even allows you to conduct a search of these databases right from the Bighub site.

Web Clearinghouses and Pointers

Because there are so many sources of information on the Net, some of the most useful sites are those that attempt to gather and organize them. Here are three of my favorite business-information clearinghouse sites:

✔ **Source: Business Information Sources on the Net, Sheila Webber**
http://www.dis.strath.ac.uk/business/
Pointers to economic statistics, company profiles and financial statements, country information, news, and more. There are many business pointer sites. This one stands out as superior.

✔ **Source: A Business Researcher's Interests**
http://www.brint.com
Provides links to business directories, media sites, marketing related resources, and much more.

✔ **Source: Fuld's Internet Intelligence Index**
http://www.fuld.com/i3/index.html
Created by the prominent competitive intelligence firm Fuld & Company Inc, this site provides links to about 600 business intelligence sites on the Web.

5

The Internet

QUICK PREVIEW

- The Internet is an interconnected network of computers that includes the World Wide Web. Key terms to know if you are new to the Internet are these: Internet service provider, online service, browser, search engine, and e-mail.
- The Internet has become the preferred place to conduct most research, as it provides access to a huge amount of information, including new sources, traditional sources, non-mainstream views, obscure data, digitized versions of primary source materials, searchable databases, government information, and international information. It's also very fast, timely, and offers multimedia and hyperlinks.
- The downside to using the Internet for research includes its potpourri of sources, the difficulty in conducting effective searches, lack of historical material, lack of context, lack of permanence of Web pages, and selectivity of coverage.
- Some of the most useful sources on the Internet for researchers are: news and newspapers; magazines and "e-journals"; books, "e-texts," and directories.

(continued)

- There are five major tools for finding information on the Internet: heirarchical indices, search engines, meta search engines, offline search utilities, and databases.
- Problems with search engines include: their ability to index only a portion of the Internet; their inability to categorize sites by content; their slowness in updating their indexes; and their vulnerability to "spamming." There are alternatives to traditional search engines such as AskJeeves, Google, and NorthernLight.
- A database is a related collection of structured information searchable by computer and is a powerful research tool. Searching a database is not the same as searching the Internet, although some databases are available through the Internet. Some of these are free and some are fee-based.
- In order to conduct an effective search you need to: figure out what you are really researching; come up with keywords and synonyms; and use phrases, truncation, Boolean, and field searching when appropriate.
- Problems in getting good results from a search engine include: too many Web pages retrieved; not enough or no Web pages retrieved; and irrelevant Web pages retrieved. You can take steps to remedy each situation.
- Another valuable resource on the Internet is the discussion groups. You can use them to search archives of previously posted messages, to read current messages, to ask questions of members of the group, and to identify experts. There are two types of groups: mailing lists and Usenet groups.
- One drawback with signing up with a mailing list discussion group is getting too much e-mail. You can reduce the amount by subscribing to a "digest" version, setting up a separate e-mail account, or by sorting discussion group messages into their own folder.
- There are some ethical issues to be attuned to when using discussion groups as source material for your research.

WHAT IS THE INTERNET?

Although this book is not geared to be a general introduction to the Internet (if that's what you need, see the list of books recommended in the appendix), it's useful to include a very brief and basic explanation. If you are new to the Internet, or feel you never really learned the basics, be sure to read this section. Otherwise, feel free to skip to page 186.

The Internet is an interconnected network of computers. More precisely it is a "network of networks." Although the term World Wide Web is sometimes used interchangeably with Internet, in actuality the Web is just one *portion* of the Internet, albeit by far the most popular part. Other components of the Internet include electronic mail ("e-mail"), discussion groups (these are the "mailing list" and "Usenet" groups discussed further in this chapter), and the older, and now less-used utility information search and download tools such as gopher, telnet, and ftp. (In this book, when I discuss the Web, I'll sometimes say "the Internet" as per the common convention, but do keep in mind the distinction.)

The Web part of the Internet is composed of sites connected on the Internet that you get to by "linking," using a special protocol called hypertext transfer protocol (http). Web pages, which are written in a language called HTML provide not just text, but graphics, and sometimes sound, video, and multimedia. The technology that enables you to click on a highlighted portion of a Web page and be linked automatically to other Web pages is called hypertext.

There are a lot of confusing terms being bandied about with this new technology, and it can be confusing to get all of them straight if you are new to the Net. Often one aspect of the Internet or of the going-online process is confused with the Internet itself. So here, in a nutshell, is what you need to know about what the Internet is *not*. The Internet is not:

- **An Internet Service Provider.**
  An Internet service provider (ISP) is a company that provides *access* to the Internet—sometimes an "on ramp" analogy is used. You pay a monthly fee (usually in the range of $9.95–$19.95/mo) to an Internet service provider for the privilege of linking to the Internet.

  Popular Internet service providers include telecommunication firms, which could be your local phone company or a national provider like AT&T, or it could be a separate company that doesn't provide phone service, but only Internet access, such as MindSpring. Some cable companies are also able to provide Internet service. Here you connect to the Internet not over your phone line, but over your cable line, which provides a much faster link than even the fastest phone connections. Another kind of Internet service provider could be an "online service" (see below) such as America Online. The most recent trend is free Internet access. Firms such as Juno (http://www.juno.com) provide access to the Internet at no charge. The downside is that you have to put up with a lot of advertising.

- **An Online Service.**
  An online service is a company that provides you with not only a connection to the Internet, but various proprietary *content* as well, such as games, chat rooms, sports, news, research, etc. Note that this content is created and made available by the online service and is not necessarily from the "open"

Internet. America Online is, by far, the best known and largest online service.

An online service, as opposed to the Internet, is a separate, usually private firm that provides various information and entertainment to its users by connecting their computers to the service's own host computer. Other services, in addition to America Online, include Prodigy, and CompuServe (America Online has purchased CompuServe), and the now defunct Delphi and Genie.

Now here's the (slightly) tricky part that confuses some novice Internet searchers. Although America Online is *not* the Internet, it does provide *access* to the Internet. In other words, although you connect to the Internet via an online service, the service is only a *conduit* to the Internet and *not* the Internet itself. The Internet consists of networked computers that nobody really owns and nobody really runs.

Note that there are also what are called "professional" online services. These are different from consumer online services like America Online in that they are expensive and provide data-rich services geared primarily for professional users such as lawyers, businesspersons, journalists, and librarians. Some of the best known of these services include Dialog, Lexis-Nexis, Dow Jones Interactive, Thomson Financial Services, and The Gale Group (actually a division of Thomson).

- **A Browser.**
A browser is a piece of software that your computer needs to have loaded in order to view the information and documents on the Internet. The two major competing browsers are Netscape's Navigator and Microsoft's Explorer. If you are an America Online user, by default you are likely using the Microsoft Explorer browser to view the Web. Browsers are provided free by Internet service providers and can be downloaded free on the Internet.

- **A Search Engine.**
A search engine is software that resides *on* the Internet that you can connect to (normally for free) that lets you conduct *searches* of the Internet. Some of the most popular search engines include AltaVista, Excite, Google, HotBot, Lycos, and Yahoo

(though, technically Yahoo is a hierarchical index and not a search engine, but we'll discuss that later in this chapter).

- **E-Mail.**
  E-mail is an *application*—something you *do* on the Internet. It's when you send messages from your computer to another person's computer. E-mailing is one of the most common things that people do on the Internet. If you are connecting to the Internet via America Online, you automatically will use America Online's built-in e-mail service. If you are connecting via a different Internet service provider, you can either send e-mail by using your browser (both Netscape and Explorer have a built-in e-mail function) or you can buy a separate piece of software (such as Claris E-Mailer) that is designed just for sending and receiving e-mail.

So, putting this altogether...we could say that you:

Connect to the *Internet* via your *Internet service provider* (America Online or another provider), you can then *send e-mail*, or do research on the *Web* using a *search engine*, which you linked to for free via the *browser* that resides in your computer. Get it? If so, great. If not, you know something? It's not really that big a deal. Let's move on.

One other clarification that novice users should know about before we start digging into the nitty gritty of doing research on the Internet is how the Net is "divided." Much of the Internet is completely free and accessible to anyone at anytime. But there are parts of the Internet that require a paid subscription, or are only open to qualified users. For example, you can read the *Wall Street Journal* online, but in order to gain access to that site, you would first need to sign up and pay a subscription fee—just as you would if you wanted the paper itself delivered to your home. *The New York Times* doesn't require you to pay, but it does require you to "register"—that is, provide some data about yourself and get a user name and password before you will be allowed access. And other sites are only open to persons affiliated with the institution behind the site. For example, many university libraries make their home pages available on the Web, but only those who are affiliated with the university, and have been issued passwords or are recognized by other means, can take advantage of some of the special services available on the home page, such as access to fee-based database search services.

WHY USE THE INTERNET FOR RESEARCH?

Why use the Internet for research? Isn't that kind of like asking why use a kettle to boil water? Well, yes, since going online to do research and going on the Internet are becoming virtually synonymous. But this hasn't always been the case. As recently as the mid-1990s, there were many professional researchers who eschewed the Internet as a source for online information—if one was to go online to do research, one would choose one of those professional online services mentioned above. The Internet was seen as kind of a lightweight—filled mostly with trivia that was, to top it off, very hard to find. (Kind of like Woody Allen's story about the food at a resort that was awful and—to top it off—served in such small portions!)

While research on the Internet still has its inherent frustrations and drawbacks, it is now legitimately the preferred means of conducting not just online research but virtually *any* kind of research. Yes, there is still trivia—lots of it—but there is also an incredible amount of valuable information, including scholarly works, electronic journals, books, news analyses, obscure facts, in-depth business information, governmental data and reports, health and medical advice, and much more. And, while searching the Internet can still be tricky, there are now a variety of search tools and friendly search engines that were not available, at least in any effective manner, until the mid-1990s.

So there may no longer be a real need to explain why it's necessary to use the Internet for research—it has come into its own as *the* place to turn to for finding almost any kind of information. There is, though, an enormous need for understanding what exactly is on the Internet and how to best pinpoint just what you need, and this is the topic of much of the rest of this chapter.

BENEFITS AND DRAWBACKS OF THE INTERNET AS A RESEARCH SOURCE

Despite the fact that turning to the Internet has become an obvious choice when doing research, the Internet, like any tool, has unique characteristics that create both benefits and drawbacks. On the positive side, the Internet offers the following:

- **Access to new and valuable sources of information** that came into being *because of the Internet*. These include electronic journals (e-journals) and Internet discussion groups.
- **A more efficient route for accessing certain standard information sources** such as newspapers, particularly overseas papers and electronic versions of existing print journals.
- **Access to an enormous *amount* of information.** Currently it is estimated that there are about 800 million pages of information on the Web.
- **Access to non-mainstream views.** Fringe groups and those without access to the media or a printing press can now make their opinions known on the Internet.
- **Access to obscure and arcane information.** Because there are so many people with such diverse interests on the Internet, a search can often turn up the most unusual and hard-to-locate nugget of data.
- **Access to digitized versions of *primary* sources.** Some libraries are digitizing (making electronic versions) of primary research sources such as personal letters, official government documents, treaties, photographs, etc. and making these available for viewing over the Internet. The same is true for audio and, in some cases, video.
- **Access to searchable databases and datasets.** There are many sites on the Internet where you can search a collection of statistical data, such as demographic or social science data. While some databases on the Internet are fee-based, others are free. (An excellent compilation of free Internet databases covering a wide range of topics is made available by a site called Bighub [http://www.bighub.com]).
- **Access to government information.** The U.S. federal government is one of the largest publishers in the world and it is utilizing the Internet as its preferred method for disseminating much of its information (see chapter 3 for much more on this).
- **Access to international information.** Not only can you easily find official data from other countries by connecting to

embassies, consulates, and foreign governmental sites, you can also search other countries' newspapers, discuss issues with citizens from around the world on the newsgroups, and locate Web sites established by individuals from other nations.

Other key benefits that the Internet brings to the researcher include:

- **Speed.** Doing a search on the Internet can take just seconds.
- **Timeliness.** On the Internet you can find information that has just been made available a few minutes earlier.
- **Multimedia.** The Internet delivers not just text, but graphics, audio, and video.
- **Hyperlinking.** The ability to click between Web pages can facilitate an associative type of research, and make it easier to view citations and supporting data from a text.

On the downside, the Internet, despite its real and seemingly growing benefits to the researcher, still presents certain drawbacks. Among the most significant are:

- **Diverse collection of information.** The Internet is truly a potpourri of information—that's one of its strengths, but it's also one of its weaknesses. On the Net you can come across everything from a scholarly paper published on particle physics to a 14-year-old's essay on her summer vacation; there are newswire feeds from respected press organizations like the AP and Reuters, as well as misinformation from a Holocaust denial group; there are commercials and advertisements, and there are scientific reports from the U.S. Department of Energy. All of this diversity makes it difficult to separate out and pinpoint just the *type* of information *you* want.
- **Difficult to search effectively.** A traditional electronic database that you might search in a library may take a little learning and practice, but once you get the hang of it, you can become an effective searcher. But on the Internet, even if you know all the ins and outs of searching, because of the built-in limitations of Internet search engines and the way Web pages are created, you'll only be able to search a small percentage of what's on the Net. You also won't be able to easily distinguish

the valuable from the trivial pages; and you can obtain unpredictable results.

- **Emphasis on new information.** The Web came into being in the early 1990s, and, consequently, most of the information available on the Internet postdates that time. However, this is changing as certain Web site owners are loading older, archival material.
- **Lack of context.** Because search engines will return just a single page from a multipage document, you can miss the larger context from which that information was derived.
- **Lack of permanence.** Web pages are notoriously unstable. They appear, move, and disappear regularly. This can be of particular concern for academic researchers, who need to cite a stable page for reference purposes.
- **Selectivity of coverage.** Despite the size of the Internet, the vast majority of the world's knowledge still resides in print. So a search for information on the Internet in no way represents a comprehensive search of the world's literature or knowledge.

  Similarly, a good deal of what's on the Internet is "off-limits" to search engines and is not retrievable. These off-limit sites include those that are accessible only to those who register, input a password, or pay a subscription fee. These include most of the major commercial fee-based databases and online services that have a presence on the Web (e.g., Dialog, Lexis-Nexis, SilverPlatter). Other "off-limit" sites include newspapers that require subscriptions or registration, professional association members-only sites, and so forth.

SOURCES OF INFORMATION
ON THE INTERNET

As discussed earlier, you can find almost anything you need on the Net. But there are certain kinds of information sources available on the Net that are of particular value to the researcher. These include:

News and Newspapers

For some, the Internet is becoming the preferred way to obtain the day's news. Many major U.S. daily newspapers put out an online version, and there are thousands of newspapers published in other countries that are now available on the Web.

Online newspapers offer two primary advantages. One is immediacy—by going online you can find out what happened literally seconds ago. The second is the easy availability of papers from other countries, which previously were often extremely difficult to locate, and sometimes impossible to search electronically.

For research purposes, though, keep in mind that accessing *breaking* news is rarely of great use. Researchers typically want to search *archives*—the older, previously published issues, sometimes going back several years. You can do this at a library, or on a professional online service like Dialog, for example. But it is tricky to do this on the Web for several reasons. First, some newspapers that have put their papers on the Web are not making their archives available; in other cases, publishers are indeed making their archives available but only the past few weeks. Other publishers may make their archives available but charge a fee to access and read any articles. Also, from a researcher's point of view, the benefits of searching newspapers' archives is the ability to search not just a single newspaper's archive, but to be able to search dozens or even hundreds at once, as one can do on a professional database. On the open Web, such searchable databases of newspaper archives are difficult to find. The end of this chapter lists a few useful sites that provide this capacity.

Magazines and E-journals

Like newspapers, many magazines and journal publishers are putting electronic versions of their publications on the Web. Again, the real value of these for the researcher is not necessarily finding the current issue (though this is nice and can be useful in some circumstances), but in being able to search the back issues. Again, like the newspapers, publishers' policies for searching their archives vary. See the end of this chapter for sites that can help you uncover the names and URLs of magazines that have a version of their publication online. You normally need to link directly to a publisher's own site to access its previous issues, and you can't count on finding them via a search engine. (One good site for searching thousands of magazine and journal archives, many for free, is called powerize.com.)

Keep in mind that the electronic version of a journal is not necessarily the equivalent of its print cousin. Some publishers leave some articles off their electronic edition, others add extra articles for their Web users, and some do both. You can't assume, then, that you've fully covered a journal—or newspaper—print version if you're able to read its Web version.

E-journals—Defining/Finding and Searching

A type of digital publication worth noting is called an e-journal. Although there are some varying definitions, I would say that an e-journal is a scholarly journal, but one available in electronic form on the Web.

Although e-journals can be very valuable research sources, they can easily be missed by a researcher, since they are a new, and many libraries have not yet catalogued them and the basic periodical directories and indexes do not always list them. Although lesser known and harder to find, some of these e-journals are of very high quality and of great value. Some of my favorite e-journals and sites for finding them are listed at the end of this chapter.

Some e-journal publishers have also introduced an interesting concept called "seamless linking." This allows users to link from a purely bibliographic database to the publishers' own site in order to view and read the entire article (the fulltext), with all of its images and graphics intact. This is an example of how hyperlinking is changing the process of scholarly research. Similarly, you can now use *hyperlinked* citations, so that after reading an article, if you are interested in tracking down a cited reference, you don't need to go to the trouble of trying to find the article in the library, or via an interlibrary loan, or through additional internet searching, but can just click on that citation and be linked directly to that article on the Internet. One major academic publisher that is leading efforts in this area is the Institute for Scientific Information (ISI), in Philadelphia, Pennsylvania via its ISINET site (www.isinet.com).

If you're an academic researcher, you'd also be interested in a project called JSTOR. JSTOR has created a digital archive of a core set of scholarly journals. It's done this by scanning in complete sets of specified journals, beginning with the first issue of publication, graphics, and all. This offers, in some cases, the first time that archives of certain older journals have been made available electronically. This allows for new scholarly research possibilities such as keyword searching to do word analysis and other scholarly tasks. To use JSTOR, though, your library needs to have subscribed to the organization.

Books, E-texts, and Directories

The Internet has something of a mixed record when it comes to making books and directories available.

For books, perhaps that best feature are the online bookstores, such as Amazon.Com and BarnesandNoble.com, as well as the many smaller and specialty online bookstores that have made it simple to find a book by keyword, and then place an order. There's little question that this has been a tremendous boon for researchers trying to find titles on a particular topic or by a particular author.

But the comlete text of actual books are rarely found on the Internet. There are several reasons for this. A major one is copyright. Another is that most people simply don't want to read 300 pages of text on their computer screen. A publisher called FatBrain has received some attention for attempting to create a new model by publishing shorter works on the Internet with its e-matter service.

One specific type of book that is represented to some degree on the Web is called an e-text. Most of these e-texts are classic humanities texts—works of Shakespeare, Homer, Wordsworth, etc. These works appear in full on the Internet more frequently than others for a few reasons. First, their copyright has expired. Secondly, they are in demand by scholars and students of literature and other humanities disciplines. Thirdly, they offer scholars the possibility of conducting word analyses—something that really wasn't easily available until these works were digitized. For example, a scholar of Shakespeare could read the Bard's works in digital form and determine how often he referred to Italy in his works; or an English-language scholar could try to find the first occurrence of a certain word, and so on.

See the listing at the end of this chapter to find the names of sites for locating e-texts.

Directories

As we discussed earlier in this book, directories are one of your most important and valuable information-finding tools. Certain directories are migrating to the Internet, but many are still only available in hard copy at a library. There is, though, a free site on the Web called dNET (http://www.d-net.com) that will help you locate the existence of both print and CD-ROM based directories. This is a very helpful source for determining what directory exists electronically that could be of assistance to you in your research.

Other Valuable Sources on the Internet

In addition to newspapers, magazines, and so forth, the Internet has also made it easier to find other sources. For instance, you can now easily get the names and descriptions of upcoming conferences and trade shows (these were described in chapter 2). What's nice about finding out about these events via the Internet is that many of the event organizers post a preliminary program on the Internet, and, in some cases, even provide a written or audio transcript from the conference itself!

TIP: Encyclopedias on the Web
One type of information that has migrated very comfortably to the Web is reference works. An all-around excellent, and free, site is Britannica.com, which offers a searchable version of the complete Encyclopedia Britannica and related reference sources (http://www.britannica.com).

Another kind of information source that the Internet has facilitated easier access to is the think tank—an organization that studies and writes about issues of some public or social nature, and sometimes from a particular political perspective. Many of the better known of these think tanks have put some of their work up on the Internet.

Finally, the Internet is a phenomenal source for all sorts of government and business information. We treat these very important areas separately, as their own chapters in this book.

FINDING AIDS

Okay, now that you know about all this good stuff on the Internet, how do you go about finding it all? Here's a rundown of what you need to know, so that you can cherry pick the best off the Net.

The first thing you need to understand is the difference between the various kinds of finding aids that are on the Internet. Basically, there are five major tools you can use to search the Internet for information:

1. A hierarchical index
2. A search engine
3. A metasearch engine
4. An offline metasearch engine utility
5. A database

The most common ways that we search the Internet are the first two, but we'll look at each of these in turn.

Hierarchical Index

A hierarchical index is a site that organizes and lists Web sites by broad categories, subcategories, sub-subcategories, etc. By far the best known hierarchical index is Yahoo!.

Yahoo! is sometimes mistakenly thought of as a search engine, but there is a very important difference in how a hierarchical index like Yahoo! works versus how a search engine works. In a

Two Hierarchical Indexes: Yahoo and LookSmart

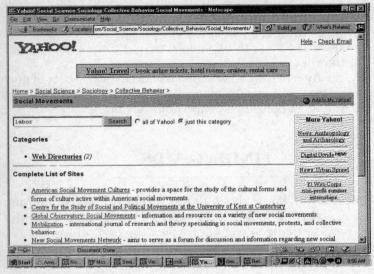

Sample Yahoo Search

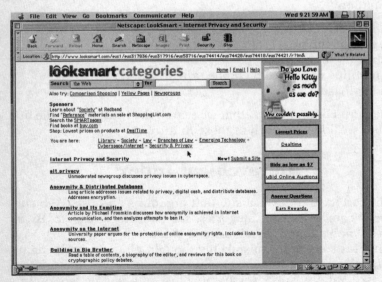

Sample LookSmart Search

nutshell, the difference is that a search engine sends out a special piece of software called a "robot" or a "spider" to "crawl" the Web, and mechanically index every site it comes across. A hierarchal index uses actual people—librarians, indexers, people who are trained to categorize information, to look at sites on the Web, and place them into an appropriate category.

That difference has an important ramification: hierarchical indexes are *selective*. Because human beings cannot index as much of the Web as a spider program, they list many fewer sites than a search engine. From a researcher's standpoint, this is both a drawback—using a hierarchical index means that your search of the Internet will be much less comprehensive—as well as an advantage—what you *do* find, should be a substantive site, and relevant to the category it was placed under.

Because of this difference, the wise researcher will turn to a hierarchical index when his or her subject is broad in order to find just a handful of relevant, well-catalogued sites and avoid the information deluge that can occur when using a search engine.

One confusing aspect of Yahoo!, though, is that although it is basically a hierarchical index, the creators of Yahoo! have also integrated a search engine function. This is actually just a partnership with a major search engine that allows their search software to be used on the Yahoo! site. So, when you input your search terms into Yahoo!, you will get back both a list of Yahoo's hierarchical category matches, *as well as* a list of sites directly on the Web turned up by the search engine portion. These distinctions are pretty well delineated, so you should be able to tell the difference.

In addition to Yahoo!, there are many other hierarchical indexes. See the end of this chapter for the names of others that you may find useful.

Tip: Refining Yahoo! Searches
When you conduct a search on Yahoo!, you are shown your results, and then given a choice to rerun another keyword search, either in "all of Yahoo!" or in "just this category," meaning running the search only in the pages of whatever category Yahoo! found was appropriate to your search. By selecting the latter, category choice, you are refining your search so that your next search should be targeted towards more relevant sites, which should improve your results.

Search Engine

Perhaps more so than any other aspect of the Internet, it is the search engine that holds out the most promise, but also presents the most frustration. Search engines promise you pearls from the Internet's sea of data, but too often just dredge up the muck. But with a little knowledge, understanding, skill, and practice, you can direct these search engines to make them work for you.

One caution. As fast as the Internet changes, search engine features and technologies change about the fastest! For this reason, although all of the principles and general advice that you read here will remain valid, the actual capabilities and workings of some of these search engines will have evolved by the time you read this.

How Search Engines Work

The first thing you should understand is how a search engine works. A search engine is a piece of software that is programmed to travel the Web and link from page to page in order to create an internal index of all of the pages that it finds. So when you input your key words into the search engine, it compares those words to the pages it has indexed, and returns to you those pages that it has determined most likely to be relevant to what you are looking for.

The way that the search engine decides *which* of its indexed pages are most relevant varies from search engine to search engine. Each has its own mathematical formula, or algorithm for making that determination. But in general, the major factors are how often your keywords are found in a page, where they are located on the page (if they are in the title or near the beginning they are typically considered more likely to be relevant), and how unusual the word is (pages that contain less common words that you've entered are sometimes given a higher ranking). Some search engines will also look at other factors, such as the number of other pages that link to a site, and rank those pages highest which have many other pages linking to them.

There are dozens of search engines that you can link to on the Web, but only a handful of really popular ones. The best-known ones are AltaVista, Excite, HotBot, Infoseek, and Lycos.

Because features of search engines change so quickly, it is not helpful to describe each of their capabilities in a print book. The

---

Tip: Choosing the Right Search Tool
- If your subject is broad or your keywords are ambiguous use a hierarchical index.
- If your subject is narrow or your keywords are unambiguous, use a single search engine.
- If your subject is extremely obscure or you need to make sure you cover as much of the Internet as possible use a metasearch engine.

---

key is to find one search engine you like and get proficient at it. One way to do this, of course, is to practice over and over, but you should also be sure to print out a copy of the search engine's "help" pages and read these carefully. You might also want to keep a copy close to your computer to consult when conducting a search. This is generally a lot easier to do than trying to find the specific help you need online.

You can check some of the sites and sources listed in the appendix under "Search Engines" to keep up to date with changes, or visit the author's Web site.

Metasearch Engine

A metasearch engine is another kind of search engine altogether. The difference is that it is a search engine that searches *other* search engines. Since no single search engine can search the entire Web, by using a metasearch engine, you can search *more* of the Web at one time.

There are many metasearch engines. Popular ones include Dogpile, InferenceFind, MetaSearch ProFusion, and SavvySearch. Each one works differently, and each searches a different set of search engines. In addition, some allow you to input advanced search terms, while others do not.

There are pros and cons to using a metasearch engine. The main advantage, as already mentioned, is that they let you search a larger portion of the Internet. The downside is that your searches generally cannot be as sophisticated or focused as they could be when searching a single search engine. This is because in order to make it possible to search multiple search engines simultaneously, a metasearch engine must transform each searcher's search statement into a kind of lowest common denominator that can be understood and translated into the protocols of each of the

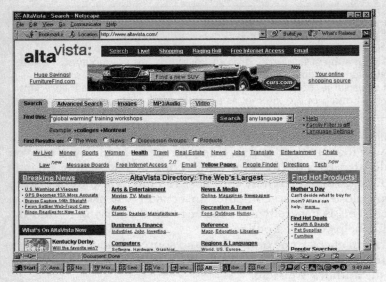

Sample AltaVista Search

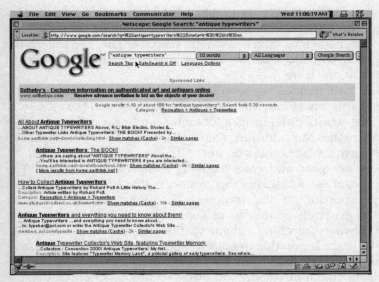

Sample Google Search

search engines. This prevents, or limits, the possibility of using advanced search statements on a metasearch engine site (e.g., Boolean operators, field searching, etc).

Metasearch engines are your best choice when you need to search as *much* of the Internet as possible: for example you are looking for a very obscure piece of data. It's not a good choice when you need to use any special or advanced search engine features.

Problems with Search Engines

Although we all need to rely on search engines to find what we need on the Internet, they all suffer from certain inherent drawbacks. Some of the biggest problem areas are:

- **Search engines can only index a portion of the Internet.** Even the most powerful search engines cannot index the entire Web, only a percentage of it. There are several reasons why. As discussed earlier, some Web pages are off-limits to search engines—these include sites that require the user to enter a password, to register, or to pay a fee, those that have forms to be filled out by the user, those that are purely graphic. Web page creators can also create a robots exclusion command that prevents search engines from entering the site and indexing the pages. But search engines also miss millions of other pages as well, simply because they may be smaller sites that were not found by the search engine.
- **Search engines do not categorize sites by content.** Unlike a traditional database, which contains data only on a certain defined set of information, the Internet is filled with all types of information, ranging from advertisements and pornography to peer-reviewed journal articles and government reports. Search engines, when they return results, cannot determine the actual content of what they have returned, leaving it up to you to slog through the pages to find the substantive, informational ones. [1]
- **Search engines can be slow to update their indexes.** When you run a search on a search engine, you are not conducting a live search on the Internet as it exists at the moment of your search, but of the index that the engine has created of the

[1]One search engine, NorthernLight, does incorporate a limited level of recognition by tagging returned sites by certain broad categories.

pages it had found on its most recent crawl. Search engines vary on how often they refresh their index. Some are very fast, but for others, the newest site that can be retrieved may be a few weeks or even a month or two old.

- **Search engines get spammed.** Most Web searchers have by now had the experience of conducting a search on some innocuous term, but getting back a batch of irrelevant hits, many of which are obviously money-making come ons, pornographic sites, and other unwanted pages having nothing to do with your search. Why and how does this occur?

There are several reasons how this happens. Some Web page creators consciously set out to try to create their page to trick search engines into thinking that they are about something altogether different than what they are. One way that these unscrupulous firms do this is by writing misleading "metatags." The metatag is the section of a Web page where the creator is supposed to describe what the page is all about. That section is invisible to the searcher when the page is actually displayed, but those metatags are used by search engines as a factor in determining how to index that page, and therefore how relevant it will be for specific searches. There are other, even more sophisticated tricks that some Web site owners use, such as creating alias (or "bridge") pages whose only purpose is to capture a high ranking on a search engine.

Search engine vendors have come up with defenses and counters to a lot of the spamming techniques, and it may be getting more difficult for these shady operators to fool search engines. But like an arms race, as soon as the search engines have blocked one method, the spammers come back with another approach.

Alternative Search Engines

Search engine technologies evolve quickly, and because so many searchers have frustrations in sorting through the great number of returns that a search engine retrieves, several new technologies have been developed that try to overcome these problems. A few of my favorites are AskJeeves, Google, and NorthernLight. Let's look at each of these to see what they offer the researcher.

- **AskJeeves**
  AskJeeves is a very easy to use site. "Jeeves" is a butler, and you simply "ask" Jeeves your question in plain English. Jeeves then returns with a list of sites that he thinks are going to answer your question. For example, if you enter the question, "Where can I find information on travel to Istanbul?", AskJeeves will come back with the following:

  > I have found answers to the following questions.
  > Click the Ask! button next to the best one:
  > Where can I find tourist information for ?
  > Where can I ask an "expert" my travel questions for ?
  > You may also be interested in the answers to these questions:
  > How can I find the travel Web site ?
  > Where can I find the travel guide?
  > Where can I find a guide to travel Web sites for?

  The way AskJeeves works is a bit ingenious. It has catalogued literally millions of the most common questions that Internet searchers have asked the service over the time that it has been in existence, and then has located sites that are most likely to answer those questions. So when you ask Jeeves a question, it automatically searches its bank of questions, and tries to find previous questions that either match or closely resemble the one you asked. In fact, it will ask if you do, indeed, want to find information on certain topics that, based on your question, it thinks you perhaps want to ask. And if one of them looks like it's on the mark, you can click on it and get linked directly to that site.

- **Google**
  Google is another innovative search site. Google is different than other search engines in the way that it ranks sites and determines which ones are most relevant to your search. Google's rankings are based on a site's "popularity," which Google defines and calculates by how many other sites link to a particular site, *and* how many sites link to *those* sites. The premise is that, if people visit a certain site often, then it is probably a good one—kind of like choosing a restaurant that's crowded rather than empty. It's not a perfect solution, but it

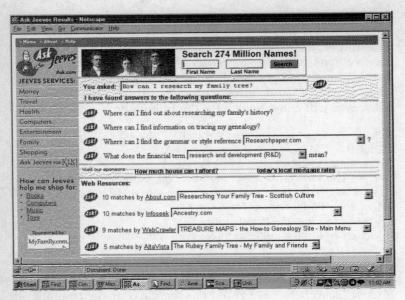

http://www.askjeeves.com

AskJeeves contains a bank of frequently asked questions, so when you make an inquiry, like this one on genealogy, AskJeeves tries to determine what you are asking and point you to useful sites.

has been effective enough that it is now my personal search engine of choice.

Google, then, is a particularly good choice when you want to find "official" sites, those that are popular among users; or want a way to filter out less relevant and peripheral sites. It is, overall, an excellent choice for battling the information overload that occurs with other search engines.

- **NorthernLight**
  NorthernLight bills itself as a research engine because it has added a few interesting twists. First, returned sites are categorized and grouped into relevant "folders." These folders are labeled by topic and by subtopic, and in various categories: by type of information (e.g., whether the page is a press release,

a job posting, etc.); by subject; or by type of page (e.g., whether the page is derived from an educational site, or a governmental, or commercial one). These folders can help narrow a search and provide some direction to your research. They don't always work perfectly and you can't rely on them completely, but they are a welcome attempt at helping you sort through the deluge of pages that a typical search engine often returns.

Another unique feature of NorthernLight is its "special collection," a searchable collection of millions of articles published from thousands of major trade magazines integrated into NorthernLight's database along with the Web sites. So when you search NorthernLight, you not only search the Web,

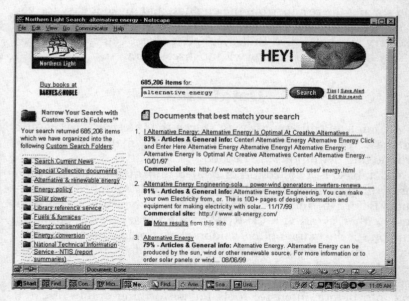

http://www.northernlight.com

Northern Light groups the Web pages it has retrieved into related folders, to make it easier for you to determine which pages are most likely to be relevant to your needs.

but a database of published articles. (Note, though, that although it is free to conduct the search on these trade magazine articles, NorthernLight charges a modest fee if you want to actually view or print them.)

Offline Metasearch Engine Utility

Another finding aid that some Internet searchers use are offline search utilities. These are software programs that you don't link to via the Internet, but download onto your own computer, just like other software. When you connect to the Internet, these go into action and, like a metasearch engine, search multiple search engines at once. The difference is that they also help in organizing and sorting the results from the engines, and make it easy for you to store and find sites you've come across. One that I've used and like very much is called Bullseye, and it's free! You can download a copy by linking to http://www.intelliseek.com

Databases

A completely different way to search the Internet is to search a database. Before discussing this important matter, some background and definitions are needed.

A database is a collection of related information, in electronic form, that is structured so that it can be easily searched by a computer. Before the Internet, researchers would typically access databases either by using a CD-ROM at the library or by signing up with one of the major online vendors that supplied remote (online) access to hundreds of databases. These included firms like Dialog, Lexis-Nexis, and Dow Jones. While these vendors are now putting their databases on the Internet and still remain the most powerful and information-intensive tools for performing online research, they can be quite pricey, and as such are typically out of reach of the budget for nonprofessional searchers. However, if you need the very best that the online world can offer, you may wish to look into them—contact information is provided at the end of this chapter.

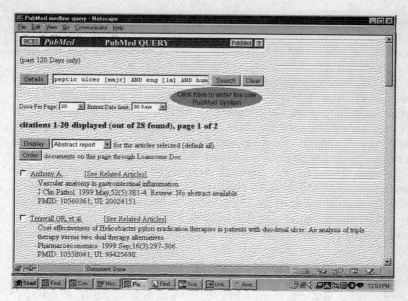

http://www.nlm.nih.gov/medlineplus/pepticulcer.html

Searchable databases, like this health and medical database from the federal government, are a powerful way to perform sophisticated searching on a collection of substantive, information-oriented pages, without the trivia, spam, and irrelevant pages typically returned on general Web searches.

Well known databases, such as ABI/Inform, Periodicals Abstracts, Academic Index, and many others have been made available for some time from database firms like UMI (renamed Bell & Howell Learning and Information), H. W. Wilson, and SilverPlatter. Their products still represent the most powerful information search tools available, since they allow for fast searching through literally millions of items of structured, scholarly, substantive information.

There are key differences, then, between searching a database and searching the Internet. The first is that although the Internet can be viewed as a giant database of sorts, as we've discussed, the information on the Internet is *not* all of the same type—that is, it is not only, say, newspaper articles, chemical formulas, descriptions of movies, market research reports, psychology studies, etc., as a traditional database would be. Instead, it is *all* of those things, and millions of other things as well. A traditional database, in contrast, is limited in its scope: e.g., PsychInfo is a database of *only* articles from psychology journals; ABI/Inform is a database of articles *only* published in business and trade journals; Newspaper Index is a database of *only* newspaper articles. So when you use a database, you know *precisely* what you are searching.

Another key difference is that Web pages, for the most part, are "unstructured." What does that mean? In a traditional database, each item in the database is called a "record." And those records are split into sections, or "fields." For example, a newspaper database record's fields might include: author name, title of the article, date of the article, name of the newspaper, and keywords that describe the main subject of the article. The searcher, then, can choose to conduct a search on one of those fields, in order to do a more precise search. For example, if I am searching a newspaper database, and want to find articles on "distance learning" but only want to read those articles that were published in the *Los Angeles Times*, I could limit my search by instructing the database to search distance learning for only those records that have been tagged with "source name: *Los Angeles Times*."

Many databases have several or even dozens of such fields, created specially to capture the key terms and categories used in a particular discipline (for example, a database of company directory data may have a field called "stock ticker" so you can search by stock ticker; a database of astronomical journal articles may have a field called "peer-reviewed articles").

Unfortunately, because the Web contains so many different types of documents, it can't be structured very precisely. Also the HTML format in which Web pages are created does not make it easy to create subject fields.

That's the bad news. But the good news is that you *can still access* and search thousands of databases that reside on or are accessible via the Internet. In other words, you can *connect* to these databases by using the Internet as the medium for establishing your online connection. This is different than using a search engine to search those disparate, unstructured individual Web pages that make up the open Internet. The Internet, then, has given researchers the convenience and ease of getting easy access to searchable databases without having to visit a library or sign up with an expensive fee-based vendor.

Some of these databases that you can access over the Internet are fee-based. Most often your best bet for using these is to go to your library, which may have a subscription to those databases (some libraries will allow patrons to connect as a user remotely from their own home by entering a password or by using another method of authenticating authorized users). There are also thousands of *free* searchable databases accessible over the Internet. While their quality and trustworthiness are more variable than the fee-based databases, many represent very valuable substantive collections of data, very useful for focused research. An excellent site that can help you locate free databases is called Isleuth. Some of the most popular, useful, and free databases on the Web are listed at the end of this chapter.

SEARCH STRATEGIES

Understanding how search engines work, and how they differ is the first step in performing precision research on the Web. But you also need to know about the art and skill of conducting a keyword search.

The search engine vendors do make an effort to make searching simple. You can, for sure, type a few words into a search engine's box, and, lo and behold, quite often get back some pretty decent stuff, and even some real winners. And the search engines' technologies have integrated some pretty neat and useful methods for turning a few words into a decent search, much of the time.

However—and this is a big however—tapping in a few words haphazardly is too much of a hit-or-miss method for doing effective searching. It does result in the occasional success, but all too often will retrieve nothing at all, or a confusing mixture of the useful and not so useful sites. Here's what you need to know in order to be an effective searcher.

Figure Out:
What Are You Really Researching?

Before you begin to create your search statement or go on the Net, it's a good idea to take a few minutes to think about what exactly you are looking for. Can you write it in a sentence? Are there other ways of describing what you are seeking? A key to good searching is the ability to come up with synonyms for your query. Let's look at one research inquiry, and how you might turn it into a search statement.

Say that you were researching the effect imposing the death penalty on minors has had on a state's crime rate. How would you turn that question into a statement for a search engine? The first step would be to write a search statement in plain English. For this example, that might be:

> What is the impact that the imposition of the death penalty on minors has had on crimes in states that have imposed it?

It's not a pretty sentence, but it is a potentially useful one, since you can examine it to create your keyword search statement. The next step would be to identify the most important or key words and phrases in the sentence. These would be those that are the most substantive, unique, and best describe the focus of your research query. (Some search engines that allow "natural language queries" would let you enter your query as a plain English statement or question, as above. But the accuracy of natural language search engines is quite variable, and most of the time it is better to translate your research query into a keyword search statement.)

As a first rough search, you might link to a search engine, and enter these key words and phrases:

> "death penalty" [phrases are normally enclosed in double quotes]
> minors crimes states impose

This would be a reasonable search, with a decent chance that you'd end up getting back some relevant results. However, to increase the odds of success, it's normally important to *think of synonyms* for your key words, and enter these in the search box too. In this case you might come up with these:

"death penalty":	"capital punishment" execution
minors:	youthful, young, teenager, children, juvenile
criminal:	defendant, accused
crimes:	offenses
states:	jurisdictions

Coming up with good synonyms is something of an art, and you need to use your judgment. What you want to do is to come up with *common* synonyms, and add those words to your search statement. You don't want to break out a thesaurus and try to find *every* possible synonym, only those that are likely to be used by someone who wrote a Web page. In this case, you can make a reasonable case for some of the above synonyms, but not those that seem obscure or off the mark. You also generally want to focus on coming up with good *nouns*, when possible, as these are more descriptive and precise than verbs or adjectives, and can help in retrieving more relevant Web pages.

A new, expanded search might read something like the following:

"death penalty" "capital punishment" impose juveniles crimes offenses criminal states

Two Important Search Strategies

There are two other very important search strategies everyone should also know about. One is called truncation, and the other is field searching.

Truncation is the technique of inputting a special symbol after the root of your keyword so that you can find all variations of that rood word. The truncation symbol, for most search engines, is an asterisk. So, for example, if you enter the truncated word *smok**, you'd get pages that contained the word smoke, smoker, smoked, smoking, etc. This way you don't have to think of all variations yourself, nor bother entering all of them in. Be careful, though, where you put the truncation symbol—put it at as far to the end of the word as possible. For example, if you wanted to pick up

---

TIP: Scan Pages for New Key Words

When you do find a relevant Web page, it's a good idea to read it over carefully to look for any terms, buzzwords or phrases that you may not have used in your search statement but would be helpful in your next search. For example, perhaps you find that three of your best pages contain the name of a legislator who is introducing a death penalty bill to apply to minors. Well, it would be a good idea to rerun the search, but this time add that person's name to pull in those items on the Web that also contain his name. This kind of iterative process is one of the professional searcher's tricks to refining the search process and progressively locating more precise results.

Here are some other techniques for improving your searching:

- When you are conducting a standard, non-Boolean search, the more words that you enter in the search box, the better your search results will generally be.
- When possible, use words that are unusual, unambiguous, and specific. For example, you'll likely have better results on a search on "typhoons" than you will on "weather"; more luck with "Jewish genealogy" than with "genealogy" alone.
- When you can, look to use multiple-word phrases rather than single words. Phrases are inherently more focused than single words and will normally return more precise results. For most search engines you need to enclose phrases in quotation marks to indicate a phrase, e.g., "borderline personality disorder."

---

variations on the word *walking*, you'd use *walk** but not *wal** because than you'd pick up words like *wall* or *walrus*.

Field searching can be another very useful technique for making your searches much more precise. Normally, when you enter a keyword, the search engine looks at the *entire* Web page to find matches—the title, the date, the whole text, the URL, etc. But field searching allows you to tell the search engine to only look at a certain *portion* (or, in information science lingo, "field") of the items. On the Web, typically the most useful kind of field searching is to search the "title" field.

By limiting your search to just words in the title, you help ensure that the matches that are made by the search engine are likely going to be more relevant to your search. For example, if you were looking for information on the country of Ireland and entered just that word into the search engine, you'd get a huge number of hits for Web pages that really aren't about that country, but just happen to mention or reference Ireland somewhere in the text. But if you instruct the search engine to only search the "title" portion of the Web pages, and return to you only pages where the word *Ireland* was found in the title, you vastly increase the odds that those pages are specifically focused on the country.

Search engines vary in if and how they allow you to perform field searching. In AltaVista, for example, to instruct the search engine to do a title field search, you would enter: title: Ireland.

Another kind of field searching that can prove to be useful is to search the URL field, which contains the address of a Web site. There are certain situations where this could be helpful:

- When you want to restrict your search to pages that were created by a certain type of organization—specifically, a business/commercial enterprise, a nonprofit organization, an educational institute, or the government. Each of these entities have their own three-letter URL suffix that signifies who they are: business sites end in "com"; nonprofits in "org"; educational institutes in "edu" and governments in "gov". (Other less common URL suffixes are "mil" for military and country abbreviations for sites that come from outside the United States.) Note, though, that the entity in charge of assigning domain names has relaxed its rules for distinguishing between commercial "com" sites and nonprofit "org" sites. So you can no longer fully rely on those two domain suffixes anymore.

  So, say that you were doing some research on biotechnology, and were trying to find studies on the topic, but only wanted to see studies that came from universities. You might, then, limit your search to those with the "edu" suffix. (You'll need to read the specific instructions on the search-engine's help pages to find out how to do this for each one. For example, on AltaVista, you'd enter the command: url:edu)

- You might also want to use the URL field when you want to limit results to just a specific institution's Web site. So, let's say you were interested in what Sony's sites contained on the topic of HDTV. Well, you might then add the phrase, on AltaVista for example, url:Sony to retrieve only sites with that URL. This is a bit tricky because you first need to know what the

URL of the institution is; you'll also be missing lots of other relevant pages that are about Sony and HDTV but just aren't from Sony itself, and you might pull up other sites that just happen have "sony" somewhere in the URL.

Boolean Searching

A Boolean search can help you create more effective searches by establishing more precise relationships between your keywords. Most search engines allow for at least some limited Boolean searching. The basics are as follows:

The primary Boolean operators are AND, OR, and NOT and work like this:

- the AND operator requires that *all* the words or phrases surrounding the AND be present:
    e.g., diabetes AND children AND treatment
    requires that all those words be present in any Web pages retrieved
- the OR operator requires that *any* of the entered words or phrases be present:
    e.g., "heart attack" OR stroke OR "high blood pressure"
    tells the search engine to bring back pages that have any of those words or phrases.
- the NOT operator requires that a word or phrase NOT be present
    e.g., computers NOT IBM
    tells the search engine to look for Web pages with the word "computers" but to then exclude any that also have IBM in them.
    (Note: in AltaVista, in order to activate the NOT operator, you must use the phrase AND NOT. The above statement would then, read: Computers AND NOT IBM.)

Alternate Boolean Operator: NEAR

Although NEAR is not technically a Boolean operator, it is similar to one, and can be an extremely useful strategy for making your searches more precise if you are using the AltaVista search engine. AltaVista has made it possible for searchers to use this operator to establish an even closer relationship between your keywords than the AND operator. By using the NEAR operator, you instruct the search engine that the keywords must be no more than ten words apart.

For example, suppose you were looking for the impact of global warming on icebergs. You would want to find references to global warming that specifically relate to icebergs. A very good search that you could conduct on AltaVista would be:

"global warming" NEAR icebergs

This strategy, along with title field searching, comprise two excellent weapons against search engine overload.

When should you use Boolean searching? Even though Boolean is considered an advanced search, contrary to what some might assume, it is not automatically superior to an ordinary non-Boolean search. Very often a good non-Boolean search can out-pull a Boolean search because a Boolean search overrides the search engine's relevancy ranking algorithm. However, you may wish to choose the Boolean mode in these circumstances:

- you want to establish a specific and close relationship between your keywords, e.g., cats NEAR seizures.
- your search is long and complicated with different relationships between words or word sets.
- your search attempts in the ordinary search mode were unsuccessful.

Advanced Searchers Tip

Often, Boolean searches are used when you have constructed a long and complicated search statement. These often need to integrate parentheses in order to clarify to the search engine which keywords are supposed to be linked with which. For example, say you were searching the Web to find a discussion of how the Euro is impacting Germany or France. In a Boolean search, you might enter:

Euro AND France OR Germany

However, the problem with that search statement is that the search engine cannot tell if you mean to search:

> Euro AND France [the page must include both these words] OR Germany [any pages that contain the word Germany]

With this search, any page that contains the word "Germany" is going to qualify as a relevant hit, which isn't what you want.

Or if you mean to search:

> Euro AND [the page must contain the word Euro] France OR Germany [and it must contain one of these words, too]

This search will return Web pages that fulfill the following requirements: they contain the word Euro *and* they also contain either the word France or Germany. This *is* what you want.

The way to make the distinction clear is to use parentheses to group those items together that are supposed to be acted on together. So in this case, your search statement should actually read like this:

> Euro AND (France OR Germany)

Troubleshooting

Let's say you've followed all the advice I've given you so far in this chapter, but you are still running into problems in your Internet searching. What can you do?

The first step is to diagnose the difficulty. Problem searches typically can be grouped as falling into one of the following categories:

1. Too many Web pages retrieved
2. Not enough or no Web pages at all retrieved
3. Irrelevant Web pages retrieved

If your problem is the first, too many Web pages, then the problem is likely that your search is too *broad*; that is, it is too general.

You can probably improve your search—in this case that means narrowing your search—by trying one or more of the following strategies:

- Look at your keywords. Are they specific enough? For example, don't look for information on simply "cars" or "comput-

> **Tip: The First Hits are the Best Hits**
> Most search engines return Web pages in order of relevancy, so your best results are going to be found in the first few screens. So just because the search engine returned 15 screens worth of Web pages doesn't mean that you should feel obligated to go through and read all of them.

ers," but name a model or style of a car or the specific issue of a computer.

- Did you remember to enclose all phrases in quotation marks?
- Consider performing a Boolean search where you can use the NEAR operator (in AltaVista).
- Consider using a title field search to narrow your search just to those sites in which your key words or phrases appear on the Web page's title field.
- Consider using a hierarchical index rather than a search engine.
- Consider using the Google search engine, which specializes in returning a few highly relevant sites, as opposed to a comprehensive list.

If your problem is that you are getting too few or no responses from the search engine, consider trying these strategies instead:

- Check for typos in your search. A misspelled word can completely throw off your search and eliminate matches.
- Look carefully at your keywords. Can you use broader ones to cast a wider net? (e.g., if your search for Laotian art didn't turn up any Web pages, how about searching for a site on Asian or international art? And then you can scan those returned pages for anything about Laos.)
- Consider using a metasearch engine, as this will search multiple search engines and cover more of the Internet than a single Internet search engine.

Keep in mind too that conceptual queries—e.g., How do parents' personalities impact their children's behavior?—are much trickier than concrete, unambiguous questions such as Where can I go scuba diving in New Jersey? For the former type of question, you may not even want to search the open Web, but instead go to a site (e.g., Psychweb at http://www.psychweb.com) or a Usenet group.

This is a tricky search for the open Web; I'd recommend finding a broad-based psychological site—there are many if you search for "psychology" on Yahoo!, for example—and then, once you're on the general psychology site, doing a keyword search for your particular topic. It's kind of like going to a library or bookstore and getting a general psychology text, and then looking up your narrow topic in the index, rather than trying to look at an index of the entire library's holdings. Get it?

In Summary

1. Be sure you know what you are searching for—write out your search statement ahead of time to get it clear in your mind.
2. Circle the most important or key words in the sentence—use primarily nouns, and/or obscure, less frequently found words or phrases.
3. Think about whether there might be common synonyms or other ways to express the same concept (e.g., if one of your keywords is "jobs", a common synonym would be "careers").
4. Enter all the words and synonyms into your search engine of choice. Put phrases inside quotation marks. (If the search engine allows it, put a plus mark in front of any word or phrase that absolutely must appear in a returned Web page in order for the page to be relevant.) Use truncation to obtain relevant variations on the word stem.
5. Review your results. If you are not happy, check for typos and try again with slightly different keywords or more or less plus signs. Consider trying a Boolean search, but first read the search engine's help pages to find out the correct protocols for doing so.

DISCUSSION GROUPS

So far this chapter has discussed doing research on the Internet by using the World Wide Web portion of the Net. However, this does not represent the entirety of what's available to you on the Internet, by any means. Another very valuable source of information and expertise are the various discussion groups, where users from around the country—and around the world—discuss, debate, and share information and resources on topics ranging from aviation and bottle collecting to yellow fever and zoo management techniques. In other words—on most anything you can think of!

Here, for example, are some questions that members of the "business librarians" (or BUSLIB) list have asked their colleagues—and successfully found answers:

- When was the first corporate stock split?
- Where can I find information on a Brazilian plant called *Coulteria tinctoria* used for hair straightening?
- Does anyone know how to get a videotape that Bill Gates used in his opening talk at the Comdex conference?
- Where can I get a videotape of the Challenger disaster?
- I need a list of worldwide producers of yellow phosphorus.
- What would be the value of $100 today, if invested in the S&P 500 in June of 1993?
- How many golf carts and forklifts are operating today in the United States?
- I need to find information on companies or plants that bottle liquor or beer.

I personally have had many, many success stories in finding answers and/or leads to information that I thought would be impossible to track down. For example, for many years I had tried unsuccessfully to track down a copy of an old, relatively obscure (early 1960s) MGM children's 33$\frac{1}{3}$ album that my brother and I used to listen to before going to bed when we were children. I tried secondhand stores, catalogues, special clearinghouses, MGM itself, resellers and distributors—but nothing. Ah, but this was before the Internet. But this was tough even for the Net! I posted my question on some "vinyl LP" and collector discussion groups, and though I got some helpful leads, none led me to the actual record!

Then I heard about a list called "stumpers"—an eclectic group specifically designed to help people who were stumped by a particular question! So I posted my question there, and among the leads I got were messages from two people who suggested that I call Bowling Green University's library of popular culture, which, amongst its collections, contained thousands and thousands of recordings. After tracking down the phone number, I was connected to a very helpful librarian, who looked up the title in his computer catalog, found that indeed it was included, and then for just $9.95 or so sent me a cassette tape of "The Bear That Wasn't" along with a photocopy of the album's cover. Eureka! (To contact Stumpers, send an e-mail message to Stumpers-L@crf.cuis.edu.)

How can you use these discussion groups in your research? There are actually several ways:

- Search the archives of *previously posted* messages from one or several groups.
- Read *current* messages being posted on newsgroups in order to learn of and stay abreast of the latest issues and concerns arising in your field of study.
- *Ask questions* of the members of the group in order to find a fact, get a referral, obtain advice, etc.
- *Identify experts*, who you may later wish to interview in depth for your research project.
- Obtain *anecdotes and personal experiences* from members on the list.
- Conduct an *informal survey* of discussion group members.

Types of Discussion Groups

Now, before getting into the specifics of how to find and search these discussion groups, a little background and some definitions are in order.

There are two major kinds of Internet discussion groups: mailing-list groups and Usenet groups.[2]

The mailing-list type, which is commonly (though technically incorrectly) called a listserv, is a discussion group to which you

---

[2]There is actually a third type of Internet-based discussion group, called a forum, that, unlike a mailing list or a Usenet newsgroup, is Web based. Forum message boards are typically created by Web site owners as a means to set up chat and discussion groups, and are employed as a way to create and extend a sense of community to the subscribers and visitors.

need to officially subscribe. After subscribing, you then receive messages from the other members of the group, which come to you in the form of regular e-mail messages. If you want to send a message to all the members of the group, you would compose an ordinary e-mail message and send it to a special mailing-list address.

The other type of Internet discussion group is a Usenet newsgroup. Like the mailing-list groups, joining a Usenet group is a way to conduct an Internet-based discussion on a particular topic with other interested Internet users. It differs, though, primarily in the mechanism that you'd use for reading and posting messages. Instead of receiving and sending e-mail to communicate with the group, members of Usenet lists post messages on what might be called a giant electronic bulletin board. To read and post messages it's necessary to use a special newsgroup reader (which normally can be activated via your Internet browser software).

While there are exceptions, another difference between mailing-list groups and newsgroups is that the level of discourse that occurs via the mailing-list groups, especially moderated ones, tends to be more focused, and relevant to serious research. While there are some Usenet groups that are substantive and scholarly, they are more prone to posts that are of a trivial nature, to flames, and to more "noise."

Finding Newsgroups

The strategy that you devise for finding and searching newsgroups depends on *why* you want to use them as a research source. Although six different ways that Internet discussion groups can be utilized as a research source have been listed above, these can actually be grouped into two major categories:

1. for searching the discussion archives
2. for monitoring current conversations

Searching the Discussion Archives

One way to utilize Internet discussion groups in your research is to search *previously* posted messages—or a discussion group's archives. In this case, you are searching a database that consists of the messages posted by members of the group. There are sites available on the Web that allow you to perform this searching *without* having to sign up and join a group. The names of these sites are listed at the end of this chapter.

Monitoring Current Conversations

You may wish to monitor the current conversations of an ongoing discussion group for a variety of reasons. It can help you get up to speed on a new topic, alert you to some of the current issues of concern among persons in the field you are researching, assist you in identifying experts, allow you to find anecdotes and personal experiences from members on the list, and even provide the opportunity to conduct an informal survey of list members.

In order to be able to perform any of these tasks, though, it is necessary to first locate a discussion group (or groups) relevant to your research, and then actually sign up with the group.

How might you go about finding a discussion group that is devoted to your research area? Often the best way is if you are referred to the name of a group by some trusted source. But often you'll need to scour the Internet yourself to try to find one. Luckily there are several sites that are geared to providing just this service, such as Kovac's Directory of Scholarly and Professional E-Conference, Liszt, TileNet, and others. Their sites are listed at the end of this chapter.

After you've found a relevant group, you'll want to join it in order to view the current conversations, and even participate. If the group you want to join is of the mailing-list variety, you need to actually subscribe to the list, which involves sending a "subscribe" command to the list address. Specific subscription instructions are normally provided by the discussion-group finder sites listed above. If the group you've found is of the newsgroup type, then you don't need to send a subscription message, you join by using the "newsgroup reader" function that is part of your Web browser.

Once you have joined a mailing list or Usenet group, you are then a part of that community, and will be able to receive and send messages to the group. Although the first few days of reading messages may seem confusing—since it is like jumping in the middle of a conversation—the "threads" of the messages will soon become clear, and you'll be able to begin following the various topics being discussed by the members. Once you start feeling comfortable with the flow of the newsgroup, you can then start thinking about how the group might assist you in your research. Here are some ways it can do so (I will use a listserv group as an example).

- Get you up to speed on a topic. An interesting way to get an "instant education" on a subject is to join an Internet discussion group. While this is not really a recommended way to begin building your knowledge of a new subject, you will, once you are able to follow the conversation, begin to discern and learn what areas are of most concern and importance to this group, and are therefore some of the most critical issues in the field. Here you don't actually need to participate in the conversation (nor should you if you are not yet knowledgeable), but just listen in, or in Internet parlance, "lurk."

- Find knowledgeable sources. After lurking awhile on a newsgroup, you'll eventually notice that some people in the group consistently seem to have the most knowledge on the topic and that their postings exhibit the most insight. This is an excellent way to locate names of expert sources, who you may later wish to contact personally to interview for your research (see chapters 6–9 on interviewing experts).

- Obtain anecdotal reports. While researchers need to be careful about how much stock they put into personal anecdotes, the fact is such reports can be very helpful for most kinds of research. You'll likely hear many anecdotal reports and stories as a member of an Internet newsgroup, and these can provide the kind of fresh, live case study material that you just can't obtain from other sources.

- Conduct informal surveys. An Internet newsgroup automatically is a predetermined selection of a certain type of person. These groups bring together affiliated users, be they lawyers, librarians, or lion tamers. As such, they can make for an ideal target group if you need to gather data from that kind of person. And it can be much easier—and cheaper—to distribute a survey to persons via the Internet than via traditional mail, phone call, or in-person surveys.

However, you need to be very careful when conducting a

> **Tip: Summarize for the Group**
> You can often encourage responses to your questions by letting the group members know that you will summarize the responses you receive and post them to the group for the members' benefit. It's good Internet etiquette to do this anyway.

survey, whether it be over the Internet or via any other medium, since polling is both an art and a science that involves the use of statistics and appropriate methodological rigor. If not done properly, surveys can produce invalid and even worthless results. There are additional and special concerns when performing surveys over the Internet that relate to whether or not the group you are polling is truly a representative sample of the larger group you are trying to survey. These issues go beyond the scope of this book. (If you are interested in this subject, you should check a standard research-methods text.)

For these reasons, the best surveys done on Internet discussion groups are the more informal ones. Such a survey might take the form of a couple of open-ended questions that would have been designed to give you anecdotal material and a flavor of what the members of the group think and feel, rather than any statistically reliable results.

Ethical Concerns in Discussion Group Research

When using newsgroup participants' postings as source material for your research, you need to be attuned to potential ethical considerations and implications. There is a long tradition in the social sciences that researchers must avoid harming their subjects, and harm can include a lack of obtaining informed consent as well as intrusion into private matters.

Each particular discipline's own professional body has created their own ethical guidelines, and it is still murky as to how the general injunctions should be applied to Internet discussion groups. Some of the difficulty arises from determining whether conversations that occur in these groups take place in a public or private

---

Tip: Handling E-mail Overload

One of the pitfalls of signing up with listserv discussion groups is that you can quickly find that your e-mailbox gets clogged with dozens of messages from members of the group each day. Here are a few strategies to help deal with this problem:

• Many lists allow you to subscribe to a digest version that consolidates all of the day's various e-mail messages into one long one. While this does help keep your e-mailbox uncluttered, it does mean you'll have to read through a very long e-mail to see what's inside that may be of interest to you.

• You may want to set up separate e-mail accounts for each list. If you are an AOL subscriber, for example, you can use different screen names to sign up with different lists. Or you can sign up with one of the free e-mail providers (such as Hotmail) and just use that.

• Some e-mail software programs, such as Eudora Pro and Claris Emailer, allow you to set up a program whereby specified e-mails are, as they come in to your e-mailbox, routed into their own folders. If, for example, you signed up with a group about business ethics called busethics, you could then program your reader so any e-mail that contains "busethics" is routed into a separate folder that you've given the name "Business Ethics List".

---

space, since those in a private space would require the greatest degree of restraint on the part of the researcher. In any case, you should always understand and respect the norms of the "culture" of the group you are studying. On the Internet, there has been a tradition that you "own your own words" and, therefore, it is not normally considered appropriate to lift others' messages without obtaining permission.

WEB SITES AND REFERENCES MENTIONED IN THIS CHAPTER

Searchable Newspaper Archives

- **Hermographic Press**
  http://www.hermograph.com
  Publishes a print directory called *Net.Journal Directory* that identifies, describes, and provides useful material on newspapers, journals, and other media that are on the Web.

- **Howard County Junior College District Libraries**
  http://www.hc.cc.tx.us/library/newssrch.htm
  Maintains a site that tracks newspaper archives on the Web.

- **The Library of Congress**
  http://lcweb.loc.gov/rr/news/oltitles.html
  Runs a site called "Newspapers Indexes" that lists, provides links, and identifies which newspapers' archives are free and which are fee-based.

- **NewsHunt**
  http://www.newshunt.com
  Quite comprehensive in its coverage and includes a link to newspapers around the world that have free searchable archives; these are all searchable directly from NewsHunt's own page.

- **NewsIndex**
  http://www.newsindex.com
  Searches the current issue and archives of 300 news sources.

- **TotalNews**
  http://www.totalnews.com
  Particularly good at covering international newspapers. It is broken down into Business, National, World, Local, Sports, Politics, Life, Entertainment, Weather, Opinion, and Sci-Tech.

- **U.S. News Archives on the Web**
  http://sunsite.unc.edu/slanews/internet/archives.html
  A site belonging to the Special Libraries Association News

Division, is a superb and frequently updated compilation of which newspapers have searchable archives on the Web; it also has information on fees and knowledgeable comments on the usefulness of each site. There are links to international newspapers, as well as other sources for finding newspapers on the Internet.

Finding Magazines and Journals on the Web

- **AJR/Newslink**
  http://www.newslink.org
- **Editor & Publisher's MediaLinks**
  http://www.mediainfo.com
- **Oxbridge Communications MediaFinder**
  http://www.mediafinder.com

E-Journals

Samples of high quality e-journals:

- **D-Lib**
  http://www.dlib.org
  Analyzes digital libraries.

- **FirstMonday**
  http://www.firstmonday.dk/
  Peer reviewed analysis of the social implications of the Internet.

- **Journal of Computer Mediated Communication**
  http://jcmc.huji.ac.il/
  Analyzes how we communicate differently when doing so through and with the aid of computers.

Sites for finding and searching e-journals:

- **Access Project**
  http://www.coalliance.org

- **FatBrain**
  http://www.fatbrain.com

- **John Labovitz E-zine List**
  http://www.meer.Internet/~johnl/e-zine-list/index.html

- **JSTOR**
  http://www.jstor.org

- **NewJour**
  http://www.newjour.com

E-Texts

Popular:

- **Project Gutenberg**
  http://www.promo.net/pg

Scholarly:

- **Rutgers University Center for Electronic Texts in the Humanities (CETH)**
  http://www.ceth.rutgers.edu/

- **University of Virginia, Electronic Text Center**
  http://etext.lib.virginia.edu/

Directories

- **D-Net**
  http://www.d-net.com

Hierarchical Indexes

- **AlphaSearch**
  http://www.calvin.edu/library/as
  Geared for academic researchers; includes databases, search engines, and other sources in addition to Web pages.

- **Argus Clearinghouse**
  http://www.clearinghouse.net
  A selective listing of Internet-based guides, with ratings of 1–5 stars.

- **BUBL Link**
  http://bubl.ac.uk/link
  Contains over 10,000 resources very carefully placed into categories and subcategories, and has advanced searching options.

- **Librarians Index to the Internet**
  http://Sunsite.berkeley.edu/InternetIndex
  Over 4,600 resources extremely well organized and catalogued by librarians.

- **LookSmart**
  http://www.looksmart.com
  A Yahoo-like hierarchical index.

- **The WWW Virtual Library**
  http://vlib.stanford.edu/overview.html
  Consists of 285 "virtual libraries" on a broad range of topics.

Search Engines

- **AltaVista**
  http://www.altavista.com

- **Excite**
  http://www.excite.com

- **FastSearch**
  http://www.alltheweb.com

- **Google**
  http://www.google.com

- **HotBot**
  http://www.hotbot.com

- **Lycos**
  http://www.lycos.com

- **NorthernLight**
  http://www.northernlight.com

Metasearch Engines

- **Dogpile**
  http://www.dogpile.com

- **MetaCrawler**
  http://www.metacrawler.com

- **Profusion**
  http://www.profusion.com

- **SavvySearch**
  http://www.savvysearch.com

Professional Online
Database Vendors

- **Dialog**
  http://www.dialog.com

- **Dow Jones Interactive**
  http://www.askdowjones.com

- **Lexis-Nexis**
  http://www.lexis-nexis.com

Free Database Finder

- **BigHub**
  http://www.bighub.com

Useful and Popular Databases on the Internet

- **EDGAR:**
  http://www.sec.gov/edaux/searches.htm
  The official site from the U.S. Securities and Exchange Commission (SEC) for searching and downloading financial and other information submitted by public firms.

- **Eric**
  http://ericir.syr.edu/Eric/
  Eric is the largest source of information on education, including nearly a million abstracts of various documents and journal articles.

- **Internet Movie Database**
  http://www.imdb.com
  Fun and educational site for finding out about movies, actors, directors, and anything else you need to know about films.

- **Jobs Database**
  http://www.careermosaic.com/cm/usenet.html
  One of the more popular databases for locating jobs online.

- **Medline Plus**
  http://www.nlm.nih.gov/medlineplus/
  Derived from the National Library of Medicine, this site helps you obtain answers to health-related questions.

- **Patent Database**
  http://www.uspto.gov/patft/index.html
  A very handy source for searching and viewing images of patent documents filed with the U.S. Patent and Trademark Office.

- **PubMed**
  http://www.ncbi.nlm.nih.gov/PubMed/
  Another service from the National Library of Medicine, this one is a search service that provides access to the 9 million citations in the respected MEDLINE database, and includes links to participating online journals and other related databases.

- **UnCoverWeb**
  http://uncweb.carl.org/
  A service that will allow you, at no cost, to search a database of millions of journal articles to obtain bibliographic information, and get tables of contents of specified journals delivered to your own e-mail box, again at no charge.

Internet Discussion
Group Finders

- **Directory of Scholarly and Professional E-Conferences**
  http://www.n2h2.com/Kovacs

- **Liszt**
  http://www.liszt.com

- **Publicly Accessible Mailing Lists**
  http://www.neosoft.com:80/internet/paml

- **Talkway**
  http://www.talkway.com

- **TileNet**
  http://www.tilenet.com

- **Topica**
  http://www.topica.com

Internet Discussion Group Archive Search Sites

- **AltaVista**
  http://www.altavista.com (select "discussion groups" then "messages")

- **Deja.com**
  http://www.deja.com

- **Remarq**
  http://www.remarq.com

- **Talkway**
  http://www.talkway.com

Performing Surveys

- **The Center for Applied Social Surveys (CASS)**
  http://www.scpr.ac.uk/cass/docs/fr_casshome.htm
  How to.

- **The Joint Program in Survey Methodology**
  http://www.jpsm.umd.edu/home/other/other.htm
  General how to.

- **University of Maryland, Survey Research Center General**
  http://www.bsos.umd.edu/src/
  How to.

Further Resources:
Keeping Up with Search Engines and Web Searching

The following sites are highly recommended for keeping up with changes in Web research, new search-engine features, and changes in the search-engine industry:

- **Greg Notess**
  http://www.notess.com

- **InformationToday**
  http://www.infotoday.com

- **OnlineInc**
  http://www.onlineinc.com

- **Research Buzz**
  http://www.researchbuzz.com

- **Searchenginewatch.com**
  http://www.searchenginewatch.com

- **Webforia**
  http://www.webforia.com

Further Resources:
Internet and Technology

- **Educom Review**
  http://www.educause.edu/pub/er/review/erAuthorListing. html
  Excellent bibliography on works related to future technologies.

- **New York Times Navigator**
  http://www.nytimes.com/library/tech/reference/cynavi.html
  Guide to useful sites on the Internet (must register first).

PART II

Experts Are Everywhere

6

Identifying Experts
Who They Are, Where to Find Them

QUICK PREVIEW: IDENTIFYING EXPERTS

An expert is simply a person with in-depth knowledge about a subject or activity. For most information-finding projects there are ten types of experts worth tracking down and contacting:

- **Book authors** are solid sources, but be sure those you speak with have stayed up to date with their subject.
- **Periodical staff writers and editors** can be excellent information sources. Technical and trade publication staffers are typically more knowledgeable in a specific field than are journalists who work on popular interest newspapers and publications.
- **Experts cited in periodical articles** make excellent information sources.
- **Convention speakers** are another potential top information source.
- **Federal government personnel** may take time to track down, but once you do, you'll find them to be surprisingly helpful.
- **Association staffers** are superb information sources—knowledgeable, helpful, and very easy to reach.

(continued)

- **Experts at private companies** are often valuable sources, but they may be hard to find and reluctant to reveal their knowledge.
- **Consultants** are often very knowledgeable, but typically not fruitful resources for the researcher, because they normally charge a fee for sharing their knowledge.
- **A "hands-on" expert** actually performs the activity you need to find out about.
- **"Non-expert experts"** are ordinary people who've had some personal experience in what you're trying to find out. They can offer interesting anecdotal reports but you need to be careful in assessing these person's credibility.

Despite the plethora of electronic information and answers now so easily available over the Internet, finding and talking to experts and real live people is *still* the most important part of the information-finding process. Here's why:

- Reading print documents or information that you've found on the Net means wading through piles of published materials or scanning scores of Web pages to try to isolate the information you need. But talking to an expert gives you the opportunity to pose questions and zero in on specific issues that concern *you*. In essence, the information you receive from the expert is "custom designed" to meet your needs.
- If an expert makes a point that's confusing, you can ask a question to clear it up—not so easy to do with a magazine article or book!
- When you talk to an expert, you receive the timeliest information possible. You can find out what has happened in the last couple of days or couple of hours.
- Talking to an expert is simply more interesting and fun. You get the kind of live opinions and candid remarks not ordinarily found in published materials.

But before you begin, you need to learn the best techniques for getting to the "best" experts.

LOCATING THE EXPERTS

Experts are everywhere. An expert is anybody who has in-depth knowledge about a particular subject or activity. A few of these experts are famous—someone like a Jane Goodall or Julia Child—but the overwhelming majority are not. The experts that you'll be talking to are most likely to be businesspersons, government workers, technical writers, shop foremen, teachers, and other ordinary persons with special know-how, skills, or background.

Here is a quick overview of ten of the best types of expert to track down and talk to. The pros and cons of each type are examined; and strategies are provided on how best to make contact.

✔ Book Authors

PRO: Book authors typically have a solid and in-depth understanding of their subject. They possess a broad view of their field and can provide excellent background information.

CON: A book author may no longer be up to date on his or her subject. This can be especially true in fields that change very rapidly (such as computer technology). Book authors can also be hard to find.

How to Reach:

The standard approach for contacting an author is to send a letter in care of the book's publisher. The publisher is then supposed to forward your letter to the author. This can be a slow and unreliable approach to making contact: It's possible that your letter will sit for days, weeks, or even months at the publishing house before it's mailed out—especially if the book is an old one. It's better to call the publisher and talk to the book's editor to find out where *you* can contact the author.

TIP: Tracking Down a Book Author

• You can often find the editor's name mentioned in the "acknowledgments" section in the front of the book. If you don't find it there, you can call the editorial department of the publisher and ask for the editor's name. Just be sure to make it easy for the publisher to help you. This means providing complete information on the book title, author, and date of publication. (If you cannot reach the editor, the next best person to speak with is probably someone in the publicity department.)

Will the publisher give you the author's address and phone number? Although many publishers have house rules prohibiting the release of this information, these rules are flexible. One key to getting the information is to make it easy for the editor or other staffer to help you: Again, be sure you have as much information about the book as possible. An editor at a major publishing house told me that her decision on whether to release information about an author often depends on *why* someone wants it. So think a little beforehand about whether your reasons for wanting to contact the author sound legitimate and important.

If you are trying to find the author of a paperback book, first check the book's copyright page to see if a different publisher put out a hardcover edition. If so, it's best to contact that publisher instead.

✔ Periodical Staff Writers and Editors

PRO: Staff writers and editors of magazines and journals are typically nontechnical types who are easy to get hold of, easy to talk to, and very helpful. They usually keep up with developments in their field and are good at pointing out other places and people to contact for information.

CON: While an editor or staff writer for a *technical or trade* publication may be quite knowledgeable about a field (such people have often covered a specific field for so long that they become experts themselves), newspaper journalists or writers or editors of publications geared for the general public (*Time, Good Housekeeping,* etc.) may not be. They may indeed write an article on a technical topic, but their knowledge of the field can still be somewhat sketchy, because they are usually journalists first and subject experts only through their contacts and interviews. But they can still be helpful sources. For example, I recently contacted a popular magazine's staff writer about an article he wrote regarding the overnight delivery services industry. Although the staffer had a good working knowledge of the field, the real value of speaking with him was getting his referrals to the true experts in the industry that he spoke with when researching the piece.

How to Reach:
When you read an article that's of interest to you, look for the writer's byline at the beginning or end of the piece. Then turn to the periodical's masthead (normally found in the first five pages of the magazine) and search for the writer's name. Contact the publication and ask to speak with that person. If the person is not on the masthead, he or she is probably a freelance writer. The editorial department of the magazine will be able to tell you how to make contact.

Another way to utilize magazine staff members as experts is to look at the masthead of a publication devoted to your subject of interest and try to zero in on a specific department editor (e.g., "technology editor" or "new products editor") who sounds as though he or she covers the kind of information you need. If you can't pick out a specific department editor but want to speak with someone on the magazine, ask to speak with the editor or the managing editor. If you are a subscriber, or at least a regular reader, it will help your cause to say so.

✔ **Experts Cited in Periodical Articles**

PRO: Virtually all periodical articles quote experts when examining an issue. For example, an article about a decline in the public's attendance of movie theaters, published in *Theatre Industry News*, quotes an industry expert on why moviegoing is declining, what can be done about it, what may happen in the future, and so forth. This makes your job of finding a knowledgeable source easy. The magazine has already done the necessary research to find an

---

TIPS: Zero in on the Best Expert
• Take special care to note those articles that are written concisely and clearly enough to be easily understandable for the nonspecialist (i.e., you!). Chances are that the writer of these articles will be equally clear and enlightening to talk to.
• An excellent source of experts on lesser-known and privately held companies are editors and reporters of regional business publications. You can get a free listing of these publications by contacting the Association of Area Business Publications, 202 Legion Avenue, Annapolis, MD 21401; 410–269–0332. Ask for a free copy of its *Directory of Members*.

expert and bring his or her opinions and expertise to its readers. All you need to do is make contact. Such people are typically leaders in their field and can be extremely valuable sources. They can provide you with a wealth of information and are one of my favorite types of expert.

CON: Occasionally, you might run into a very knowledgeable source who is not so adept at communicating his or her expertise. This can make for a confusing information interview. If you encounter a confusing source, try to get the person to define any buzzwords or jargon.

How to Reach:

When an article quotes an expert, the piece normally provides the reader with his or her name and place and city of work. It is then a simple task to call up directory assistance in that city and obtain the phone number of the organization. (You can get the area code of any city by calling the operator.) If the article does not provide the expert's place of work or the city, call the publication directly to ask for it.

✔ Convention Speakers

PRO: People who are invited to present technical sessions at professional conventions are often real leaders and innovators in their field. They should be intimately informed about the topic of their presentation.

CON: Again, you may encounter a top-notch authority who is not as talented at communicating his or her expertise. Otherwise, there is no real drawback with this sort of expert.

How to Reach:

You can find out where conventions are being held on your subject by checking a library copy of the *Directory of Conventions* or by scanning an "upcoming events" column in a relevant trade publication. (See page 59 for more information on conventions.)

✔ Federal Government Personnel

PRO: Many experts in government view sharing information with the public as an important part of their job. What is surprising to many is that government experts are sometimes the most helpful of all sources. In fact, there is actually a law requiring government personnel to be helpful to the public!

CON: If you don't have an expert's name, it can be time-consuming and frustrating to track down the person you need. If you do telephone, be prepared to be transferred around a bit.

How to Reach:
See pages 116–118 on finding your way around Washington, and chapter 3 for an overview of obtaining information from the government.

✔ Association Staffers

PRO: As explained earlier in this book, people who work at professional associations are one of the very best sources of information. They are normally very knowledgeable, helpful, and easy to reach.

CON: An association executive might slant his or her remarks to advance the association's particular industry or cause. In addition, some association personnel are true experts in their field, while others are more oriented toward administrative or public relations work. Be sure you dig for the real experts. (Sometimes the true experts do not work in the association office itself, but work in private industry while maintaining a position with the association. It's fine to contact these people at their regular place of work.)

How to Reach:
Simply look up your subject in a library copy of the *Encyclopedia of Associations.* Call the association and ask your question.

✔ Company Personnel

PRO: Whether it's the person who buys tomatoes for Ragu, or the employee in charge of computer keyboard quality control at Texas Instruments, sometimes the "inside" information you need can be provided only by a specific person at a particular firm. If you're researching a type of *product*, a good place to start getting information is a company that makes it. I've found that salespeople for manufacturers are more than happy to educate interested people about their product, and they don't mind if your questions are elementary.

CON: It can be hard to identify the precise people you need to reach at a company, and if you do find them, they may be reluctant to reveal what you want to know. (See page 274 on obtaining "sensitive" information.) When interviewing company personnel, you also have to be on guard against receiving information that's biased toward promoting their firm.

How to Reach:

To find the names, addresses, and phone numbers of companies, consult Dun & Bradstreet's *Million Dollar Directory* or Standard & Poor's *Register,* found in the library. Once you have a company's address and phone number, you can try to get the information you need by calling its public affairs or public relations office; if the people there don't have the answer, they should be able to connect you with someone who does.

✔ Consultants

PRO: Some consultants are outstanding experts in their field and can provide a great deal of inside information, advice, and in-depth knowledge.

CON: There are a number of disadvantages in using a consultant in a research project. First, it can be difficult to determine how good a particular consultant truly is (however, see chapter 9 for tips on evaluating a source's expertise). An even bigger drawback is that unlike the other types of expert described in this chapter, most consultants will want to charge a fee for sharing their knowledge. This is understandable, because a consultant's livelihood is based on selling access to his or her expertise. However, few researchers are in a position to spend a great deal of money in gathering information, and in fact, as described in this chapter it is normally not necessary to do so!

How to Reach:

To locate a local consultant, you might just check your Yellow Pages. To find others located nationwide, check either a library copy of *Consultants and Consulting Organizations Directory* (Gale Research Company) or call a trade association of consultants by checking the *Encyclopedia of Associations* and asking for referrals.

✔ The "Hands-On" Expert

PRO: This is the person who actually performs an activity that you want to learn about—the fashion designer, master chef, computer programmer, and so on. Such people understand the subject in the intimate and detailed way that comes only from hands-on experience. You can really get a sense of the nitty-gritty by talking with them.

CON: These people's opinions will naturally be based on their own unique experiences. They are not like the journalist or industry observer who forms conclusions by gathering data from a wide variety of sources. You might receive a narrower, more limited view of the subject.

How to Reach:

Sometimes a professional association can refer you to a member who is a hands-on expert. Or just use your ingenuity. Ask yourself the question, Who would know? Let's say you wanted to talk to a top-notch auto mechanic. Try and figure out what type of organization would need to have a top-flight mechanic on its staff. You could call up United Parcel Service, ask for the fleet department, and then talk to the head mechanic. Or let's say you needed to learn about custodial techniques and products. Maybe you'd call Disneyland's director of grounds maintenance. Experts *are* everywhere.

✔ The "Non-Expert" Expert

PRO: The non-expert expert is simply another person who has had some personal experience with whatever it is you are researching. For example, say you were scheduled to have a hip replacement operation and were wondering how much mobility you'll likely have after the operation. If you can speak to one or more people who had this operation, you will likely learn some useful information and get some helpful advice.

CON: When you obtain anecdotal information like this, you need to be particularly careful in evaluating it for reliability and credibility. Obviously, it can be hazardous to draw broad conclusions from one person's personal experiences. However, if you

---

TIP: Directories of Experts

• Here are a few interesting sources. *The Yearbook of Experts, Authorities and Spokespersons,* published by Broadcast Interview Source in Washington, DC, is used by journalists to find experts on scores of subjects ranging from adult education to zoos. The reader looks up his or her subject of interest, and the directory provides the name of the association, company, school, or other organization that has volunteered to be contacted as an information source. For example, if you look up anti-Semitism, you find the Simon Wiesenthal Center and a person who can be contacted for information. The guide is free to working journalists ($37.50 to everyone else) and is available from Broadcast Interview Source, 2233 Wisconsin Avenue NW, Washington, DC 20007; 202–333–4904. Anyone can search the information for free, though, over Broadcast Interview Source's Web site at http://www.yearbooknews.com

Other useful lists of experts are available on the Web, including http://www.experts.com, the University of Southern California's Experts Directory at http://uscnews.usc.edu/experts/index.html, AllExperts at http://www.allexperts.com and JournalismNet at http://www.journalismnet.com/experts.htm. You can find an updated list of experts by browsing the LookSmart directory (http://www.looksmart.com) under the hierarchical category of: World—Reference & Education—Reference Desk—Ask an Expert.

---

hear the same reports from many people who appear to be trust-worthy, then you may determine that such anecdotal information is worth paying attention to. A full discussion on the uses of anecdotal information and strategies for assessing credibility is provided in chapter 9.

How to Reach:

Probably the best way these days to quickly and efficiently tap into the experiences, opinions, and views of "non-expert experts" is to post a message to a relevant Internet discussion group ("usenet" and "listserv" groups). See the discussion regarding "Groups Discussion" in chapter 5 to find out more on how to find the right group.

TIP: Internet Expert Sites
One of the newest sources of "non-expert" experts are sites on the internet that are staffed by volunteers and others who will answer questions on almost any toic. Popular sites include about.com, ExpertCentral (expertcentral.com), KnowPost (knowpost.com), and Abuzz (abuzz.com), among many, many, others. In fact, there is a list of dozens of these on this all-in-one expert locator site: http://www.redesk.com/expert.html. And on some sites, the "expert" is siply the comments of the various visitors to the site.

The quality and reliability of the answers you get on these sites, as you might imagine, varies quite a bit and depends on the knowledge of the particular person wh is the self-appointed expert. In order to try to help searchers identify those persons who have been most helpful to question-askers, some of these sites are asking visitors to rate and rank experts, to provide some guidance on whose advice to trust.

7

Making the Connection
Getting Access to an Expert

QUICK PREVIEW: MAKING THE CONNECTION

- Prepare for your talk with the expert beforehand. Do some reading on the subject, make a list of questions, and think how to best probe each particular source's specific area of expertise.
- Don't contact the leading expert first. Instead, talk to someone who is not too technical and is accustomed to explaining concepts to nonexperts. One such source could be a journalist.
- Decide if you will tape-record your conversation or take notes.
- Although it has become more difficult in recent years to get hold of experts, as they have become busier and more pressed for time, you can do so with the right attitude and a few strategies.
- Telephoning rather than writing the experts is normally the best way to make contact. It's quicker, and you can ask questions and have a dialogue. E-mail is another option for contacting people who are very busy and hard to reach.
- Tips for reaching a busy expert: Select the best means of making contact. Set up an appointment to talk. Make your questions short and succinct. Don't be afraid to keep trying. Call a related office.
- If you call an organization's general phone number to try to identify an expert, figure out how to get the switchboard operator to help you.
- Don't be too quick to accept an "I can't help you" or "I don't know" response to your request to talk to an expert. If necessary, call and try again some other time.

How do you best prepare for your talk with the experts? What's the best way to track them down? What should you actually ask? Here's what you need to know:

GETTING READY BEFOREHAND

It's important that you don't contact the experts without first doing some preparation. One expert in library science who is frequently interviewed for information told me that if the inquirer has done some reading and checking around first, it makes her job a lot easier, and she can be much more helpful.

As mentioned earlier, you should first do some reading. Although it would be helpful to find and read anything the expert you're about to speak with has written, it's not absolutely necessary. It is important, though, to have done some kind of reading and research on the subject first; otherwise, you won't know what questions to ask and you may end up wasting your time and the expert's.

Before you contact an expert, also take a couple of minutes to think about how best to present what you're doing to this

---

TIP: You May Be Helping the Expert
• Think about any ways you may be helping the expert. For example, if the information you gather is going to be published, or presented to a group of influential people, let the expert know it. If you quote or cite an expert, or include the person in a list of sources of further information, it may be an aid to his or her reputation or business. This point is especially important to get across when you interview a vendor or consultant of some kind. These people normally charge for their expertise but will usually give you their information for free in hopes of getting customers through your information report. (This technique works equally well when you need assistance from an organization. Think of ways you will be letting others know of that firm's services.)

So be sure to figure out in advance exactly how your work can help publicize a person. And offer to send a final copy of anything you put together so that the expert can add it to his or her professional credential file.

---

particular source to encourage help. What should be stressed? What should be downplayed?

It's important that you spend a few minutes thinking about the best kinds of questions you could ask. These questions should reflect:

• Matters that are confusing and unclear to you after you've read information on the subject.
• Areas in which you need more detailed information.
• Problems or subjects unique to your needs that have not been addressed in any materials you've looked at.

Also, be sure to use this opportunity to probe for a deeper analysis of your subject and to search for the significance of the information you've acquired so far. For example, if your research on the airline industry turns up the fact that "currently, corporations do not negotiate with airlines for volume discounts," you'll want to find out *the reason why not* from the experts. If, in your study of the problems of the elderly, you discover that Medicare payments are planned to be reduced, you'll want to dig out *the implications of that policy* once it's instituted.

When you make up your questions, you should also consider what kinds of queries best probe a particular source's specific area of expertise. Let's say you had to find out everything you could about the subject of tents. If you are interviewing a product design expert at a leading manufacturer, a question about the characteristics of various tent materials would be very appropriate to that source's expertise. If the next expert you interviewed was a top-notch camper, then a question about efficient strategies for quickly setting up a tent would be very productive. Of course, if you value a particular source's overall knowledge, there is nothing wrong with asking questions outside his or her exact expertise. But it is important to think carefully beforehand about what a particular source's real specialties are, and then try to zero in on them.

I've found that it's helpful to actually write up a list of all your questions and have them in front of you when speaking to an expert. (If you plan to contact an expert by mail, you can write up and send the questions; see page 245 for more on phone versus mail contacts.) The purpose of writing up your questions is to allow you to do all your planning and thinking ahead of time. This way, during the conversation, you'll have time to concentrate on what the expert is saying. You won't have to worry about what to ask next, or whether you've asked all your questions, because they will be written out on a sheet of paper in front of you. Each time you ask a question, just cross it off your list.

TIP: Sound Natural
• Try to avoid making your discussion sound like you're reading a list of questions—it's better to sound natural.

Once you've written up the questionnaire, you're ready for the talk.

SELECTING THE FIRST EXPERT TO SPEAK WITH

How do you decide which expert to talk to first? I've found that it's usually not a good idea to contact the leading expert in the field first. It's normally better to wait until after you've spoken with some other people. This way, by the time you speak with the premier expert, you'll know enough about the subject to ask the most incisive and probing questions, rather than basic questions you can get answered by other sources.

A good type of first source to contact is often a nontechnical person—for example, someone who has written a clear and concise article that provides an overview of the field or someone in an association's educational division. As you learn more and become more confident, you can speak with the more technical experts in the field.

NOTE TAKING VS. TAPE-RECORDING

Finally, the last decision to make before you actually talk to the expert is whether to take notes or tape the conversation. This decision really comes down to a personal preference. I prefer note taking; to me, it seems like a bother to set up a tape recorder and then play back the tape to hunt through the whole conversation to find significant statements. I find it easier and more efficient to quickly jot down the important points as the expert makes them. The information is then right in front of me on a piece of paper, ready to be used whenever I need it. But if you prefer taping, you can buy devices at electronics stores that attach to the phone receiver and tape the conversation. You should inform the person that you are making a tape. (That's another reason I'm not crazy about taping. Many people get nervous and withhold information.)

A couple of strategies on note taking: Try not to make your notes too cryptic. Write them as if you were penning them for another person. Otherwise you may later find yourself desperately

---

TIP: Tapes Plus Notes

• If you do decide to tape, you can make it easy to find specific statements by using a tape recorder with a numerical indexing counter. Whenever the expert makes an important remark, just jot down the number displayed. Later you can locate those statements simply by fast-forwarding the recorder to the numbers you noted.

trying to decipher your own handwriting. Also, it really does help to read over your notes immediately after the interview is over; they will make a lot more sense to you than if you read them a day or two later. Another benefit of reading notes immediately is that sometimes during an information interview you'll be writing so fast that you won't be able to write full sentences. Immediately after the conversation the details are still fresh in your mind, and you'll be able to fill in the gaps.

MAKING CONTACT

When I first wrote this book in 1986, it really wasn't all that tough to contact and interview an expert for information. It really just took some strategizing—and a bit of nerve. But starting in the hectic and fast-paced 1990s, it became more challenging to actually reach the person you need. In today's high-tech dominated business world, people have very little, if any, spare time—so it's getting tougher to actually make contact and get someone to spend a few minutes with you. As Herbert Simon, the Nobel Prize winner in Economics has succinctly put it, "What information consumes is rather obvious: it consumes the attention of its recipients. Hence, a wealth of information creates a poverty of attention...."

But it's not impossible to get the attention of others. All it requires is that you think carefully about how you are going to do it. You need to consider which means of contact to use (discussed later in this chapter) and make sure you follow the strategies outlined in the chapter on getting the person to cooperate with you. It used to be that you could almost assume that once you had the name and contact information, the vast majority of experts would talk to you without your doing all that much, but now you have to work a little harder to get results.

Finding Phone Numbers, Addresses, and E-mail Addresses

What do you do if you read an article that cites an expert but does not tell you where he or she works or can be contacted? If you run into this problem, you'll want to contact the magazine or journal and have a little patience. For example, I recently was researching the subject of "finding free software" and found a very interesting article in *Inc.* magazine that quoted an expert on the topic. Unfortunately, the article did not say where this person worked or where he could be reached. And to top it off, there was no writer's byline accompanying the article.

I decided to call up *Inc.* magazine to try and track down the expert. I found *Inc.*'s phone number by checking the masthead and then called the magazine and asked to be connected with the editorial department. A woman answered the phone, and I gave her the issue's date, the page number of the story, and the headline. She then checked her files, found the writer of the piece, and gave me that reporter's direct phone number. I called the writer and told her what I was trying to find. She was able to look up the story in her files and inform me that the expert was a professor at the University of Texas. She gave me his phone number.

The lesson is, if you have trouble figuring out where to find an expert, don't be afraid to contact the source that cited that person to get the necessary information to track him or her down.

The Internet has also made it extremely simple to find phone numbers, addresses, and e-mail addresses for persons and businesses located around the country, or even around the world. Some even offer "reverse" directories: that is, you enter a phone number, and you are then given a name and address.

There are several sites that allow you to enter the name of a person or a business, and then get contact information. Note that nearly all of these sites use ordinary telephone directory phone books to compile their address and phone number listings, so if the person you're trying to find has an unlisted number, you're unlikely to find them this way. Also keep in mind that sometimes these directories can be slow in updating their listings. And e-mail listings are spotty at best. Despite these flaws, these sites can still prove to be very helpful. Here are the names and URLs of the best known of these:

- **Four11**
  http://www.four11.com
- **Switchboard**
  http://www.switchboard.com
- **InfoSpace**
  http://www.infospace.com
- **InfoUsa**
  http://www.lookupusa.com

TIP: When to Write
• There may be certain cases in which a letter is more appropriate. If you want to reach a superstar celebrity, for example, you're not as likely to get that person on the phone. If you do write, keep your letter simple and short, and don't ask for a lot. Make it as easy as possible for the person to respond. Enclose a stamped, self-addressed envelope. Another tip is when writing to an organization or business for information, write to the top or one of the top people. Your letter will then be funneled to the appropriate office "lower down" and will receive more attention since it came down from a higher office.

For international directories, check LookSmart's hierarchical directory at World—People & Chat—People Finders—Int'l White Pages. Link to: http://www.looksmart.com

Phone Calls vs. Letters vs. E-mail

As discussed earlier in this chapter, because so many people are badly pressed for time and often stressed at their jobs, you need to think more carefully than ever about what is the best and most appropriate means of making contact—a letter, e-mail, or a phone call.

The general principle, though, is always the same—you should use whatever approach will stand out the most, get attention, and not get lost. When e-mail first became popular in the early 1990s, it became my preferred way of reaching someone, because I found that people would respond so quickly. While I still often use e-mail, it has lost the "novelty" quality it had for a short time. And, in fact, the danger today is that, with so many people getting swamped with e-mails, your note won't be answered at all, or get buried and lost among all the others. And so now it seems that getting a phone call seems more unusual than getting an e-mail. But then you run into the voice mail problem . . . !

What to do? Here are a few tips for tracking down busy people:

- Despite the increasing problems with e-mail, I still often find it the best way to get a response. I think this remains true because the nature of this medium is such that it makes it very fast and easy for a person to respond. So I often use e-mail for my an initial contact, even if only to set up a phone-call appointment. Another plus to e-mail is that it gives the recipient a chance to think about your questions ahead of time and come up with more thoughtful responses.

- If you call someone and you're lucky enough not to get voice mail, don't assume that, because the person you wanted to speak with picked up the phone, it is a good time for him or her to talk. Explain why you're calling, and then ask if you might be able to set up a specific phone appointment to ask questions sometime in the next week or so.

- When you speak with an expert on the phone, make your questions succinct and quick. And never read a long list!

- If you send an e-mail, make sure the header is clear, inviting, and personal. It might even make the recipient a bit curious. But don't, at all costs, make it an overly cute "lure" that may make it appear to be some kind of come-on or spam—many people (myself included) delete these before even reading them!

- More than ever before, you may need to make multiple attempts to reach a person—three or four times is not uncommon. Consider using more than one medium—phone *and* e-mail, for example. Don't be a pest(or not *too much* of one!). Remain polite—but be persistent.

- One excellent strategy for gaining an inside track to a group of experts is by joining a relevant Internet discussion group. You'll be able to spot who are the experts and approach them as another member of the list. If you remain on the list long enough, and begin to make contributions, then you truly will become a member of that community and will be able to tap into others' expertise on a regular basis.

- Consider sending a personal letter. The reason: a handwritten or even typed letter is less common these days, so it will get attention. Overnight-delivery packages get attention too, so if you want to pay the cost, you might also consider that option. In the letter you should include an e-mail address for the person to respond to, because it takes time and effort to write back—and most people don't have time these days!

Sometimes you know *where* you're likely to find an expert (e.g., a particular company or association), but you don't have anyone's name. Here are some strategies for finding an expert in these cases:

- If you know the name of the department in a company that can help you, ask to be connected with the "director" of that office. If you don't have a department in mind, ask to be connected with "public affairs" or "public relations." Although a spokesperson there will probably give you fewer details than someone who works in another department, you may still get some helpful information. Calling the public affairs or public relations department is also helpful when your inquiry relates to something that affects the company as a whole; for example, if you wanted to find out about a company's new product line or the closing of a branch office.
- When calling an organization's general phone number, be careful how you phrase your information request to the switchboard operator. This person is usually very busy and will not have the time to help you figure out who you want to speak with.

Let's say you need to find out about new technologies in lightbulbs. An excellent information source would be a major lightbulb manufacturer like General Electric. If you called up GE's main number and asked the switchboard operator, "Who can I speak with that can help me find out about new technologies in lightbulbs?" you risk getting a discouraging "Sorry, I don't know" or, if you're lucky, "I can connect you with someone who can take your name and address and mail you some of our sales brochures." That's not exactly what you wanted. So, instead, try to help the switchboard operator by providing some guidance as to where to send you. For example, you might say, "I have a technical question on your incandescent lightbulb products. Which department can help me?" Now the operator can feel more comfortable switching your call to a technical or engineering department. Or describe by function the "type" of person you want to reach: for example, "the person in charge of selecting new store sites" or "the manager of your computer systems." You can even try to guess the department you need—for example, by asking for "new product development"—and you may discover that the firm actually has a department like the one you guessed! Or the operator may find a similar-sounding department—for example, "planning and development"—and ask if he or she should connect you there. If it seems close, you should agree. Once connected, ask to speak with a manager or director of that division and pose your question. If that individual can't help you, he or she may be able to refer you to the appropriate division.

If you're calling a professional association, nonprofit organization, or public institution, there are certain departments common to many of these bodies that are especially fruitful information sources. For example:

- The in-house library. The reference librarian is an excellent source of information and can search published resources for you.

- The education department. This department is typically found in associations. Its role is to inform members and the public of the resources of the organization.

- The publications department. Here you can usually get an index of what the organization publishes, and sometimes what's about to be published.

There is one final important point to keep in mind when you're trying to make contact with an expert. When you talk to the switchboard operator, an administrator, or whoever else picks up the phone, don't be so quick to take "We can't help you" or "I don't know" as an answer to your request for an expert. Often the problem is just that you've been unlucky enough to catch someone in a bad mood or someone who is not too knowledgeable about the organization's resources. Try politely rephrasing your question a couple of times if necessary to get some help or ask, "Is there another person in the organization I can speak with who might know?" If this does not work, then consider calling another time, when someone else may answer.

The person you speak with initially may want to turn you over to a publications department. This may not be so bad, because you may find that there indeed are some relevant publications available that will help you. But do not feel obligated to end your search at this point. You should still ask to see if there is an expert available.

8

Talking with Experts
Strategies for Getting Inside Information

QUICK PREVIEW: TALKING WITH EXPERTS

- Never assume an expert won't talk. Most of the time the person will be happy to help you.
- Present yourself properly to the expert by identifying who you are and by asking if it's a good time to talk. Be serious, get to the point, admit any ignorance on the subject, and ask *specific* questions. Let the expert steer the conversation; put off tough questions until later.
- Think of ways you can heighten an expert's interest in what you are doing. For example, can you publicize his or her work to others or share any information that you come up with?
- During the conversation, question things that don't make sense to you, ask for definitions of technical terms, and see if the expert can help you define what it is that you really need to find out.
- Once the conversation is moving, get control and steer it to where you want it to go.

(continued)

- At the end of the conversation, ask if there is anything important that hasn't been discussed, request written information, and ask for the names of other experts.
- As you learn more about the subject, update your questions. Periodically review your overall goals and strategies.
- Always keep the "big picture"—your ultimate objective in the information-finding project—in mind as you proceed.
- If you encounter an expert who's suspicious of you, try gaining his or her confidence by revealing more about yourself and by offering to show a copy of anything you write up.
- If you encounter a hostile source, try to build up trust. Consider sending a written inquiry, share your findings, be as nice as possible, and let the person know how he or she is acting.
- Use the strategies outlined in this chapter to handle those experts who say, "I don't have time" and "I don't know," and who "tell no evil."
- You can try to obtain "sensitive" information by rephrasing questions, asking peripheral questions, asking for "feelings," taking a position on an issue, and keeping the conversation "off the record."
- You may confront ethical dilemmas when attempting to obtain "inside information" from knowledgeable sources. Often these dilemmas involve the issue of misrepresenting your affiliation and/or the purpose of your project. If faced with such ethical concerns, you should first make sure you've exhausted all public sources, identified easily interviewable experts, and confirmed the importance of the data you are seeking. Don't assume you need a ruse to get information—the truth usually works fine. Misrepresenting yourself is not advisable.

As discussed in the previous chapter, people *are* becoming increasingly pressed for time and harder to get hold of. But you should never assume that people are not going to talk to you.

Whether the topic is fine china, poodle breeding, or Norwegian economics, experts have a great interest in their topic, and they enjoy discussing it. Remember, these people have devoted a great portion of their lives to learning and exploring their field. When someone approaches them needing information, they're almost always pleased to oblige.

Adding to their inclination to talk is the fact that, no matter how mundane a subject may seem, there is always some kind of controversy that excites the experts. For example, I recently discovered in the course of researching the sexy topic of water meters that an intense battle was being fought between those favoring plastic meters and those who liked bronze ones! The important point to remember is, never assume someone won't talk to you. Always try.

Here are some other, more general strategies for approaching experts to smooth the interview procedure and encourage their cooperation.

PRESENTING YOURSELF TO THE EXPERT

Okay, the secretary has just told you that the boss will be on the line shortly. The expert picks up the phone and says hello. Now what?

No, don't hang up. Here's what to do to get the conversation off to a smooth start:

Identify Yourself. You've got to identify yourself—clearly and precisely—and explain why you are calling. This is very important to do to allay the natural suspicion we all have when a stranger contacts us. Don't start off your conversation by saying, "Hello. Can I ask you some questions about oil futures trading?" Infinitely better is, "My name is Karen Johnson, and I'm calling from (hometown or firm and city). I'm currently collecting information on the benefits of oil futures market trading (for a possible book or for a report for my firm or to learn about career opportunities), and I read your recent article titled 'Why Trade Oil Futures?' I wonder if I could have just a couple of minutes to ask you a few questions?"

It's also helpful to explain your goals and which sources you've already checked. The more information the expert has on why you're calling, the easier his or her job will be, and the more you'll get out of the conversation.

Ask the Expert If It's a Good Time to Talk. You don't want to interview someone who's in a rush to get it over with. If it's a bad time, set up an appointment for a formal phone interview at a specific time a day or two in the future. This gives importance to your phone interview and legitimizes it. In fact, it may not be such a bad idea to make an initial call solely to set up an appointment for a future formal phone interview.

Be Serious. You need to convey the impression that your project is important to you, not a lark or a trifling matter.

Get to the Point. People want to know why you're calling. I find it's more relaxing and enjoyable to save friendly conversation about the weather and so forth until after the interview is completed.

TIP: Be Sensitive
• When presenting yourself, don't make the mistake I once did of conveying the impression that you're attempting to become quickly knowledgeable in the expert's field. I had about eight weeks to write a comprehensive report on the topic of micrographics. I explained this to one of my first expert sources. He refused to help and told me that such a project couldn't be done. He was wrong, but I learned my lesson. It's kind of insulting to say to somebody who's been in a field for twenty, maybe thirty, or more years that you are going to become an "instant expert" in a matter of weeks. Instead, it's much wiser to say that you're *collecting* information and advice from experts in the field, or reporting on what the experts are saying, or anything along those lines. In essence, that is really what you are doing anyway.

Admit Your Ignorance. If you are unsure about your subject and do not feel confident, it is *much better to simply admit that to the expert up front.* It's fine to say something like "I am just starting to learn about this subject, so please excuse me if my questions sound elementary." The worst mistake you could make is to fumble around trying to sound knowledgeable with a lot of "uhs," "well I guess sos," and so on. These only serve to arouse suspicions—the expert may think you are trying to hide something! If you are asked a question to which you don't know the answer, simply say "I don't know" rather than trying to make believe you do know! Don't feel embarrassed or guilty that you do not know more—the whole idea of finding information is to learn! Also, once the expert knows that you are a novice, he or she is more likely to avoid using jargon and buzzwords and will attempt to explain concepts to you more clearly.

Be Specific. This is quite important, especially at the beginning of the conversation. Here's an example of what I mean. Suppose the topic you need to find out about is the "future of baseball in this country." If you began your conversation by posing such an overwhelmingly broad question, you'd be starting off on the wrong foot. It's too difficult and vague a question to answer, and your source will feel on the spot. Instead, start off with a more specific question that can be answered easily, such as "Do you think that the drug problem in baseball has lessened during the last few years?" or "Are the followers of the baseball scene pre-

---

TIP: Be Nice!
• Another important point is attitude. The importance of politeness should be obvious, but it's a point worth stressing. Your attitude really will make a difference. Don't ever be demanding or impatient. Try to sound confident, cheerful, and professional—present yourself as though you were interviewing for a job.

---

dicting that a new commissioner will have an impact on the players' rising salaries?" Even if these questions are not vital to you, they will get the ball rolling, which *is* vital to the conversation. Later, especially toward the end of the conversation, when a rapport has been established, you can throw in the "future of baseball" question. By then, the expert is warmed up, and the answers given to your earlier questions make him or her more responsive.

Follow the Expert's Lead. At the beginning, let the source take the lead in directing the conversation. If the person feels comfortable talking about something that's not exactly on the right track for you, show interest anyway. Later on in the discussion you can redirect the conversation to cover the precise areas you are interested in.

Delay Tough Questions. Don't begin the conversation with questions that may stump your source. If you think you've asked such a stumper, don't press for an answer. Drop it, and go to another question. Later on in the conversation you can try bringing it back up. Similarly, if you think any of your questions could be considered offensive, save these for the end, too.

GETTING THE EXPERT INTERESTED

Everyone wants to feel important. You can help the discussion along by making the source feel good. Show some sincere appreciation, give some praise, and tell the expert how helpful the information and advice is.

A good way to get experts to open up is to heighten their interest in what you are doing. Here are a few strategies:

TIP: Don't "Survey"
• People normally don't like to be "surveyed," but they like to give "opinions" or their "thoughts" on a matter. It's more personal.

• As mentioned earlier, be sure you figure out in advance any way the expert will be helped by talking to you.
• If you work for or are on assignment for a well-known publication or company, it may help to mention it. Often people feel excited about being consulted by a prestigious organization. This doesn't mean that experts always prefer talking to someone calling from a well-known organization. Some people are actually *less* disposed, either because they prefer to do a "public service" and help out an amateur information seeker or because they do not want their remarks to be widely circulated. It's a personal preference that will vary among your sources.
• A good way to heighten the expert's enthusiasm is to let the person know of any interesting bits of information you've come up with so far in your research. Often the information you've discovered could be used by the expert for his or her own purposes. Similarly, you should offer to share your final findings with the expert. Remember, you're doing a lot of in-depth digging in the expert's field; what you ultimately come up with should be of interest to that person. (Note: Again, this can be a sensitive area. Don't make it sound as though your research will be groundbreaking. Just humbly offer to send whatever information you come up with.)
• Attempt to interest the expert enough so that he or she really *wants* to help you. For example, if you wanted to interview an interior design consultant about some art-oriented question, you could get the person interested in talking to you by letting him or her know that talking to you will enable the viewpoint of a representative of the profession to be "heard" in your pro-

---

TIP: Be Persistent
• If your first couple of interviews don't go as smoothly as you hoped, don't despair. It's really a numbers game, and the process is such that some interviews will be great, some good, and some not so good.

---

ject. A different approach is to appeal a bit to ego. When you let a source know that your work is identifying the very leading experts in the field, it is very flattering, and the source will naturally want to be included in such a listing. It's also complimentary to ask for someone's ideas on a subject, especially if you mention that you'll be passing along those thoughts to others as expert opinion.

• Finally, try to get a feel for whether your expert would be excited about being quoted or would prefer to remain anonymous.

GETTING THE MOST OUT OF THE INTERVIEW

Here are some specific pointers to keep in mind during the actual conversation:

Question Things! If an expert says something that doesn't sound right, or that contradicts something else you've been told, ask for more information. (For example, if an expert tells you matter-of-factly that so-and-so's theory on the link between attitude and illness is preposterous, ask the expert *why* he or she does not believe it. What are the *reasons?*) Questioning statements with a "why," instead of accepting them at face value, is one of the very best ways to deepen your understanding of any subject. Don't let questions "hang" unanswered. Politely press for reasons and explanations.

Probe for Specifics. Try not to accept general, unproven statements. If an expert on computers tells you that IBM makes the best computer on the market, ask him or her to tell you *why*. If you're then told that it's superior because the firm provides better service, ask *how* it provides better service. If the expert tells you that IBM's service is better because its response time to problems is quicker than that of its competitors, find out *how much* quicker. Again, if an expert tells you that it would be extremely unlikely for someone to get sick from eating too much of a certain vitamin, ask whether, in fact, it has *ever* happened; if so, what was the situation or condition that made it occur.

Ask for Definitions of Technical Terms. If the expert throws in any terms or buzzwords you don't understand, ask for a definition. Asking for explanations is nothing to be embarrassed about. It may be important for you to know the definitions of certain words, as they may be standard terminology in the field. Tell the expert that you want to define the term precisely but in layman's language.

Ask for Help. Early on in your project, you'll be trying to figure out exactly what you need to know to understand your field. You can enlist the experts' assistance in better defining exactly what you need to find out. If you have a good rapport with an expert, you can ask that person to help you isolate the critical issues on which you need to become knowledgeable.

Let's say you're digging up information on dream research. Initially you probably do not know what the important issues are in that field and may not even be sure what questions to ask. But an expert will know the issues. He or she may say something like, "Well, if you want to find out about the latest in dream research, you should ask experts about some recent findings in 'lucid dreaming' and discoveries about the Senoi Indian dream techniques." What you're doing here is asking the expert to tell you which issues are important in the field, and what *questions* you should be asking other experts. In a sense, you are trying to find out the answer to the question, What should I be finding out? And there's nobody better qualified to tell you than the experts themselves. (Because this type of question is somewhat offbeat, you should not begin your conversation with it, but work it in toward the middle or end.)

Keep in Control. You've got to keep the interview on track. Occasionally a source may think that you are interested in a subject that is actually of no concern to you. He or she will try to be helpful but may go off on a tangent and talk a blue streak about something of no interest to you. Listen politely, but soon you'll have to rein the expert in and ask a question you *are* interested in. It's up to you to keep the conversation on course. You have a limited amount of time for each discussion, and it's important to make the most of it. Otherwise you'll be wasting your time and the expert's time. (Note: As discussed earlier, at the *very beginning* of a conversation you may want to allow the expert to talk about almost anything just to get the ball rolling. But soon you've got to move in and get the conversation on track.)

Wrap it Up. *At the very end of an information interview*, there are three questions you should ask:

- *"Is there anything important we haven't discussed?"* It's possible that your source has some additional important information to discuss but hasn't mentioned it because you didn't ask. This provides the expert with the opportunity to talk about it.
- *"Do you have any written information you can send me?"* Often the expert has written articles on the subject or keeps clippings of relevant materials.
- *"Who else do you recommend that I speak with?"* This is an extremely important question that you should be sure to ask all your sources. There are many reasons why this is such an important question. One is that it is a quick way to get the name and phone number of another expert. Even more important, however, is the fact that you now have a referral person you can cite when you contact the new expert. Be sure to let that person know that you were referred by the mutual acquaintance. If you leave a message for the expert, it's worth mentioning the contact's name in the message to encourage a call back. There's almost no better way to reach someone than through a direct referral like this.

Another reason that it's so important to ask to be referred to other experts is that often the more people you are referred to, the more likely it is that you'll be speaking with someone who has the specific expertise you seek. Say that you have to find out all about new technologies in camera light meters. And say that you've

---

TIP: Confirm Your Facts
• The end of a conversation is a good time to clear up any confusing points the expert may have made during the discussion. You can use this time to confirm important facts, state your understanding of the issues, and get them verified.

decided to call a camera manufacturers association to try to find the information. Well, maybe the association's technical staffperson Tom will tell you that he keeps up only with general industry developments. But when you ask him for a contact, he refers you to his friend Pat at Nikon, who is involved more in day-to-day technological advances. You thank Tom and give Pat a call. Well, it turns out that Pat does have some good technological know-how, and you get some information from her, but she's not a real specialist in light metering components. She refers you to Bill, who heads that division, and he, in turn, refers you to the expert, Joe, on his staff.

So the process is such that when you get referrals, you often zero in on someone whose expertise is more appropriate to your inquiry. (The process can be frustrating, too: It often results in your best sources coming at the very *end* of your information search, when you are trying to wrap it all up!)

STAYING ON COURSE AND REDIRECTING FOCUS

Throughout your interviews, it's important to keep on the course you've charted. To do so means asking the right questions and directing your energies to get you where you want to go.

The questions you pose to the experts will need to be constantly revised and updated as your interviews progress. Some of your simpler questions will be answered the same way by everyone, and it won't be necessary to keep asking them. At the same time, you'll also find that you'll have to add *new* questions as you go along and experts bring up issues that you weren't aware of. You'll notice as you speak with the experts that the important issues will emerge automatically as their conversation gravitates to critical matters. You'll then be able to incorporate these issues into your questionnaire. You'll want to create questions about these new issues and ask them of future sources. So your questionnaire will be a flexible one, and it will be modified throughout your information search to reflect the major issues as you see them emerge.

If you come to a point where you start to predict the answers

---

TIP: Read Your Old Notes
• Reading over the notes you've taken during interviews up until this point will stimulate you to think of new questions and fresh angles you haven't yet pursued.

---

from the experts, it's a sign that it's time to step back a little from the information-gathering project and assess where it's going. Think about whether it's necessary to alter the direction you're heading in and, if so, in what way. Think about whether your goals have changed since you began the project and, if so, how. Are there gaps in your information that need to be filled? Are there new angles to explore? Think about any new types of sources that you haven't tried yet that should be approached. Take stock of where you are and how things are going.

For example, let's say you're digging up information on careers in journalism. After interviewing a dozen or so experts, the time is ripe to assess where you stand in the project. As you step back, maybe you realize that, although you've interviewed people in the newspaper and magazine industry, you haven't spoken with anyone in television journalism; your efforts can now be directed toward reaching those sources. Maybe you'll discover that your overall goals have changed, too. When you started the project, you were interested in finding information about all types of journalism careers. Now, after a dozen interviews, you realize that you want to pursue information specifically about the career of newswriting. So you redirect your questions and choose sources to reflect that new goal.

Keep the "Big Picture" in Mind. At all times during your project, keep your ultimate goal in mind as a guiding force. Try not to get sidetracked into pursuing routes that have nothing to do with why you are conducting your information search. If, for example, your goal is to find information that compares the quality of the various long-distance carriers, and you're talking to a telecommunications expert, try to avoid being led into a long discussion on, say, the legal precedent behind the breakup of AT&T. Although that topic is related to long-distance service, it really is not pertinent to your specific goals. It's fine to change your goals as you go along, but just be sure that all your activities serve that goal.

CRACKING THE TOUGH NUTS

Now, what do you do if you have a source who's really a tough nut to crack and it's important that this person share his or her information?

The great majority of experts *will* talk to you and give you the answers you need. But it's possible to run into someone who is not so helpful. There are a number of reasons why someone would be unhelpful. Maybe you've called at a bad time. Maybe the person is simply someone who is not the helpful type. Or maybe you've encountered someone who is protective of his or her knowledge and doesn't want to share it.

Whatever the reason, if you encounter someone like this, sometimes the easiest thing to do is to abandon the interview and move on to the next one. As mentioned earlier, not *all* of your conversations with experts are going to be perfect, so it's no big deal to drop a difficult one. But what if this one is important to you? In that case, you shouldn't give up. There are a number of strategies you can use to turn a difficult interview into a productive one.

In this section we'll examine the ways to get through the rockiest interviews. This includes strategies for dealing with reluctant sources and strategies for dealing with difficult questions and topics.

Building Up Trust

A source who is unwilling to talk to you is often suspicious. Even if you've identified yourself clearly and explained why you are seeking information, the person may still be suspicious of who you *really* are and what you're going to do with the information. From the expert's perspective, you are just an anonymous voice on the phone; you could be a competitor or someone up to no good.

One strategy you can take to help allay suspicions is to simply stay on the phone longer and keep talking. Reveal more about yourself and why you're gathering information. Slowly, the expert will get a better feeling for who you are, and you'll become less anonymous and less threatening. As you reveal more about yourself and what you're doing, the unhelpful expert often loosens up somewhat and starts to talk.

Another way you can calm the fears of a suspicious source is by

---

TIP: Handling a Hostile Source

• How do you handle a hostile source? It's very rare to encounter someone who is outright belligerent, but it can happen.

Chances are, the person is hostile because he or she is a little nervous and suspicious of you. One thing you can do to help allay suspicions is to explain as specifically as possible *who* will be receiving the information that you are gathering.

Another strategy is to offer to send a written inquiry on your letterhead or your company's letterhead. There are a couple of reasons why a letter is more reassuring to a hostile source. For one thing, an expert who sees a specific letterhead feels more certain that you are who you say you are—letters are more "solid" than phone calls. In addition, letters provide the person with time to think. One reason a source may act hostile is fear of saying something later regretted. Now a response can be made more carefully.

It's possible that your source is hostile because you're being viewed as a competitor of some kind. There are a couple of ways you can try to overcome this problem. One strategy, if your work really does compete in some way with the expert's, is to be sure to offer to share your findings. Another strategy is to downplay the competition by emphasizing those aspects of your project that differ from the expert's.

What if all these strategies fail and your source is still hostile? Be *extra nice.* I've found that if you are unrelentingly nice—even if it kills you!—most of the time you will disarm the hostility. It may not be easy to do, but if a hostile source's information is very important to you, just grit your teeth and smile.

If this fails, too, you have little choice but to politely let the source know how he or she is acting. You might say something like, "It sounds like this is a bad time for you. Would it be better if I call back?" Or you can be blunt. One time I was interviewing a vice president of a major tobacco company in hopes of finding out more about its innovative use of copiers. For some unknown reason, the vice president was very belligerent toward me. Finally, I just asked, "Why are you so hostile?" That question confronted the issue in a nonaggressive way and let the man realize how he was being perceived. He then became much more helpful.

Remember, hostile sources are *rare.* The great majority of people are very helpful.

---

offering to send a copy of anything you write before it's published or presented to anyone. A big concern for some people is being misquoted or misunderstood. Some experts feel better if they know that they can correct errors or have some control over their remarks. In fact, their review can benefit you, too, because it should serve as a check on the accuracy of your information.

Specific Problem Areas

Here are ways to handle some common tough interview spots:

The "I Don't Have Time to Talk" Expert. What do you do if your source says he or she doesn't have time to speak with you? One strategy is to ask to be given just a minute or two. This will reassure the source that the whole morning won't be used up on the phone with you. But an interesting thing you'll find is that once that expert starts talking, most of the time he or she will continue to talk for twenty, thirty, forty minutes, or more!

Another way to reassure experts is to tell them to tell *you* when they want the discussion to end. If you give them the control of stopping the conversation, they're likely to be reassured.

A different tactic is to set up a future day and time for a formal phone interview. This enables the source to budget some time to allow for a few minutes with you.

The "I Don't Know" Expert. How do you handle a source who is answering a lot of your questions with "I don't know" and you think the person really does know. Sometimes the "I don't know" syndrome occurs when an expert does not want to mislead you with an answer that's not precise. But often all you're really looking for is a general idea. If this is the case, try asking for a "rough estimate" or a "ballpark figure." This will take the pressure off your source to be exact, and it may yield the general information that you're looking for.

The Expert Who Will Tell No Evil. Sometimes in your information interviews, you'll need to find out the negative or bad side of an issue. For example, you are interviewing a trustee of a college, and you want to find out what the school's problems are. Or let's say you're interviewing a representative of the American Advertising Executives Association, and you want to find out the negative aspects of a career in advertising. In both of these cases, the sources will probably feel uncomfortable giving you this negative information. In general, people prefer telling you the good, rather than the bad. It's safer, especially when one is representing a particular institution, product, or cause.

Here's a way to make it easier for the expert to reveal the negative. Ask for "the best points and the worst points," or the "strengths and weaknesses" of the matter in question. By asking experts to talk about—and indeed emphasize if they wish—the good, you allow them to dilute the bad, making it easier to divulge.

The "Too Smart" Expert. Occasionally, the very leading expert in a field may be so intimately knowledgeable of all the details of a subject and so aware of all the permutations that affect it that the person will sincerely have difficulty answering basic questions. For example, once I was writing a report on how companies can reduce their travel and entertainment expenses. One of the premier experts in the field answered many of my questions with, "That is too complicated a matter to respond to simply" or "There is no one answer to that question" or "It really depends on the situation." Although he was technically correct, he was unable to come down from his lofty plane and work a little to provide some kind of help. If you get an expert like this, don't give up. You should still be able to glean some good information out of the conversation and get a feel for what the "big picture" looks like.

Obtaining "Sensitive" Information

In many information searches, it becomes necessary at some point to ask an expert about some controversial or sensitive matter. Although you'll be surprised at how often people will freely discuss this type of information, you'll want to have some strategies for getting as much cooperation as possible.

Don't Begin with Sensitive Questions. You should not begin your conversation with a controversial or sensitive question. These are best situated in the middle of a conversation when the expert is warmed up a bit and feeling more relaxed. It's also best not to end with a very sensitive question, unless you feel it is so sensitive that it may cause the expert to terminate his or her conversation with you.

Rephrase Questions. If you've asked a controversial question that the expert is unwilling to answer, try posing it in a different form. Let's say you received a "no comment" to your question, "Will Bill Jones be next in line to be president of the National Restaurant Association?" You could then try asking something like "Is Bill Jones a leading contender for the presidency?" or "Will Bill Jones be playing an important role in the association during the next few years?"

Go from the General to the Specific. This is one approach for getting answers to sensitive questions. For example, once I needed to find out how much money, if any, a particular company saved by implementing a "telecommuting" program—that is, a system where employees can work at home via the use of a computer and a phone line hookup. Instead of asking the company how much money the program had saved, I asked a series of questions: Overall, was the program a plus for the company? Did it save the firm some money? Was it a significant amount? Roughly, about how much did it save?

Ask "Peripheral" Questions. This is a strategy to get bits and pieces of information that may shed light on your query. Again, in the Bill Jones example, you could ask questions about the vice presidency, previous association voting patterns, and so forth to try to piece together a picture.

Ask for Ballpark Figures. When you need to find out some sensitive numerical fact, you may find that it's easier for experts to provide rough estimates or a "range" rather than precise numbers. Another strategy for getting sensitive figures is to suggest a few numbers yourself to get a reaction. Often an expert won't volunteer the information, but will respond to your estimates.

Ask for "Feelings." You may find it easier to get an answer if you try to elicit an emotional response. Ask the person how he or she *personally feels* about a controversial topic.

Take a Position. This is an old news reporter's trick. Suppose you're trying to find out from an oil company executive whether there's any truth to the rumor that the firm is lowering its imports by 2 percent next year. If you bluntly ask the question, you're likely to get a "no comment." Instead, try taking a position on the

---

TIP: Negotiate an Agreement
• If you do need to quote a source or write up certain sensitive information, you can often negotiate with the expert how much or what type of information you may use. For example, although an expert may want remarks to be off the record, you might ask to use only one particular statement made during the conversation. Many times you'll discover that the expert will agree. Similarly, you can negotiate exactly how you will identify the source. For example, the expert may not let you use his or her name, but may not mind being identified as "an employee of Jax Manufacturing in Boston," or something similar. The more choices you can give the expert, the more in control the person will feel, and the more comfortable he or she will be about agreeing to some type of attribution. But remember, most of the time it's not necessary to work out attribution arrangements. All you need to do is to get the source to share expertise with you.

---

question—state it as a fact—and continue the conversation. You might say "Since your company will be reducing imports by 2 percent next year, will there be a corresponding increase in domestic production?" Your source may have to bite his tongue to let your assumption go unanswered—especially because he may fear that you will later think you got the information from him! You may not get a definite answer on the subject through this ploy, but you may get more than if you just asked the question bluntly.

Keep Your Conversation "Off the Record." Sometimes an expert source won't mind talking about controversial topics but doesn't want to be identified as the source or see the remarks in print. If you think this is the case, be certain you assure the expert that his or her remarks will be off the record, if so desired. Most of the time, it doesn't matter a bit to you if a source speaks off the record—you just want to have the information for your own knowledge.

If you decide that under no circumstances will your source divulge the sensitive information you want, you should consider contacting other people who may have access to the same information.

Offensive Questions

What do you do if you have a question or remark that you think may offend the source? You should always try to phrase your questions diplomatically to avoid insulting the expert. For example, if someone tells you "It's a scientific fact that wearing wool hats causes baldness," you can express your skepticism politely. You might say ,"Do you think your opinion on this is in the minority? Why don't you think there is more support for this view?"

Here are two other strategies to keep in mind. First, if you think the question is offensive enough to cut off the interview, save it for near the end to prevent the conversation from ending early on. Second, use another reporter's trick: Pose the question in the third person. Don't, for example, ask, "Since you have never been invited to present your research results to the scientific community, isn't your information of dubious value?" Instead say, "Some people have said that since you have never been invited . . . "

ETHICAL ISSUES IN OBTAINING SENSITIVE INFORMATION

What do you do if you need to interview someone for information but do not want to tell the person who you are or why you need it? Sometimes this happens when you want "insider" information on a specific firm or competitor company—and the only place to find that information is by talking to individuals who work at that company itself!

This is an issue that professional researchers who conduct "competitive intelligence" have recently been grappling with. (There is even a trade association of competitive intelligence professionals!) It's a tricky issue, because it revolves around the definition of what is and is not misrepresentation. There may be gray areas where the researcher does not out-and-out lie, but is tempted to withhold the "whole" truth out of fear that such disclosure would discourage the source from sharing his or her knowledge.

What should you do if faced with this type of situation? There are a number of questions worth asking yourself:

- Have I truly exhausted all public, published sources? As outlined in this book, there are scores of government documents, computer database records, trade magazine articles, and other public information sources available just for the asking. Make sure you have thoroughly researched the existence of all these potential sources.
- If you are sure no published information exists that can answer your question, try to identify persons you can interview where you feel more comfortable revealing who you are and the purpose of your project. For example, if you need to find out facts about a company's future strategic plans, you can obtain insights by interviewing Wall Street analysts, trade magazine editors, and other types of experts.
- If those persons still do not have the information you need, ask yourself how vital it really is that you find that specific piece of information. Are there related data that could be helpful? Is there peripheral information from which you can piece together a picture?
- If you are sure that you still need that precise information, you may be convinced that the only way to get it is to misrepresent yourself. But this is not always so. Say, for example, you need information on a competitive company. You just might find that if you call the knowledgeable source, are up front, polite, and gracious, you may get unexpected cooperation! The source may help you for any number of reasons: He or she might have questions to ask you; the person may just enjoy talking; or he or she doesn't think what you are asking is particularly sensitive—who knows! The point is, don't assume you need to make up some ruse—as Mark Twain said, "When in doubt . . . tell the truth." You may be pleasantly surprised at the results!

If, finally, you are certain that the only way to obtain the information you need is by hiding who you are or by making up a story, you should ask yourself whether you really want to take that approach. Here are my arguments as to why misrepresenting yourself or even withholding relevant information (e.g., the nature of your research project) is *not* advisable:

Self-interest

- An unethical research activity may eventually be revealed to others. How will this affect you or your organization's reputation?
- Unethical data-gathering activities will eventually cause organizations to become so suspicious of researchers—with good reason—that sources of information will dry up. The job of the researcher will become much more difficult.
- With no standards set in this area, you and/or your own organization can become a target for unethical information gathering.

Personal Ethics

- Take a hard look to see if any research activity you are considering will violate your own personal code of ethics. For example, most of us would not consider telephoning someone and misleading them into sending a check for $500. But today, information is as valuable a commodity as money. We would all like an extra $500, but we recognize legitimate boundaries in how to obtain it. Don't the same standards hold true for precious information? You should put yourself in the other person's shoes and ask yourself how *you* would feel if you were the recipient of what you are considering. Would you feel that you were dealt with fairly?

Finally, it is important to remember that just because there are ethical guidelines to follow, excellent research can still be performed by legitimate methods and by intelligent and thoughtful analysis of data.

9

Information Quality
Evaluating Sources and
Determining Accuracy

QUICK PREVIEW: DATA QUALITY

- While the Internet has increased awareness of the need to evaluate information sources, the matter actually transcends the Internet.
- When evaluating published documents, consider the *type* of document (whether it is a primary or secondary one) and the purpose of its publication.
- You should also scrutinize what you read to determine whether you are getting all sides of the story and whether the author is attempting to influence you with loaded words and other techniques.
- Other important considerations: How was the information collected? Is it logical and well-organized? How is it presented?
- Polls and surveys are fraught with hazards. You should check whether the sponsoring organization is nonpartisan, what type of selection criteria were employed to obtain the sample, if any of the questions were "loaded," and whether the placement of the questions could have affected the answers.

(continued)

- You can also evaluate experts. Watch for bias, narrow scope of expertise, out-of-date experts and those too far removed from their subject, and confusing sources. Be aware of an expert's affiliations and loyalties. Try to supplement potentially biased sources with more objective ones.
- Evaluate experts by noting whose names are cited frequently in leading trade publications. Ask experts for their opinions of others' work, use certain sources as "yardsticks," and probe for facts behind general statements.
- Be a critical thinker. This means not just believing something because everyone says it's so, or because something is repeated often or is the first opinion you hear. It also means questioning, probing, and looking for connections between data until you yourself are convinced of the truth of the matter under investigation.
- Although you need to apply basic information evaluation techniques to data found on the Internet, the Net also has certain characteristics that compel additional evaluation strategies. These characteristics include self-publishing that exists without any filters or checks, the heterogeneous nature of the information found on the Net, and a blurry line between the purely informative and commercial.
- You can use a checklist of indicators to assess credibility of information found on the Internet. These should include examining: how the site was located, the organization behind the site, the author of the page, the author's demonstration of his/her knowledge, the method used by the author to present his/her work, evidence of bias, and the currency of the information. You can take active evaluation strategies, too, such as: searching for the author's name on the Web, contacting the author to ask follow-up questions, and confirming the information with other sources.
- Anecdotal information, which appears often on the Internet, can be of value to the researcher, but will require special care in evaluation. You need to examine whether an anecdote is an appropriate answer, if the person providing the anecdote demonstrates an understanding of the topic, the motivation of the person sharing the information, whether there is confirma-

tion of the anecdote, and the ramifications of taking action based on the anecdotal report.

Your ability to ascertain the validity of anecdotal material and other information will depend to a large degree on how much you trust that source, and your own knowledge of the topic.

EVALUATING YOUR INFORMATION SOURCES

By now, primarily because of the Internet, we have all been made aware of the problems of bad and unreliable information. There have been several stories circulating in the press, as well as via word of mouth, about persons who found some bit of information on the Internet that turned out to be either a complete hoax, misleading, or simply untrue. And so, in a matter of a relatively short time, the pendulum on the Internet as a source of information has gone from an early unquestioning acceptance, to, by some, total disparagement.

But the truth is more complex than either extreme. We'll discuss the reliability of information located on the Internet in some depth later in this chapter. The larger point, and the one we need to look at first, is that while evaluating sources and thinking critically is certainly of special concern when applied to the Internet, the concern goes beyond that medium and is relevant for all media. So, although we will discuss the special issues that the Internet presents, let's first start with some basic rules that you can apply to *any* information source, whether found on the Internet, in print, or in any other format.

EVALUATING PUBLISHED SOURCES

The following are some key considerations to note when determining the accuracy of published data:

What Is the Type of Document? There is a critical distinction between a *primary* and *secondary* data source. A primary source is the originator of the data, such as a personal letter, photograph, or original governmental document, and a secondary source secures the data from the original source, and is an account, like a newspaper article. A concern with too much reliance on secondary sources is that they often delete the methods employed in collecting data and sometimes fail to reproduce significant footnotes or comments that may qualify the data in some way.[1]

What Is the Purpose of the Publication? A source is suspect if published to promote sales, to advance the interests of an industrial, commercial, or other group, to present the cause of a political party, or to carry on any sort of propaganda. Also suspect is data published anonymously or by an organization on the defensive, or under conditions that suggest a controversy, or in a form that reveals a strained attempt at "frankness."[2]

Are You Getting All Sides of the Story? Try to determine whether the article, report, or book is presenting only one side of an issue when there is clearly more than one point of view. For example, an article that cites *only* the problems associated with, say, national health insurance, without at least referring to potential benefits could not be viewed as a balanced presentation. That piece may still be useful, however, for example, to learn of the claims of those opposed to such a program, for finding out about other stud-

[1] Nemmers and Meyers, quoted in Churchill, Gilbert A., Jr., *Marketing Research: Methodical Foundations* (Hinsdale, Ill.: Dryden Press, 1987).

[2] Ibid.

ies cited, and to obtain leads for further research. The point is that it should not be used as the sole source of information.

Note that this issue of "balanced coverage" is tricky, and it's not always easy to determine what constitutes balanced coverage. In fact, one can even make the case that presenting both sides of an issue is not always legitimate. For example, if one is writing about a clearly outrageous case of child abuse, does the best coverage give equal time to the abuser to give his or her side of the story? These kinds of questions are thorny journalistic and sociological issues beyond the scope of this book. Suffice it to say: *Be aware* as to whether you are getting all *reasonably legitimate* points of view on an issue, and if it is clear you are not, do not use that source as a definitive one.

Is the Author Trying to Subtly Influence You? It's not enough to determine simply whether coverage of a topic is "balanced"; it's also critical to be able to detect the more subtle ways that an author may be trying to insert his or her views into a piece. Choice of words, placement of names, and other techniques can be employed consciously or unconsciously by the writer to influence the reader.

For example, see how the choice of the following words that mean the same thing can connote totally different feelings and elicit different reactions.

Free enterprise	Capitalism
Persons incarcerated	Criminals
Mixed drinks	Hard liquor
Spiritually renewed	Born again
Stronger defense	More money for missiles
Increased revenues	Higher taxes

Even something as simple as the insertion of quotation marks, or the use of a different word, can subtly change connotations. For example, compare these two sentences:

- John Doe, director of public affairs, said that he was instituting the clean-up committee to make headway in cleaning up the environment.
- John Doe, director of public affairs, claimed that "helping the environment" was the reason he was instituting the clean-up committee.

By setting Doe's words within quotation marks, the writer seems to imply that his remark should not be read as a fact; it almost seems like the writer is winking at the reader. The word *claim* is another way to cast doubt on the speaker's trustworthiness. The writer could have also shown his or her skepticism by beginning the sentence with the innocuous words *according to*, which again would add a subjective element to the sentence, decreasing Doe's credibility.

Keep your antenna up and be attuned to these subtleties—again, if you detect that information is being presented in a slanted manner, it does not mean you have to disregard the material; keep an open mind and just try not to let yourself be influenced by the *manner* in which a piece is written. You will need to make up your own mind after consulting a variety of different sources.

Is the Information Presented Logically and Is It Well Organized? Are the data internally consistent? Are conclusions supported by the data and evidence presented? Look for data presented in a well-organized manner, tables clearly labeled, and lucid accompanying explanatory material. Typically (although by no means always), these elements reflect a well-thought-out study.

Is the Information Based on a Poll or Survey? The quality of individual polls and surveys vary enormously. There is a science to accurate data collection that involves technical considerations such as sample size, rate of response, sampling and nonsampling errors, and more. It's important to find out how the information was collected (e.g., mail questionnaire or phone), who was interviewed, and the other details behind the study.

Polls and surveys that purport to measure people's views and behaviors are so fraught with hazards, in fact, that some observers believe that even the finest and most well-known survey organizations cannot overcome the great number of barriers that exist in accurate reporting. For these reasons, polls, surveys, forecasts, and the like should be utilized by researchers only with a great deal of caution.

Dr. Jared Jobe, director of the Collaborative Research Program at the U.S. National Center for Health Statistics, notes that there are a number of areas where polls and surveys can be misleading or inaccurate. The following are some of the most common problems:

- **Partisan sponsoring organizations.** Organizations that have a motive to manipulate surveys to achieve a desired result are obviously suspect.

- **Selection criteria.** By what mechanism and approach was the group selected? Was it a random sampling? The key point is whether the respondents were a *representative* sample of the particular population of interest. Jobe advises researchers to watch out for mail surveys, magazine subscriber surveys, and telephone call-in polls, because these are often biased by the fact that only persons with a particular reason for responding will answer the questions (those with extreme positions on an issue may be overrepresented).

- **Loaded questions.** Jobe's research has shown that people's opinions are greatly affected by the tone, manner, and choice of words of the interviewer. Other studies have shown that people will provide totally different opinions depending on whether the words the interviewer uses contain positive or negative connotations. For example, according to one study, public opinion shifts if asked about favoring more spending "to aid the *poor*" compared to spending more for *welfare*. Sometimes, responses differ even when alternative words are used that do not seem to be loaded. For example, people were found to be less willing to approve speeches against democracy when asked whether the United States should "*allow* public speeches against democracy" than when asked whether the United States should "*forbid* public speeches against democracy."[3]

- **Placement of questions.** Question placement can affect the way people respond. For example, say a subject was asked whether defense spending should be increased by 10 percent. If he or she replied no, the subject might then be more inclined to say yes to a follow-up question as to whether the United States should increase defense spending by 5 percent. Had the respondent *only* been asked whether defense spending should be increased by 5 percent, he or she may have been more likely to have replied in the negative.

[3]For further discussion and examples, see Rich Jaroslovsky, "What's on Your Mind America?" *Psychology Today*, July/Aug. 1988, 54–59.

- **Asking for memories and recollections.** Jobe says that people are notoriously poor at remembering their past actions and activities.

- **Complex questions.** People will often answer questions they do not understand.

- **Vague questions.** Questions that are open to more than one interpretation obviously make for poor research results.

- **Sensitive questions.** Queries that ask people to admit to socially unacceptable behavior are less reliable. For example, today people often do not like to admit that they smoke.

- **Misleading conclusions.** Sometimes the survey process is fine, but the conclusions are misleading. For example, Jobe cites the commercial that says "no toothpaste gets your teeth whiter." Such a claim can simply mean that the brand is no worse than all the rest.

The best way to guard against these problems is to get a copy of the actual questionnaire utilized and study it to try to detect any of these pitfalls. Jobe advises researchers to look at many surveys, conducted by more than one organization at different times. If these surveys reveal generally the same findings, then you can feel fairly confident about the results.

EVALUATING EXPERTS

When you interview a "live" expert, how do you evaluate that person's credibility and knowledge? Here are some strategies.

Signs of a Good Source

Here are a few helpful indicators of a good source:

Peer Recognition. Has the source had anything published in trade journals or spoken at industry conferences? If so, it's an excellent sign because it signifies recognition by peers. Peer recognition is one of the very best indicators of an authoritative source. If you don't know whether a source has written or spoken on the topic, there is nothing wrong with politely asking. Use your judgment when applying this rule. If an expert has made a brand-new discovery or just finished a research project, it may take time to be recognized.

Referrals. How did you find the source? If you were referred by a recognized expert in the field, or someone you felt was a worthy source, it is a good sign. Good experts typically refer you to other good experts.

Repetition. Does the source repeat things you've heard before that you know to be true? If so, it's another good sign.

Attentiveness. Does the source pay careful attention to your questions and respond sensitively? I've found this to be a sign of a good source.

Sources to Beware Of

The Biased Source. Bias is a tricky matter. The critical thing to be aware of is where a particular source is "coming from." For example, is he or she a salesperson for a product, a political appointee, or a representative of a special cause? Take this into account when evaluating the information. This doesn't mean that people with certain viewpoints or leanings are not going to be truthful or accurate. It simply means that each person's perspective must be uncovered so that you know how to evaluate his or her information.

For example, once I was digging up information on how certain cities cut their energy costs by forming fuel-buying cooperatives. One of the people I talked to was the president of a regional association of fuel dealers. He told me co-ops were a very bad idea; he said that although the participants might cut their purchasing costs, they suffer in the quality of their service. I noted his objection seriously, but at the same time realized that because he represented a group of fuel dealers, his constituency would have the most to lose if this co-op idea really caught on. I decided to call the individual co-op members directly to find out if they had indeed encountered service problems. It turned out that none had.

You must also stay on guard against organizations that do not easily telegraph their biases. These organizations often have impartial-sounding names but actually promote a very specific stand on an issue. For example, you locate an association innocently called Citizens for Energy Awareness. The name suggests merely that the committee wants to help spread information. But it's possible that the committee's sole raison d'être is to advance the cause of nuclear energy or to ban it. To check for such biases, find out what kind of people the association is composed of. Are most of the officers of the Citizens for Energy Awareness executives at nuclear power plants? If so, you can guess why that organization has been created! Take a look at some of the organization's brochures and research reports. Do its studies and findings unfailingly reach the same conclusion and support the same side of a controversial issue? You might still get some good information from this special-interest group, but be aware that you will not get a balanced picture.

Another type of biased source that you need to be on guard against is the "overly enthusiastic" source. This kind of person is typically involved in implementing a new project of some sort. You're sure to get rave reviews from this person when you ask how the project is going. Nobody wants to express doubts about the success of his or her new ventures, so you have to be careful not to take glowing reports as gospel. In the above case of the fuel cooperatives, for example, the co-op members themselves may want to paint an overly rosy picture of their project. Probe for as many hard facts as you can.

When you run into cases in which you feel your sources have too many personal interests to be totally unbiased, try to supplement those sources with more disinterested experts. Again, in the case of the fuel-buying cooperatives, I would probably get the most objective information not from the fuel dealers or the co-op members, but from a government expert in the Department of Energy or another unbiased authority on fuel.

The Overly Narrow Source. Let's say you are trying to find information on crime trends in the United States, and you find an expert on supermarket shoplifting. You'll have to ask yourself whether that person's opinions go beyond his or her area of expertise and extend to overall U.S. crime trends.

The Out-of-Date Source. Are you looking into a field that is constantly changing? If so, you want to be sure your sources have kept up with the changes. Try to find out the last time the person was actually involved in the subject. In certain fields—microcomputer technology, for example—information from only six months ago is quite dated.

The Too-Far-Removed Source. High-level sources with very broad administrative duties are often too far removed to provide you with the nitty-gritty details you need. For example, if you are digging up information on upcoming design trends in small automobiles, the head of the public affairs department of General Motors would be able to give you only the sketchiest and most basic information. You'd be much better off talking to design engineers to get more specific details. (Calling the public affairs office can still be worthwhile, if only to ask to be referred to a technical expert.)

The Unaccountable Source. The opposite of talking to a high-level official, like a public affairs executive, is the problem of talking to someone lower down on the company ladder who is not as accountable for what he or she says. While the public affairs person may not give you the nitty-gritty that you want, the person is careful about what he or she says, and the information you get should at least be accurate. The shop foreman may not feel so restrained and cautious and will give you the details you want. But try to get those "facts" confirmed by other sources before relying on them as indisputable.

The Secondary Source. Is your source a true expert or just someone who is reporting on the experts' work or reorganizing existing information? Secondary sources *can* be helpful, but they are not ordinarily as intimately knowledgeable about the subject as primary sources.

The Confusing Source. If the person talks only in technical jargon and is unable to communicate his or her expertise to you,

you're not going to get much out of the conversation. Move on to the next one.

Evaluation Strategies

Here are a few methods you can use to help evaluate your sources:

- Note the names of people who keep appearing in the articles that you read. When you see somebody quoted often, and in a variety of periodicals, it's usually a sign that the person is a leader in the field and has something valuable to say.
- It's fine to ask experts for their opinion of other sources. Just be diplomatic about how you ask. One way is to ask if they "agree" with so-and-so's conclusions about the subject in question.
- Think about using certain sources as yardsticks. If you've spoken with someone you feel is a top-notch authority, you can measure other sources' responses against that person's.
- If a source makes a statement you're skeptical of, politely ask where the information comes from: His or her research? Hands-on experience? Something read somewhere?
- If you doubt someone's expertise, you can test the person by asking a question to which you already know the answer.
- Does the expert say something definitively that you already know is absolutely incorrect? If so, that is obviously not a good sign!
- Have you had a chance to read anything the expert has written? I have found that the most useful experts to speak with are those that can write a clear, well-organized article or report.
- Does the expert simply repeat what everyone else says or does he or she have some fresh perspective on the issue? I've found that the truly superior experts can take an issue and not just describe the current situation, but see implications and add some new angles. The best experts provide insight into the underlying "why" questions, which lead to broad implications. For example, when I was researching the topic of publishing

on the Web, one of the best experts I spoke with early on told me that the *reason* why Web publishing was going to be significant was that before the Internet, there were two strong barriers of entry that made a mass-publishing operation difficult: 1) the need for a printing press; and 2) the need for some distribution mechanism, such as delivery trucks or a satellite system. The Web eliminates the need for either of these, demolishes the barriers to entry, and therefore makes it possible for anyone with a PC and modem (or even just access to one) to broadcast their information to a worldwide audience—and do so virtually instantaneously.

- I've found that one intuitive way to evaluate an expert is simply to ask yourself after you've had your interview whether you feel satisfied.

CRITICAL THINKING

Much of the advice given in this chapter could fall under the heading of "critical thinking." Being a critical thinker is vital for a researcher. But what does critical thinking really mean?

Critical thinking means a number of things. It means:

- Not just believing something because everyone says it's so.
- Not just believing something because you have heard it repeated so often.
- Not just accepting the first opinion you hear.

Critical thinking means constantly asking questions, probing, and digging deeply into a subject to learn more and more until *you yourself* are satisfied of the truth of the matter.

Critical thinking also means looking at bits of data, pieces of information, and bodies of knowledge and searching for connections and differences. It means sitting down and simply thinking hard about all that you've uncovered and trying to figure out what it all has in common. What are the threads that link the data? How do they differ?

What about the concept of trust or faith? Can a critical thinker ever decide simply to believe what someone says just because he or she trusts a person's judgment? I think yes. However, the trust will be an *intelligently placed one*. The experienced researcher sometimes intuitively feels when to trust a source and when not to. But this is a very difficult task, and it may not always be possible to make a decision on whom to trust. But you can ask yourself certain questions to help you explore your "gut" feelings:

- Has the person proven himself or herself to be reliable and accurate in this subject in the past?
- Does the rest of his or her work show integrity?
- Does the person have an ax to grind in this case or does he or she seem unbiased?

When Evidence Is Not There

What does the researcher do when he or she does not find any hard evidence to support a claim or position? Must the researcher dismiss any conclusions or findings as simply unproven and therefore not worth accepting? Let's look at a scenario where such a situation might be faced.

Let's say I came across a scientist who claimed that his work and analysis showed that there was a strong link between levels of air pollution and the onset of heart disease. Say that currently the medical establishment had not proven any link between the two, and in fact, there was no evidence at all linking the two phenomena together. How would one evaluate the scientist's claims?

Obviously, few researchers are in a position to definitively determine whether or not this person's claim is valid. There are scientific methods of discovery that are performed extremely carefully under intense scrutiny to determine whether a reported phenomenon is indeed a reliable finding. However, you may find yourself in a position where you must make some kind of unscientific judgment on such a matter.

Although the judgment will be unscientific, it can still be of great importance, because it is these types of informal, unscientific but rational judgment that can provide enough interest in a subject to get the gears in motion for the scientists to set out and create their rigorous tests to discover truths. There is a lag time between the discovery of a phenomenon and its proof (or disproof), and the researcher can be a vital link in the process for assisting in facilitating the movement from the stage of initial theory or discovery to the stage of proof.

Going back to the example, what would you need to do to determine for yourself the likelihood of the link between air pollution and heart disease being correct? There are a number of paths you could pursue. First, you could find out the answers to these types of questions:

- What is the manner in which the person is presenting his findings? Is it in a sensational way, making claims like "revolutionary...fantastic...unbelievable," or are the claims presented in a more reasonable and rational way? Does the author of the study provide advice on how to best interpret his work or just run down a list of amazing benefits?
- Are there backup records available to document claims? If the research is very new, is there at least an attempt to carefully collect records and document findings for the future?
- In what types of outlet is the person choosing to publicize his findings? For example, does he advertise in the classifieds of *National Enquirer* and ask people to send in $10 to get his secrets, or does he approach the mainstream media and/or scientific community? What kind of audience is he trying to reach—a gullible one or one that will provide intense levels of scrutiny?
- Does this person make all of his records and findings open for anyone to inspect, or is much of it "secret formula" claims that will not be released?
- What else has this person worked on? Does the scientist show evidence of achievement in related fields? Is he respected by peers?

As you can see, most of these questions do not ask you to analyze the actual claim itself, but to look at relevant peripheral information that can be an aid in making the judgment. And, of course, it is possible that even someone who fits all the "right" answers will ultimately be proven incorrect (or vice versa, but less likely). But you may need to make a judgment call. Finally, your role as a researcher cannot be to comment on whether the claims are correct, but whether a phenomenon does or does not deserve serious scrutiny and attention from the larger community. And this is no insignificant job.

EVALUATING INFORMATION
FOUND ON THE INTERNET

My cat recently had a seizure. I went onto the Net and plugged the words "cats" and "seizures" into the AltaVista search engine to see what I could find out. The search engine returned a couple dozen pages, and one in particular looked to be right on target. And, indeed, this page contained a great deal of information: the various types of seizures cats get, possible causes, different treatments, and so forth. It was a well-organized, well-written site, with many links to related sites.

As it turned out, though, this comprehensive page was not written by a veterinarian, but by a graduate student in, of all fields, computer science. How to assess what I learned on this site? These were not the words of an expert, but simply of someone who had an interest in cats and apparently has done some research on seizures in cats. This is an example of the kinds of unusual challenges the Internet is presenting information gatherers.

The first question, when discussing information and the Internet is whether data found on the Internet should be assessed any differently than information found via a traditional source, like a newspaper or magazine article? On one level, the answer would be no, in that you'd apply the same basic evaluation standards and criteria to assess any information you come across, regardless of which media it was derived from. But at the same time, there are certain innate characteristics of the Internet that present novel problems and issues, and therefore it *is* necessary to utilize different evaluation tools and strategies.

One such characteristic is that to publish on the Internet, it is not necessary to go through any external checks or "filters," unlike being published in a traditional medium like a book, journal, or newspaper. You can, of course, find misinformation and bad data in the mainstream media. But at least the writer would still have had to have his or her work go through some kind of initial quality check—it could be by a rigorous peer review process, or less formally, reviewed by an editor, copyeditor, or proofreader. These reviews provide at least a basic level of scrutiny, which is absent on the Web.

Another unique problem to the Internet is that information is "heterogeneous." That is, the information does not consist of just one kind of information, but countless different kinds all thrown together, so to speak, in the same "vat." Yes, scholarly articles and substantive research reports are there, but mixed in will be company home pages, news sites, pornography sites, commercial advertisements, vanity pages, and "infotainment" sites. So it's virtually impossible to restrict your search to a desired set of important or substantive information.

Finally, the delineation between a pure information source and an advertising/commercial one is not always clear cut on the Internet. In our traditional media, like a newspaper, magazine, radio, or television broadcast, you can clearly distinguish the news from the ads. On the Internet, you can come across a blending of the two, in that company Web sites will also often try to provide its visitors with useful information, and online news sites may include links to commercial sites. For example, in the class I give on Research Methods, I had students do a search on cholestin, a Chinese red yeast that has been shown to be effective in reducing cholesterol levels. One of my students reported that she was linked to a site called the "Cholestin Healthcare Product Guide" that explained blood cholesterol levels and other technical matters, and she thought she had reached an objective informational site. But she discovered that it was part of the Pharmanex site, the company that sells the product. She finally determined that she was actually reading an advertisement. It was also confusing because there were references and links to *Prevention* magazine. She went on to make another interesting point to the (online) class:

> In addition to the fuzziness between content and advertising, I think one of the most insidious aspects of [determining] information validity on the Internet is the inherent vulnerability of the attention span. As you swim through vast, murky streams of nonrelevant information

on the Web, you become lulled into half-attention. When a site does come along that provides clear, coherent information on exactly what you need, you jump on it like it's the last steamboat off the river. You're begging to be advertised to!

These are fundamental challenges when using the Web for research. But in addition, there are other practical concerns, as information found on the Web often suffers from these flaws:

Missing Data

- There are no clues as to background or expertise of the author.
- There is no identification of the institution behind the author, or its mission.
- There is no contact information: no mailing address, phone number or e-mail.
- There is no date that informs you when the information was created.

Misleading and Confusing Data

- You may not have any context describing the document that particular Web page you've linked to comes from. Since you can only see a single Web page at a time, you can't see the surrounding pages that can put that one page in a meaningful context. For example, say you link to a page from a study that reports that the market for "personal care" products is growing at 5 percent a year. You don't know what the definition of "personal care" was for this study, whether the "market" is U.S. or global, how the study was performed, and so on. If you had the full report in front of you in print, you'd typically find these definitions provided up front.
- You can't be sure the site is actually associated with the institution, cause, person, etc. that its name implies it is.

So, when evaluating information on the Internet you'll need to take a two-pronged approach. You must first consider the general evaluation guidelines presented above, and second consider employing special techniques designed for evaluating information found on the Net.

And, in fact, several information experts—many of whom are librarians—have come up with very useful checklists for evaluating information found on the Internet. (I've listed a few of my favorites at the end of this chapter.) I've gone through and read through many of these, and have culled what I believe to be the major themes, and then added some of my own techniques as well. The result is this checklist of credibility indicators (you can download a copy from my Web site at http://www.robertberkman.com).

INTERNET INFORMATION QUALITY INDICATOR CHECKLIST

You can apply the following quality indicators to make an assessment of the information you find on the Net. Of course, this is not a science by any means, but those sites that meet a greater number of credibility indicators will likely be more reliable sources.

1. How did you find the site? Indicators of credibility:
   ❏ The site was recommended or referred by another, trusted source (this could be print, online, or word of mouth).
2. Who is the organization behind the site? Indicators of credibility:
   ❏ The site was created by, or is part of, a known institution of some kind.
   ❏ That organization provides complete contact information, and can be contacted by mail or telephone, or visited in person.
   ❏ The organization identifies itself as an educational (edu), or a nonprofit (org) site.
3. Who is the author? Indicators of credibility:
   ❏ The author was referred by another trusted source.
   ❏ The author's work has been quoted by others in the field.
   ❏ The author's site is linked to often on the Web. This technique for assessing credibility is something of an Internet equivalent to a standard method for evaluating authors in the academic world, called citation analysis. With this method, scholars assess an author's work by noting the

number of times his/her published articles have been cited in others' published work.

4. How does the author demonstrate his/her breadth of knowledge on the topic? Indicators of credibility:
   ❏ Author cites theory and background, where relevant.
   ❏ Author quotes and/or paraphrases others' work and writings on the topic.
   ❏ Author demonstrates knowledge of others' work in the field.
   ❏ Author builds on others' work by adding new insights and by raising new questions.

5. How does the author present his/her work? Indicators of credibility:
   ❏ Author describes his/her methods of research, and how conclusions were reached.
   ❏ Author provides or offers links to supporting evidence.
   ❏ Author identifies any limitations of his/her research.

6. In what manner does the author present his/her material? Indicators of credibility:
   ❏ Author's writing is clear.
   ❏ Author's writing is logical.
   ❏ Author's writing is organized.
   ❏ Author's writing shows evidence of thoughtfulness and analysis.
   ❏ Author's writing shows a caring, and even a passion, for the topic.

7. What evidence is there of any bias? Indicators of credibility:
   ❏ The organization and/or author behind the site has no overtly stated political/ideological or other overriding agenda that would automatically detract from the credibility of the data presented.
   ❏ If there *is* an overriding political/ideological agenda, it is not hidden in any way to disguise its purpose, either by a misleading name or by other means.
   ❏ If there *is* an overriding political/ideological agenda, any research methods utilized (e.g., polls or surveys performed, sources utilized) can stand scrutiny on their own.

8. Date and currency:
   ❏ There is a published date on the Web page

❏ The date is clear as to its meaning (e.g., date of original source, date Web site created, date most recently updated, etc.).

❏ The date is timely for the purposes of your research.

9. (Optional) For those sites where there is an existing equivalent source in some other medium (print, CD-ROM, online database):

❏ The data presented on the Web page is as complete as in the other media.

❏ If the data is not as complete, the site describes the differences in coverage.

10. A few more words about the matter of currency. Currency on the Internet is a troublesome area, because the date you view on a Web page (if the site even provides one), can signify one of many things. It could indicate the date the information was first created, it might mean when that information was uploaded to the Internet, it could mean the date of the most recent complete update, or it could mean the date on which a few minor additions were made. In some cases, where the Web master has installed a calendar update program that automatically posts the current date, the date you see could mean nothing at all!

A final way to evaluate Internet information is to rely primarily on sources that have already been prescreened and selected by one of the hierarchical indexes, such as Yahoo, or a more specialized index like AlphaSearch. See the notes in chapter 5 for the names and URLs of these.

11. Active evaluation strategies:

In addition to utilizing those credibility indicators listed, another important way to evaluate the credibility of information found on the Net is by taking certain *active* evaluation strategies. I recommend doing the following:

❏ Perform a keyword search on the author's name (use quotation marks) to find out what, if anything, the author has had published on the Internet. Do a search on DejaNews to find any messages the author may have posted on Internet newsgroups.

❏ Contact the author and ask follow-up questions. This is useful both for making a better evaluation of the person's

knowledge as well as having the opportunity to ask your own questions.
❑ Confirm/check the author's information with at least one other source.

(The above checklist has been reprinted in part from the September 1999 issue of *The Information Advisor*, a monthly publication that I edit. It is excerpted here by permission of the publisher, FIND/SVP, a global business advisory service, 625 Avenue of the Americas, New York, NY 10010, http://www.findsvp.com)

MY FAVORITE INTERNET QUALITY CHECKLISTS

There are scores of checklists on the Web for evaluating information on the Internet. Here are the ones I like the best:

- **Evaluating Internet Research Sources**
  Robert Harris Professor of English at Southern California College, Costa Mesa, California
  http://www.sccu.edu/faculty/R_Harris/evalu8it.htm

- **Evaluating Information Found on the Internet and Practical Steps in Evaluating Internet Resources**
  Elizabeth E. Kirk
  http://milton.mse.jhu.edu:8001/research/education/net.html

- **Evaluating Quality on the Net**
  Hope N. Tillman
  http://www.tiac.net/users/hope/findqual.html

- **How to Critically Analyze Information Sources**
  Jack Corse, Simon Fraser University
  http://www.lib.sfu.ca/kiosk/corse/libguide5.htm

- **Evaluating Web Resources**
  Jan Alexander and Marsha Ann Tate, Widener Univeristy
  This is my favorite of the evaluation checklist sites. Alexander and Tate have gone the extra mile and come up

with specific evaluation strategies for six different types of Web pages, and have established a different set of measurement criteria to apply to each of these. The six are: informational pages, advocacy pages, business/marketing pages, news pages, entertainment pages and personal pages.

http://www2.widener.edu/Wolfgram-Memorial-Library/webeval.htm

ANECDOTAL AND OPINION PAGES

There is a specific type of information that is frequently found and used on the Net that presents its own special problems. This is the "anecdotal report"—a story, experience, or point of view that a user shares with the rest of the world. Such a person makes no claim to any special expertise or authority, but presents his views and make his points drawing primarily from his own life experiences. Anecdotes are found all over the Internet, but are particularly prevalent in the forums and discussion groups, especially in online support groups.

How should you evaluate this kind of information? Should you even bother paying attention? Opinions will vary, but based on my own experiences (okay, that means this is anecdotal!), I believe that these are, in fact, valuable, and represent a fascinating new kind of information resource.

While it's true that science traditionally looks askance at anecdotal information, in our own lives, we rely on it, and reasonably so. You wouldn't, for instance, require a double-blind test when you ask your neighbor whether so and so is a good dentist. And if you're driving down a road, and you see several cars heading the other way, and the drivers of those vehicles all tell you to turn back because a tree is down and blocking the road, you can be pretty sure that you'd better go back. So, whereas if you were a scientist you would not send anecdotal stories to your professional journal, the fact is we regularly rely on anecdotal reports. We do so every day, and they provide a primary (though hardly infallible) source of knowledge for how we make our way around the world.

And the fact is that sometimes science, because of its (rightly) rigorous demands, can be late in making confirmations of what many people already know. I have an example from my personal life to illustrates this. In the late 1970s, my father was diagnosed with angina pectoris and was told that his arteries were severely blocked. His doctors prescribed the drug Inderol, and he was told there really wasn't anything he could do, except eventually have bypass surgery. The notion that diet and exercise could halt, let alone reverse, years of built-up arterial plaque was considered out of the question. And, that, indeed was the state of the science at the time.

But my father had just heard some very encouraging reports—anecdotal reports—from persons that attended a center in Santa Barbara run by a man named Nathan Pritikin. Pritikin's clients, persons who were diagnosed with arteriosclerosis and other heart problems, spent a month at the retreat on an extreme low-fat diet and performed regular exercise. By the end of their stay, nearly all reported that they felt so much better they were able to go on long walks without pain, and many were even able to give up their medications. My father decided that he didn't have too much to lose and, given the alternatives, he made a decision to give the center a try. And so, like virtually all of the other attendees at the Pritikin Longevity Center, within a week or so he felt better than he had in years, and was soon off his medication.

As we all now know, the science and the medical professions have determined that a low-fat diet and regular exercise are effective approaches for halting and even reversing the progression of this kind of disease.

My point is not that you now should believe every story and report you come across—just that you need to be skeptical of those who dismiss the value of all anecdotal reports—be skeptical of the skeptics! Things are complicated and it takes time to look at them closely. Later in this chapter I'll provide some evaluation strategies to apply to specific anecdotal reports.

So, while it is clear you have to be very careful in assessing an unknown person's views and comments on the Internet, that's not really the "big story." The big story is that for the first time it is possible to instantly query and tap the knowledge of millions of people. These are people who have a passionate interest in some topic, have spent a great deal of time involved in some phenomena, and have something valuable to say.

Under what circumstances is using one of these nonexperts as a source most appropriate? I think that they are particularly useful in a couple of circumstances. One is for researching a very obscure topic, when you are looking for an enthusiast. For example, I have a small collection of antique typewriters. Before the Internet, it would almost be impossible to dialogue with other collectors—there just aren't enough of us, and we're spread out all over the world. But now there are several sites on the Internet devoted to typewriter collectors, and I can learn from others in the field and share information.

Another situation in which anecdotal reports are useful is when you want to obtain the experiences of other people who are going through the same thing you are. For example, the Internet is filled with support groups for all sorts of health and medical issues—from attention deficit disorder to whooping cough. Based on my own experiences and those I know, the majority of people that have used these health- and medical-support groups have benefited enormously. You can get views on everything from coping strategies to doctor referrals, possible drug side effects, and dealing with family members. Anecdotal reports are also quite valuable when you want to learn of the experiences others have had using various products or companies.

But still, the question remains, How do you actually evaluate a *specific* anecdotal posting? Here are a few tips:

- Consider whether an anecdote is an appropriate *type* of answer for what you are looking for. Anecdotal information is best for "softer," and "fuzzier" knowledge. For example, I'd be more prone to take the advice of someone on a hip-surgery recovery list who told me about a sleeping technique for reducing nighttime pain, than I would be to take someone's advice to try a powerful drug.

  Similarly, think about whether an opinion is an appropriate and valid information source for what you are researching. For example, someone's opinion of the quality of a rental truck company's customer service would be valid because as long as this person was a customer, he or she would have been in a position to have an opinion. But that same person's opinion on, say, flaws in a recent physics experiment, would be worthless unless he/she showed evidence of in-depth knowledge of that science.

- How deep and long-standing is the person's understanding of what they are discussing? Is there evidence that the person has been immersed in the topic and has taken time to understand what he is talking about? Or is he just ranting, giving opinions off the top of his head, or jumping to conclusions based on a single incident?

- What is the possible *motivation* of the person sharing this advice? Again, I'd be more likely to believe someone on an astronomy list who tells me of a good time and location to see a meteor shower than I would be to trust some unknown person's stock tip. In the first case, there isn't much of a reason for someone to provide incorrect or misleading information; in the latter, there certainly could be. (In fact, one section of the Internet that is notorious for unreliable advice is the various investor message boards.)

- Do other people reinforce the anecdotal information? If someone really is onto something interesting (e.g., sleeping with your legs in a certain way reduces pain after hip surgery), then other people on the list or elsewhere, on or off the Net, should be able to confirm that this works.

- How serious are the ramifications of following the person's advice? What are the costs if it turns out to be wrong? If you go looking for the shower and no meteors appear, you haven't lost that much. But sinking $1,000 in a stock based on a tip or taking a drug because someone reported good results with it have obvious ramifications.

Ultimately, this all comes down to a matter of trust. And the hard part is that trust on the Internet can not be made on the same intuitive and gut level that you make when you trust Tom at your office but not Gary; or the advice of your neighbor Janet, but not Bill. On the Internet, you are missing the cues that help you make those judgments—subtle things like a person's body language, their expression, their past record, and their true interest in your welfare. That's why you need these additional guidelines.

Finally, your ability to ascertain the validity of somebody's information will also depend greatly on how much you already know about the subject. The more knowledge you have, the better position you'll be in. For this reason, if you are researching an unfamiliar topic, and you are wondering about the reliability of some information from an unknown person, it could be helpful to forward or show that person's comments to a colleague or friend who *is* knowledgeable.

10

Wrapping It Up

Organizing and Writing Up Your Results, with the Benefit of the Expert Review

---

QUICK PREVIEW: WRAPPING IT UP

- You'll know it's time to conclude your talks with the experts when you can predict the answers to your questions and when you're putting out a lot of energy but not receiving much new information.
- Before you consider your project complete, have one or more of the best experts you've spoken with review your work for accuracy. This is a *critical* step in the process.
- Organize the information you've collected by subject rather than by source. This will make it easy to arrange your final work.
- When deciding what is worth including in your final report, select information that's relevant and reliable.
- Make conclusions whenever appropriate.
- Always remember to be fair—search for opposing views and be complete and honest.

Eventually you'll come to the point in your interviews when it is time to start winding down your information search. But there are a number of critical steps that still need to be attended to at this late point. Here are the things you need to know.

KNOWING WHEN TO CALL IT QUITS

How do you know when you've done enough work? Here's a guideline you can use: Be aware of when you can predict how the experts are going to answer your questions. As discussed earlier, when this first occurs, it's a good time to step back and redirect your focus. But if you've redirected once or twice already, and you can't think of any new paths to pursue, it's usually a sign that you've covered your subject well, and you don't have to go any further.

Another guideline you can use to decide when it's time to quit is when you discover that you are putting in a lot of work but not getting much new information. When you reach this point of diminishing returns, it's also probably time to wrap it all up.

One other rule you may decide to use: If you are approaching a deadline and you're out of time, you may have no choice but to quit! I've found that you need to budget something along the lines of 80 to 85 percent of your total allotted time for research and 15 to 20 percent for writing up the results.

Be aware, though, that typically the very best information in a research project comes more toward the very end! The reason is that as you do more and more research, you naturally learn more and more about your topic. This then allows you to better define your project's scope, better refine your questions, and get referred to people who have increasingly more of the specific type of expertise you seek. So don't wrap things up too fast if the good stuff is just starting to roll in, either. It's better to have completed an excellent research project that's a little late than a mediocre one that's in right on time.

MAKING SURE YOUR FINAL INFORMATION IS ACCURATE

After you decide to end your talks with the experts, the next critical step is to make sure you've covered your subject effectively and that the information you've gathered is accurate and complete.

The first thing you should do is to think back to your early expert contacts. Were there top-notch sources you spoke with but did not know at that early stage what kinds of questions to ask? Now that your knowledge of the subject is deeper and clearer, it might be worth going back to those people to talk to them again. Write an outline of your findings. Where do gaps still remain? Think of which sources you could consult to fill them.

Another step you might take at this point is to confirm the accuracy of certain discussions. Say, for example, that you spoke with an expert but you're not quite sure you understood the person completely. Jot down your interpretation of that source's points and send it off for confirmation.

The next step is very critical to complete this whole talking-to-the-experts process and make it really work. This is the "expert review" procedure and it works as follows.

If you are writing up your results, write a draft. If you are not writing up your results, write a rough draft anyway. Now go back and review all the different experts you've spoken with during the course of your information interviews. Select one or two that were especially knowledgeable and helpful—your very best sources. Get in touch with these people again and ask them to review your work for accuracy. Tell them that all their comments, suggestions, and criticisms are welcome. Be sure to tell the reviewers that they have indeed been specially selected. Ninety-five percent of the time these people will be flattered that you've singled them out, and they will be more than happy to take a few minutes and read your draft. You can even type in questions at locations in your draft where you are unsure of certain points.

If you are going to be writing up your results, you should acknowledge the expert reviewers' assistance somewhere in the work, and tell them that you plan to do this.

Your reviewers will almost never ask for a fee to do this job for you. A big reason for this is that you have been very selective in your choice of reviewers. You'll find that in any information-finding project you will always "hit it off" with at least a couple of experts along the way. The process is such that about 10 to 15 percent of the people you talk to will not be too helpful or knowledgeable, 60 to 70 percent will be quite helpful and provide you with very good information, and 10 to 15 percent will be of superb assistance. There is always that percentage of extra-nice experts who go out of their way to help you in any way they can. *These are the people you get in touch with again* to ask for this review.

I usually prefer two or three reviewers, each with a different perspective. For example, after I wrote a report on the topic of microcomputers, I sent one draft to a computer programmer, another to a consultant, and a third to a vendor. If you know of an expert who specializes only in one aspect of your study, you can send just that particular section of your work to that person.

There are two ways you can actually carry out this review procedure. One way is to mail your draft to your reviewers and ask them to mark it up and send it back to you. This is okay, but I prefer another approach. I would recommend that you send the draft and ask them to read it and mark it with comments. Then you should get on the telephone with each reviewer, have a copy of your draft in front of you, and go over the draft page by page with the expert. This way, you can ask the reviewers questions about any of their points you don't understand, and you can explain yourself on any points in your report that weren't clear to the reviewers.

In essence, this expert review is completing the circle—the experts are now reviewing the expert information that you've gathered. At this point, if you've done a thorough job, you should feel like an expert yourself.

NOTE TAKING AND ORGANIZATION

As mentioned previously, whenever you consult a written source of information, or talk to an expert, you'll want to take notes and keep your information organized.

There are naturally many different approaches you could take to organizing information. I've found that one particular method seems to work quite well for the purpose of organizing a lot of unfamiliar information gathered from a multitude of sources.

The way it works is as follows: Get a pad of paper, and for the first batch of written-information sources you consult (say, five to eight) take your notes on a pad, clearly marking at the top the name of the source, where it can be found, and the pages consulted. After you've finished with this first batch, you should be knowledgeable enough to be able to define the key subtopic categories within your subject and fit all future information you collect (from both written sources and talks with experts) into those categories you've established.

For example, let's say I was trying to find out everything about the sport of ballooning. After reading and taking notes on a number of articles on the topic, maybe I'd determine that there were fifteen critical subtopics within the subject. These might be purchasing a balloon, setting one up, safety considerations, fuel, and so on. My next step would be to get a stack of index cards and write each subtopic on top of a different card. Then I'd go back to my pad and copy the notes onto the appropriate index card. So if one sheet of the pad contained notes about a number of subtopics (fuel, safety, etc.) but were drawn from one source, I'd break up

those notes into those categories and copy them onto the appropriate index cards. This would eventually result in my having a
stack of cards, each containing information about only one
subtopic, but gathered from a number of different information
sources. In theory, all my future notes should be able to fit into
one of those categories.

As you continue to uncover information, however, and become
knowledgeable about your subject, you may find that you'll need
to modify the categories you originally created. Some subtopics
may prove to be very minor and can be incorporated into a larger
category. Or there may be additional categories to add as new topics arise that you hadn't considered.

This method of arranging information by subject, rather than
by source, will make the final organizational steps simple. You can
just shuffle the index cards until you're satisfied that the subtopics
are arranged in a logical and smooth order. Then, if you are going
to be writing up your results or making an oral presentation, you
have an outline already created.

You may find it convenient to continue to take notes on large
pads of paper even after you've created your index card categories.
That's fine. Just be sure to copy the notes on the appropriate cards.

WRITING UP YOUR RESULTS

Here are some pointers to keep in mind if you plan to formally
write up the results of your information search.

Sort the Gems from the Junk. As you read through all the notes
you've taken—notes from magazine articles, government reports,
talks with experts, and all other sources you've consulted—you'll
need to decide which pieces of information should be included in
your report. How do you discern the valuable from the not-so-
valuable? How do you decide which fact is important and which
is useless?

Although this is a common concern among first-time information seekers, if you've done a thorough job in your search, you will
understand the subject well enough at this point to know which

information is important and which is not. But here are three guidelines that can help you make a decision:

- Pay particular attention to the information that you've gathered and the notes that you've taken during the last 10 to 20 percent of your project. As mentioned earlier in this chapter, for several reasons, the best information usually comes towards the end of a project, and you'll want to make sure that that information receives the highest priority when finalizing the scope, focus, and conclusions of your work.
- A critical question you need to ask about any piece of information is whether it is *relevant* to your investigation. Does it add information, shed new light, suggest a trend, or provide background for your subject? If a piece of information, no matter how interesting, does not advance the specific goals or fall within the scope of your project, it should not be included.
- When evaluating your information, think about who provided it. Was it from a source you considered reliable or did it come from a biased or otherwise suspect source?

Be Complete. When you write up your results, don't tease with a remark that leaves the reader hanging. It's very important to fully explain your points clearly, and preferably with a concrete example. A statement like "the Model W skis are the best because they meet all important criteria" would only be helpful if you explained what the important criteria actually are. Anticipate the questions your statements will elicit from a reader, and then do your best to answer them.

Make Conclusions. Another common question among beginning information gatherers is whether it is appropriate to state one's opinion or make conclusions on a controversial issue. Let's say you've just spent three months learning all about the racquetball industry. You've spoken to club owners, association executives, sports columnists, and equipment manufacturers. You've read articles in leading trade publications and in the general press. As you read over your information, you begin to come to the conclusion that indicators are pointing to an imminent drop in the popularity of the sport. Are you qualified to state that conclusion?

In most cases, I would definitely say *yes*—with a couple of small cautions. If you've done a thorough job digging out information on your subject, you are certainly justified in drawing conclusions and stating them. If you realize that the facts point to certain trends, or add up to certain conclusions, you should state them. In fact, findings like these are one of the most important things that can come out of these information-finding projects.

Now, although you can draw broad conclusions, it's best to quote the experts themselves on factual data and opinions. Let's say you are doing a study on the fight against some rare disease. A statement in your report like "this disease is not at all contagious" should be attributed to a particular expert, or at least preceded by words like "according to experts I spoke with . . ."

Tip: Citing Sources Found on the Internet

If you are writing up your results in a formal manner, how do you appropriately cite information you've obtained from Web pages, Internet discussions, and even e-mail correspondence? You'll need to check a current edition of one of the standard style guides (e.g., Modern Language Association (MLA), American Psychological Association (APA), *Chicago Manual of Style,* etc.) to get help. But if you don't have one, there are several Web resources you can turn to. Here are a few good ones:

 • Guide for Citing Electronic Information (APA Style)
http://www.wilpaterson.edu/wpcpages/library/citing.htm
 • Online! A Reference Guide to Using Internet Sources
http://www.bedfordstmartins.com/online/
 • "Beyond the MLA Handbook: Documenting Electronic Sources on the Internet," Eugene Kleppinger
http://english.ttu.edu/kairos/1.2/inbox/mla.html
 • A Field Guide to Sources On, About and On the Internet
http://www.cc.emory.edu/WHSCL/citation.formats.html
 • Bibliographic Formats for Citing Electronic Information
Based on Li and Crane's Electronic Styles: A Handbook For Citing Electronic Information (1996), by Information Today, Inc.
http://www.uvm.edu/~ncrane/estyles

But in any information-finding project, you are certainly permitted to step back, look at the big picture, and give your opinion. You should then indicate in some manner, however, that this is *your* conclusion. In the racquetball case, you could phrase your statement along these lines: "After investigating the industry and talking to numerous experts in the field, this author feels that the game will soon be decreasing in popularity. The major reasons for this, I believe, are . . ."

What do you do when there are arguments and evidence on both sides of an issue and you're not sure who is correct? I recently worked on a project that required finding information on potential health hazards of video display terminals (VDTs). There were two distinctly opposing viewpoints: Government and industry tests all showed that radiation levels fell well within safety standards; but unions and certain workers organizations claimed that there was little information on the long-term effects of the VDTs' low-level radiation, and they cited cases of higher-than-expected health problems among certain VDT workers.

It was not totally clear—to me at least—what the "answer" was regarding the safety of this equipment. So I decided to present the arguments of both sides as clearly as possible and leave it up to readers to draw their own conclusions.

In many information searches you'll run into these gray areas; you'll want a simple answer, but there won't be one. That's okay. Just present the facts as you see them.

Also be sure to ask yourself whenever you write about a controversial or sensitive issue whether you are being *fair*. Fairness is pretty tough to judge, but I think the *Washington Post Deskbook on Style* defines it well. According to the editor of that book, being fair includes the following guidelines:

- **Search for opposing views.** In other words, don't be lazy and accept the first opinion you hear. Get both sides of the story.

- **Be complete.** Don't omit facts of major importance. Otherwise, your reader will be misled.

- **Be relevant.** Unnecessary information will cloud an issue.

- **Be honest.**

To Quote or Not to Quote

People often wonder when it's necessary to attribute information to an expert or a written source, and when it's acceptable to use the information without attribution. Although one wit claimed that "to steal ideas from one person is plagiarism; to steal from many is research,"* the general rule is that when you use somebody's own idea or work, you must attribute it to that source. But if somebody provides facts or general information that can be obtained from many sources (e.g., Death Valley, California, has the highest recorded temperature in the United States), it is not necessary to do so.

What about obtaining permission to quote the experts that you've interviewed? If you are writing a very sensitive piece, you can play it safe and specifically ask each expert for their permission, but normally it's not necessary. As long as you've identified yourself to the expert, explained that you are writing an article or a report, and made no off-the-record agreements, the expert should realize that you are using his or her remarks for publication.

Another common question regards obtaining permission to excerpt or quote published information. Here the general rule is that you may make what is called "fair use" of published materials without seeking permission. In general, "fair use" allows you to quote a few lines of a short article or a couple of paragraphs of a longer piece or book *with attribution* but without getting permission from the publisher. If you want to use more than this, you should send a letter to the publisher explaining exactly what information you want to use, exactly where it is located, and why you want to use it. The great majority of the time, the publisher will *not* charge you for the use of the material, but will require that you print a specific credit line. The publisher may also want you to send it a copy of the final work.

These general rules are exactly that—general. Each case is different. The best rule is to use your common sense and, if there is any doubt at all about attributing information or obtaining permission, to err on the safe side.

*Arthur Bloch, *Murphy's Law Book 3* (Los Angeles: Price Stern, 1982), p. 50.

If for some reason a publisher is unwilling to grant permission, try to track down the author of the piece yourself. Then you can interview that person for information, and the expertise will be available to you without a hassle.

Libel is a much more complicated matter, and a full discussion of the topic is beyond the scope of this book. It's worth noting, however, a concise definition that was published in the *Washington Post Deskbook on Style:* "Basically, a libelous statement is a published statement that injures a person (or organization or corporation) in his trade, profession or community standing." Although traditional defenses against a libel charge have included "truth" (i.e., the information published was accurate) and "reasonable care" (on the part of the writer), it is impossible to generalize about this topic. The *Post* advises writers to again consider simply whether they are being fair. Did you give the party a chance to respond?

One last point: Be sure to show your appreciation to the experts you speak with. If you can think of any way that you can help them, or return the favor, offer it. And if someone ever comes to you with an information request, remember how much you appreciated the experts who helped you and try to do likewise.

11

Troubleshooting

Typical Questions Information Seekers Ask

Here are some typical questions I am asked by researchers who are undertaking an information-finding project.

How do I know where to begin my information search?

There is rarely any single *perfect* place to begin your research. The Information Seeker's Map on page 326 should help you get started. The key is to get started on your research and begin learning about your subject. As you begin to gather information and understand your topic, the question will become irrelevant.

How do I know whether to use print sources or the Internet when starting my research?

This can be confusing, especially since many periodical indexes and publications today can be found both in print and on the Internet. The basic rule of research stays the same, though: Start off with basic sources and build up your knowledge gradually. So, whether you choose print or electronic, your initial sources should be nontechnical and geared for the popular user. Keep in mind, too, that print sources still retain certain advantages over electronic.

I know that there must be some information on the topic, but I can't find anything!

It's extremely doubtful that *no* information whatsoever exists—especially these days in the age of the Internet. One possible cause for not finding anything is that you might be unaware of the standard terminology that your subject is categorized under. For example, say you were researching the topic "static electricity"—you would need to know that "electrostatics" is the standard scientific term for that phenomenon and that all indexes and materials will categorize the topic under that heading. Also, make sure you check as many sources as possible before you conclude there is nothing available on your subject. If you still cannot find anything, look up related or broader subjects. In the rare instance where there is truly absolutely nothing written on your subject, it could mean you are onto something interesting, and the results of your research could add to the body of knowledge!

I've found some articles on my subject, but I can't understand them.

Don't worry. Keep on researching the topic and look for articles written for a more general audience. If you can't find any at all, try finding a description in an introductory textbook or encyclopedia.

I'd like to contact some experts, but to tell you the truth, I'm afraid.

You are certainly not alone! Just about everyone gets nervous about calling strangers and asking for information the first time. But think about it—you've got nothing to lose. Chances are, the person is going to help you out, and if worse comes to worse and the phone conversation doesn't work out, you can always say "thanks for your time" and hang up. It took me almost two years of talking to experts before I felt really relaxed before making these kinds of calls, so don't be too hard on yourself!

I can never get hold of these experts—either they are out or they don't return my calls!

It's not that you can't get hold of them, it's just that you haven't made enough calls! The process of reaching experts is, to a great extent, a numbers game—call enough people and you will always reach at least a certain percentage. It's a time-consuming process, but it works! If the person is very busy, though, try calling his or her office and asking for an e-mail address, and send your queries that way. This makes it unnecessary for the person to be available when you call, and also allows the person to respond when he or she has time to reply. Review the section in chapter 7, "Quick Preview: Making the Connection."

I got the expert on the phone, but he talked so fast I don't think I wrote it all down.

Don't worry. Note taking is a skill that improves with practice. After you speak with a number of people, you'll intuitively know how to capture the key points. And it really does help to read over your notes *immediately* after the conversation, so you can fill in gaps while the talk is still fresh in your mind. If it looks like you missed something critical, just call the person back to go over those issues again.

How do I know when to stop doing research?

There is no perfect time, but, as mentioned earlier in the book, when you feel you can predict the experts' answers, have reassessed the direction of your project, and are expending a lot of research time but getting little new information, it's probably time to wrap up. You can try writing a draft of your findings to see if there are gaps still remaining that require additional research.

Help! I think I may have collected too much information! I'm swamped with articles, notes, and other data!

If you're overloaded with too many hits from a search engine, see the strategies I provide on page 212. If it's just too much informa- tion on your topic in general that you've collected, your problem is probably not too much information, but not enough organiza- tion. Start going through your notes and begin categorizing each statement of fact under a topic subheading and transcribe all related facts under each heading. This will make your big stack of information more manageable. Get rid of information that, although interesting, does not directly relate to the scope of your project or advance its mission.

Uh-oh, I've got conflicting information in my notes. How do I know whom to believe?

This is common—often there is more than one opinion on a subject. See chapter 9 on evaluating information sources. Sometimes you may simply have to present both points of view and allow the reader to decide the merits.

I really enjoy doing this kind of research. How can I find out about careers in this field?

That is a very interesting question, and it is one I have been asked many times. There are a number of different careers that involve digging up and analyzing information. The most obvious and well-known field involving finding information is library science. Some ex-librarians have started "information broker" businesses and sell their research skills to businesses and organizations for a fee. Other careers that involve heavy amounts of research include certain types of journalism (such as investigative journalism), private investigator services, new business or product development, and market research.

After reading this book, you may find that all of the sources and strategies described are a bit overwhelming, like there is just *too much* out there. But don't worry about trying to memorize the whole book. Just take a look at the Information Seeker's Map on page 326 to get a feel for the entire process, start some research at one of the "easy start" sources identified in chapter 1, then go with the flow and consult the book for help if you run into problems. And remember the basics:

- The information you seek is almost certainly available for the asking.
- There are experts around who will talk to you and answer your questions.

12

A Researcher's Road Map

Project Planning and Source Selection

As the online world and the Internet become more popular, it becomes increasingly confusing and difficult to know what type of source is best to use for what kind of research. Do you start with a book or a magazine article? Should you browse magazines in print, or try searching them on a CD-ROM? What about the fact that some magazines are now on the Internet, too? Or should you just call an expert and ask him or her your questions?

This is a complicated matter, and there is no perfect solution. However, I will try here to provide two ways to make these decisions easier. The first is to offer a general step-by-step strategy on how to approach a research project, and the second is a description of what I see as the special strengths of the major print, electronic, and other sources described in this book.

PROJECT PLANNING

Although every information-finding project is different, in most cases the process of learning about a new subject follows a similar path. Generally, the trick is to build your knowledge of the subject by first using nontechnical sources and gradually proceeding to more advanced and technical ones. Any information-finding project I undertake generally goes through six steps, outlined below.

1. DEFINE YOUR PROBLEM

√What do you need?
√Why do you need it?
√What will you do with it?

2. LOCATE YOUR SOURCES

√Pick the right library
√Check basic indexes
√Read articles and note experts' names
√Identify and contact an association

3. OBTAIN TECHNICAL SOURCES

√Check technical indexes
√Identify and obtain trade journals

4. MAKE LIST OF QUESTIONS/ CONTACT & INTERVIEW EXPERTS

√Gather expert names
√Jot down your questions not addressed in literature
√Start with non-technical experts
√Identify yourself clearly
√Be persistent but polite

5. REDIRECT FOCUS & EVALUATE PROGRESS

√Have goals changed?
√New questions to ask?
√Untapped sources to contact?

6. WRITE DRAFT/GET EXPERT REVIEW

√Send to experts
√Get comments
√Final changes

Information Seeker's Map

Although in practice these steps will overlap, I've found it useful to keep them in mind separately when planning my investigations.

1. Define your problem.

Break it down into its component parts. Determine why you need this information and what you plan to do with it. This will make your information search clearer to you and easier to conduct.

2. Locate basic sources.

Because you probably know very little about the topic at this stage, you'll first want to obtain definitions and understand basic concepts. The best information sources to consult at this early stage are nontechnical ones that explain unusual concepts and terms clearly and without jargon. Such sources can include newspapers and magazines geared to a general audience, reports published by the government for the public, and literature for consumers from manufacturers of products.

Print out any articles you've located online. Underline what you feel are the significant points.

Review what you've underlined, and try to create topic categories to help provide structure and focus to your research (see pages 311-312). Don't, though, let these categories limit the extent or scope of your research. You may need to create new categories as you continue your research.

TIP: When reading your printouts, try to conduct an imaginary dialogue with the authors as you read them—in other words, if what you read prompts a question, write it in the margin. If you agree with something, note it; if you disagree, write why. This dialoguing and questioning spurs you to advance the authors' arguments and brings you to the next, higher level of discussion.

---

3. Obtain technical sources.

Now you're ready to seek out more specialized information. After you've grasped the basic terms and concepts of your subject, you're ready to dig into more technical material. Sources to check at this point could include trade publications, research center reports, and transcripts of convention presentations.

4. **Make a list of questions, contacts, and interview experts.**
While you were doing your research and reading, you should have been noting the names of experts to interview. Once you've done enough reading to feel fairly confident in understanding the basics of your topic, you should be in a good position to come up with some thoughtful questions to pose to the experts you've identified. When you've gotten all you can from published material, you should feel confident enough to begin contacting some experts to get answers to the questions you still have on the subject.

5. **Redirect focus and evaluate progress.**
This is the time to step back and review your progress. Compare what you've learned with what you decided you wanted to learn in step 1. Make adjustments or redirect your focus, if necessary. Go back to earlier steps to fill in gaps, if needed.

6. **Write a draft/get expert review.**
Get one or more experts to review your work for accuracy. Don't neglect this very important step.

Now, congratulate yourself for having completed your information-finding project and succeeded in becoming an "instant" expert!

TIP: Identify key words and terminologies to allow for more precise searching. You can do this by simply reading about your topic and noting keywords as they pop up. For example, if you were studying how businesses prepare for the future, you would discover that key phrases in the materials you've gathered include "forecasting," "strategic planning," and "anticipatory management." Then you could conduct your searches by using those keywords.

SOURCE SELECTION

The list below is designed to help you determine how the major types of information sources discussed in this book compare in terms of special strengths and potential drawbacks. This can be useful for short projects or quick-answer research when you don't need to consult many sources and are only looking for one or two to check.

Print Sources

- **Textbooks**
  Provide basic definitions and clarify terms. Useful for obtaining a basic understanding of complex matters—especially at the beginning of a research project. Drawbacks include a possible time lag in reflecting the very latest news and movements in the field.

- **Reference Books**
  Statistical data, definitions, numerical data, and basic facts.

- **Nonfiction Books**
  In-depth coverage of a particular topic. Useful for obtaining a deeper understanding of complex topics. Drawbacks include length of time to get through and absorb an entire book during a fast-moving research project.

- **Directories**
  Lists, rankings, compilations, and addresses. Good for overviews, snapshots, and finding contact information (for companies, magazines, products, etc.). Drawbacks include the short life span of most directory data, making it necessary to find and use the latest edition (or one no more than a year old).

- **Newspaper Articles**
  Coverage of events of local significance not covered elsewhere; cites experts; usually written in nontechnical manner. Drawbacks include occasional superficial coverage of complex topics.

- **Magazine and Journal Articles**
  More depth than newspapers. Best overall general research source. Also readily available electronically, which offers the

advantage of searchability. However, print remains easier to read.

There are three major categories of magazine and journal articles: popular, trade, and scholarly. Popular magazines include those you would find on a newsstand that appeal to the widest audience. Trade magazines are more specialized and are usually targeted to those working in a particular field (aerospace, nuclear engineering, wastewater treatment) or those who have a special interest. Scholarly journals are normally written by professors and academics for other professors and academics. Though all of these types of periodicals can be useful for researchers, trade magazines most often balance depth of coverage while still being understandable for the layperson. (Another category of print periodicals is the newsletter, which contains highly focused discussions and analyses of news and events in specific industries, technology markets, products, etc. These are "insider" sources that specialize in providing implications and analyses of the latest and most significant developments in the field. They are usually very expensive and are not as commonly found in libraries as the other types of publications.)

Electronic Sources

- **Professional Online**
  Sophisticated, powerful search capabilities; massive databases. Best for highly targeted searches of major and leading popular, trade, and scholarly literature, as well as government data and other highly focused, data-intensive sources, including newsletters. Drawbacks include high cost to search and difficulty in learning system.

- **Library CD-ROMs and Online Databases**
  Free (at the library) and relatively easy access to large information databases; supports sophisticated searching of major, leading print journals in many fields. Drawbacks include occasional slow lag time to update CD-ROM, the lack of full text on some systems and the need to learn proprietary search commands.

- **The Web**
  Amazingly eclectic, diverse, and alternative information source. Great for finding obscure information, free and cheap government data, information presented graphically, and the state of the art on the Internet and related technology. E-zines, or publications available only on the Web, are coming into their own as legitimate periodicals, especially those that cover the Internet, technology, and computer-related information. Drawbacks include information overload, difficulty in conducting precision searches, the mixture of commercial and substantive sites, the amount of time it may take to find useful data, and difficulty in evaluating the credibility and actual source of some data.

- **Online Discussion Groups**
  Excellent for locating experts, up-to-the-minute developments in a field or on countless topics, and anecdotal reports. Drawbacks include a high noise-to-signal ratio and the tricky nature of evaluating the credibility of anecdotal reports.

Other Key Sources

- **Government and University Research**
  Free or inexpensive access to in-depth studies, often relating to issues in science, technology, or matters of public policy. Drawbacks can include difficulty finding what you need and the age of the study.

- **Associations**
  Free or inexpensive access to industry surveys, news, and overviews, as well as potential referrals to experts. Drawbacks include possible bias on the part of association personnel in favor of their industry.

- **Experts**
  Customized, up-to-the-minute live information. Need to assess the expert's knowledge, credibility, and potential biases.

You may wonder if it is possible to know *which* of the many information sources listed in this book will be best for *your* project. Unfortunately, it is almost impossible to know for certain which sources will turn out to be the most fruitful for a specific information-finding project. In one case you may find that your best sources turned out to be research centers and museums; in another, a specialized bookstore and a trade magazine; and in other projects, a general Internet search. The only way to know whether a particular source is going to pay off for a particular search is to try it. Dig up as many relevant library resources, "supersources," federal government sources, business information sources (if appropriate), and finally, the experts themselves, until you feel you've found what you were looking for.

This is not to say that you cannot make some educated guesses and choose sources that seem more likely to pay off. For example, if you need information on some very timely matter, it would likely be covered in a newspaper, wire service or magazine; information on a more obscure scientific matter might be found at a laboratory, research center or university. Similarly, a public-policy or consumer-oriented issue is likely to be covered somewhere in the federal government; an art-related issue covered at a museum or maybe a university; and so on. So you don't really have to fly blind. Read the descriptions of the sources in this book, and use your best judgment to try to zero in on the ones that will most likely cover your subject.

APPENDIX A

Sources of Further Information

The following is a selected listing of books, magazines, journals, and associations that can assist you in learning more about research and information finding. Most of these sources are inexpensive or free. However, the online magazines and journals are geared more to the professional researcher and information professional and will cost more.

BOOKS

General Research and Information-Finding Techniques

The following books are excellent foundations for obtaining fundamental research skills, as well as for identifying basic information sources.

BARZUN, JACQUES, AND GRAFF, HENRY F. *The Modern Researcher*, 5th *ed.* (Harcourt Brace Jovanovich, 1992; $37.50). A classic book on the art of conducting research, including an analysis of the researcher's "virtues." Provides great food for thought on the problems, dilemmas, and challenges in the researcher's quest for truth.

BOOTH, WAYNE C., COLUMB, GREGORY C., AND WILLIAMS, JOSEPH M. *The Craft of Research* (University of California Press, 1995; $12.95). A very thorough and detailed approach to conducting a research project. Topics covered include asking questions, reading critically, making good arguments, claims and evidence, drafting a report, communicating evidence visually, research ethics, and more.

BRADY, JOHN. *The Craft of Interviewing* (Random House, 1977; $12). Another classic; this one on how to conduct an interview. Aimed especially at journalists, this book provides strategies, tips, and advice on how to reach sources and then get them to cooperate with you.

FULD, LEONARD. *The New Competitor Intelligence* (John Wiley, 1994; $34.95). Leonard Fuld is one of the country's leading experts on the topic of competitive intelligence—finding facts on competitor companies. This book lists basic reference sources, provides creative information-finding strategies, and discusses the reasons for competitive intelligence activity in today's business world.

GARVIN, ANDREW. *The Art of Being Well-Informed*, 2nd ed. (Avery Publishing Group, 1996; $14.95). Written by the president of the worldwide research and consulting group FIND/SVP (and coauthored by me), this 243-page paperback is geared to raising the "information consciousness" of businesspersons. It offers advice and case studies as to why research and information-gathering systems are critical to businesses today, and provides a listing of a number of sources. The second edition also examines the role of the Internet in business research, and provides specific strategies for battling information overload.

KING, DENNIS. *Get the Facts on Anyone* (IDG Books, 1999; $15). Written by an investigative reporter, this book will help you locate missing people, locate credit and financial information, uncover court records, and use databases to find information that relates to people.

SCOTT, ROBERT. *The Investigator's Little Black Book* (Crime Time Publishing, 1998; $19.95). An intriguing little paperback book that identifies hundreds of sources for researchers. Some of these are databases and directories, but others are lesser-known or unusual sources, such as where to find very old phone books, video archives, military records, and much more.

Internet Searching

You might think that a hardcopy book is not the ideal medium for learning about Internet searching, since the technology and sites change so quickly. And you'd be mostly correct. But the fact is, there are certain fundamental online searching strategies and techniques that remain valid over a long period of time. The sources listed here are books that will stand the test of time.

BASCH, REVA. *Researching Online for Dummies* (IDG Books, 1998; $24.99). Basch is one of the country's premier information searchers and Internet gurus and she reveals many of her secrets in this outstanding book. "Dummies" title notwithstanding, this is a must guide not just for beginner but for advanced searchers as well.

Internet Rough Guide (Rough Guides, updated annually). These little books pack a wallop. If you are a newcomer to the online world and need to get up-to-speed quickly on what the Net is all about, this book will succinctly provide you with everything you need to know.

The "Super Searcher" series (Information Today, http://www.infotoday. com). This publisher specializes in books and journals on Internet searching, including an excellent series on searching the Net. Sample titles include: *Super Searchers Do Business and Law of the Super Searchers: The Online Secrets of Top Legal Researchers.*

Knowledge and Strategy

A whole slew of excellent books are available that explain not just *how* to find information, but *why* information is important, particularly for use as a strategic asset in organizations. This discipline is most frequently called "knowledge management" and it examines how firms can identify and share what they know internally as a critical strategic advantage. Below are the titles of the leading books written by the most insightful analysts in this field.

CHOO, WUN CHEI. *The Knowing Organization: How Organizations Use Information to Construct Meaning, Create Knowledge, and Make Decisions* (Oxford University Press, 1999). According to Choo, who is a professor at the University of Toronto, a "knowing organization" possesses information and knowledge so that it is well informed, mentally perceptive, and enlightened. Choo has written several outstanding books on information, knowledge, and organizations. He is particularly adept at looking at the nitty gritty of the nature and strategic value of facts, insights, data, and knowledge from an information and library-oriented focus, rather than from a purely management or IT perspective.

DAVENPORT, THOMAS, AND PRUSAK, LAURENCE. *Information Ecology: Mastering the Information and Knowledge Environment* (Oxford University Press, 1997; $29.95) and *Working Knowledge: How Organizations Manage What They Know* (Harvard Business School Press, 1997; $29.95). Davenport and Prusak are perhaps the most respected names in the knowledge management field. They have helped scores of companies implement their knowledge management initiatives and so they know what works and what doesn't from hands-on experience. I have enjoyed Prusak's lectures in person, and always appreciate his perspective that knowledge management works only when the focus is on the human qualities of knowledge creation, and not on computer systems.

HAMEL, GARY, AND PRAHALAD, C.K. *Competing for the Future* (Harvard Business Press, reprint 1996; $14.95). More than a discussion of knowledge management, this book, a favorite of mine, examines how firms can leverage information, knowledge and other resources in order to be positioned first in a market and to *create* a successful future.

HARARI, OREN, AND ULRICH, ROBERT. *Leapfrogging the Competition: Five Giant Steps to Becoming a Market Leader* (Prima, 1999). Like *Competing for the Future*, the scope of this book goes beyond knowledge management, as its focus is on business innovation and success. But Harari, who wrote another book I liked very much called *Jumping the Curve*, focuses clearly on how information and knowledge sharing can be a critical means to those ends.

NONAKA, IKUJIRO, ET AL. *The Knowledge-Creating Company: How Japanese Companies Create the Dynamics of Innovation*. (Oxford University Press, 1995; $27.50). A groundbreaking book when it was published, *The Knowledge-Creating Company* provides case studies from an Eastern perspective. It also discusses how organizations can identify and capture "tacit" or unexpressed knowledge.

SCHWARTZ, PETER. *The Art of the Long View: Planning for the Future in an Uncertain World* (Doubleday, 1996; $15.95). Another future-oriented work, in this one Schwartz analyzes how organizations can create a strategic vision by the use of scenario planning and other forecasting techniques. His chapter on "Information Hunting and Gathering" is one of the best treatises anywhere on the art of research.

STEWART, THOMAS. *Intellectual Capital: The New Wealth of Organizations* (Doubleday, 1997; $27.00). While I have not yet had a chance to read this book, I know Stewart as one of the most insightful and cogent writers on knowledge management from his regular coverage of the discipline in *Fortune* magazine. Stewart's focus in this book is on "intellectual capital"—how firms can identify, measure, and leverage their intellectual assets whether they are in documents or in people's minds.

Social Concerns and Technology Critiques

Along with the benefits that technology and the Internet have brought, there's also a downside—the "Faustian bargain" that educator Neil Postman likes to remind us we've all made. While researchers have clearly benefited from the speed, power, and accessibility of the Internet, there are wider and overlapping concerns about society's rush to embrace online technologies. The following works include both personal favorites and a select number of scholarly and probing works by some of the most respected technology analysts and social critics.

BIRKERTS, SVEN. *The Gutenberg Elegies: The Fate of Reading in an Electronic Age* (Fawcett, 1995; $12.50). Birkerts was one of the first widely published critics of life in a wired world. In this book he makes an argument as to why the printed word and our sources of literature are superior to electronic and virtual communication.

PFAFFENBERG, BRYAN. *Democratizing Information: Online Databases and the Rise of End-User Searching* (G.K. Hall, 1990; $30). While this is an older book that predates the popular rise of the Internet, Pfaffenberg, a professor at the University of Virginia, cogently analyzes how new technologies never evolve in a vacuum. Rather, their applications and uses are shaped by the social mores, values, and forces that exist at the time of their creation. He uses online databases to illustrate his thesis. Pfaffenberg is a frequent writer and speaker on the intersection of technologies and the democratic form of government.

POSTMAN, NEIL. *Technopoly: The Surrender of Culture to a Technology* (Vintage, 1993; $12). Neil Postman is my favorite critic and author and I never fail to gain an enormous number of insights from his books. Postman has a penetrating mind and is a crystal-clear thinker—he also has a great wit and sense of humor.

Because Postman is a long-time critic of technology, he is sometimes called a grouch or curmudgeon. But that's incorrect: Postman's purpose is simply to make sure we stop and think about what we are doing, and not march blindly and unthinkingly into a future that may have unanticipated consequences. *Technopoly* is his primary work on the role of technology on society. Postman has written several other excellent books, such as *The Disappearance of Childhood*, *The End of Education*, and a series of thought-provoking essays in the book *Conscientious Objections*.

Shenk, David. *Data Smog: Surviving the Information Glut* (HarperSanFrancisco, 1998; $13). Shenk's book is an interesting discussion and analysis of the causes of information overload, and the many problems that data glut is causing. Shenk has come out with a follow-up to this one called *The End of Patience: Cautionary Notes on the Information Revolution.*

There are also a few more books in this category that I haven't gotten to yet but are on my must-read list. These include *The Control Revolution: How the Internet Is Putting Individuals in Charge and Changing the World We Know* by Andrew L. Shapiro; *Digital McLuhan: A Guide to the Information Millennium* by Paul Levinson; and *Holding on to Reality: The Nature of Information at the Turn of the Millennium* by University of Montana philosopher Albert Borgmann. An article I'd like to mention that's a bit older now but that I still find an excellent read was published in the August 1995 issue of *Harper's*. The piece, titled "What Are We Doing Online?", is actually a debate among several thoughtful thinkers who discuss the benefits and drawbacks of living in a wired world.

If you have the inclination to dig even deeper into this fascinating, and increasingly relevant subject, you should read the seminal works on technology and society. This means that in addition to reading the oft-quoted Marshall McLuhan (more often quoted than read!) and his *Understanding Media: The Extensions of Man*, you should also peruse the works of Lewis Mumford, such as his *Technics and Civilization*. You'd also need to read works by Jacques Ellul, such as *The Technological Society*. These brilliant writers' analyses remain the foundation for the more modern critics of technology.

MAGAZINES, JOURNALS, AND NEWSLETTERS

Most publications that focus just on research and online searching are geared to librarians and other information professionals. The CyberSkeptic's Guide to Internet Research is excellent (published by Bibliodata in Needham Heights, MA), as is, I must say, my own newsletter, The Information Advisor (published by FIND/SVP in New York City). Both of these publications, though, are geared primarily to business research, which may or may not be your primary focus of interest.

The two leading professional trade journals, which are actually read mostly by librarians, are *Online* and *EContent* (both published by Online Inc. in Wilton, CT). Another prominent and well-respected publisher of magazines and books on research is Information Today, located in Medford, NJ. Its publications include *Link-Up*, *Information Today*, and *Searcher*. With the exception of *Searcher*, which is written by industry expert Barbara Quint and geared mainly to proficient information professionals, Information Today's publications are a bit more accessible to the casual searcher. And you can get a good European and global perspective on the information industry from a journal called *Information World Review*, published in the U.K. by Learned Information.

PROFESSIONAL ASSOCIATIONS

If you really are interested in learning more about research and information gathering, you should contact one or more of the following organizations. In addition to their regular services, all publish various newsletters or magazines and hold regular conferences.

Association of Independent Information Professionals
7044 S. 13th St., Oak Creek, WI 53154; 414-766-0421
http://www.aiip.com
This organization's membership consists of *independent* information professionals (sometimes called "information brokers") who make their living doing computer and manual organization, retrieval, and dissemination of information. This would be the organization to turn to if you are interested in learning how to start your own information-brokering firm.

Investigative Reporters and Editors Association
138 Neff Annex, University of Missouri, Columbia, MO 65211;
573-882-2772
http://www.ire.org

This organization is an excellent resource for learning how to gather information, interview sources, and perform online research. One of its books, *The Reporter's Handbook,* edited by Steven Weinberg, is a superb guidebook filled with sources and strategies for uncovering a wide range of hard-to-get data.

Special Libraries Association
1700 18th Street NW, Washington, DC 20009; 202-234-4700
A leading and highly respected organization of librarians who work in corporations, technical organizations, and various institutions outside the traditional public library. It publishes a very good journal called *Information Outlook.*

Society of Competitive Intelligence Professionals (SCIP)
1700 Diagonal Rd., Ste. 600, Alexandria, VA 22314;
703-739-0696
http://www.scip.org
SCIP consists of about 3,000 business professionals who evaluate competitors and competitive conditions and wish to improve their skills.

UNIVERSITY PROGRAMS, WORKSHOPS, AND COURSES

If you are really serious about learning more about information, technology, research, and searching, you can get a degree in a related field. The closest traditional degree would be a Masters in Library Science (M.L.S.), and the most progressive library schools are retooling their programs to meet the needs of the information age. Some excellent M.L.S. programs include Simmons College in Boston; the University of Texas, Austin; Indiana University; and Rutgers University in New Jersey. The University of California, Berkeley, has completely revamped and renamed its school so that it is now the School of Information Management and Systems. There, students look at intranets, the strategic use of information in corporations, and knowledge-management applications.

A related program is one that emphasizes the various forms of media and how we interact and relate to them. Two top-notch programs are New York University's Media Ecology M.A. and Ph.D. program (headed by Neil Postman in NYU's School of Education) and the McLuhan Program in Culture and Technology at the University of Toronto.

If you are simply interested in taking a class on searching, many Internet search workshops are available, typically from your local library, a night school, or nearby university. I teach an online nine-week, three-credit course on how to do research for the Media Studies division at the New School for Social Research (New York, NY) as well as a course on New Media Ethics (http://www.dialnsa.edu). I also conduct training seminars and workshops for organizations (see: http://www.robertberkman.com or e-mail: rberkman@aol.com).

APPENDIX B

Ten Tips for Conducting Precision Research on the Internet

For All Searches:

1. All search tools on the Web are not alike. Use a hierarchical index like Yahoo when your topic is very broad; use a standard search engine (like AltaVista, HotBot, InfoSeek) for narrower topics; and use a metasearch engine (like Dogpile or Metacrawler) for extremely narrow and arcane topics.
2. When creating your search statement, use words that are unique, unusual, and unambiguous. Use phrases whenever possible—most search engines let you indicate these by the use of quotation marks.
3. AltaVista is the only major search engine that allows you to use NEAR as a Boolean operator. This helps make your searches more precise than just using the Boolean AND between your key words.
4. You can make your searches more precise by limiting your search to words only found in a Web page's title or even in its URL. AltaVista allows you to do this, for example, via its "field searching" feature.
5. Use the Google (http://www.google.com) search engine to cut down on irrelevant, trivial pages and to find the most popular sites on the Web.

6. An easy way to remember the rules and protocols for searching various search engines is to print out a copy of the search engine's help pages and keep them handy by your PC.

7. You can take active strategies to evaluate the credibility of a Web page. For example, you can search for the author's name on the Web to find other references to his/her work, or send the author an e-mail with your own follow-up questions to ascertain expertise.

8. You can often obtain valuable research data by joining and then "listening in" to conversations that occur on the Internet discussion groups. But to encourage cooperation from the group to respond to one of your questions, you should offer to summarize the responses you receive for the full group.

9. If you're swamped with e-mail from Internet discussion groups, you can cut down on overload by signing up with the "digest" version, creating a separate user name for each group you subscribe to, and by using an e-mail software that allows you to sort incoming messages into labeled folders.

10. It normally costs money to search powerful "databases" of related information, even on the Web. But you can find a list of free searchable databases by linking to Bighub at http://www.bighub.com

For Business Searches:

1. A few popular business magazines make their archives available for FREE on the Web, even for nonsubscribers. These include *American Demographics* (www.demographics.com), Inc. (www.inconline.com), and *FastCompany* (www.fastcompany. com).

2. If you are looking for information on exporting or reaching foreign markets, an enormous amount of free market data is available from the U.S. Department of Commerce at http://www.mac.doc.gov

3. You can quickly find FREE market statistics from the United States International Trade Administration (http://www.ita.gov).

4. When using a search engine to perform market research, avoid using the word "sales" since it is too broad. Instead, consider adding the following words and phrases to your search statement to retrieve relevant pages: "units shipped," forecast, projected, "market share," shipments.

5. You can search for and obtain FREE annual reports at the Public Register's Annual Report Service: http://www.prars.com

6. The United States Patent and Trademark Office now makes their complete database of patent filings—along with images—available for free searching! Link to the site at: http://www.uspto.gov/patft/index.html

7. Normally, there is a fee to search databases of published articles, even on the Web. But you can search the archives of dozens of respected city business journals on the Web at http://www.amcity.com

8. An excellent—and free—site that summarizes and ranks business-related Web sites is the Dow Jones Business Directory—you can link to it at http://www.businessdirectory.dowjones.com

9. Expensive, Wall Street–analyst brokerage reports were once available only to clients. Now some are migrating to the Net—though these aren't free. Find the ones you need at http://www.multexinvestor.com and http://investext.com

10. You can download public companies' filings with the SEC from its Web site at http://www.sec.gov/edgarhp.htm—or try an alternative, edgaronline, which allows you more flexible searching and formatting options; link to it at http://www.edgar-online.com

For Academic Searches:

1. Thousands of libraries around the U.S.—and around the world—are putting their catalogs up on the Web. You can search them for free by linking to the Library of Congress' locator site: Library of Congress http://lcweb.loc.gov/z3950/gateway.html

2. Digital Libraries are scanning in primary materials from their collection such as letters, photographs, governmental documents, and more, but these can be hard to find. You can link to: http://www.dlib.org/projects.html, a service of the D-Lib e-journal on digital libraries to find them.

3. The world's largest archive of computerized social science data is available free on the Web—link to the Interuniversity Consortium for Political and Social Research at http://www.icpsr.umich.edu

4. Not all publications on the Web are counterculture 'zines. You can also find peer-reviewed scholarly journals—search for the ones you need by linking to http://www.coalliance.org

5. How do you cite your Internet sources in your final paper or report?—link to the Columbia Guide to Online Style at http://www.columbia.edu/cu/cup/cgos/idx_basic.html to obtain examples of proper style guidelines.
6. Traditional fee-based searchable databases are a more powerful a source of scholarly material than the free Internet. If you are affiliated with a university you may be able to search databases for free by linking to your institution's home page and logging on—even when not physically at the school.
7. Some of the basic periodical directories you use for locating names of journals are moving to the Web. An excellent free one is mediafinder.com from Oxbridge Communications Inc.
8. Yahoo is not the only hierarchical index available—others that index and categorize Web sites, but with a more scholarly and academic focus, include AlphaSearch at http://www.calvin.edu/library/as and BUBL Link at http://bubl.ac.uk/link
9. Normally, you have to pay to download magazine and journal articles, even from the Web. But one site, called Powerize.com, lets you search and view thousands of some of the best at no charge at all.
10. You can conduct research by observing and monitoring conversations on Internet discussion groups—but you'll need to be attuned to ethical concerns regarding obtaining informed consent and getting permission to use others' words.

Index

Index

Index

Index

National Bureau of Economic Research, 152

National Center for Health Statistics, 95

National Computer Systems Laboratory, 89

National Criminal Justice Reference Service, 100

National Directory of Nonprofit Organizations, 41

National Endowment for the Arts and the Humanities, 113-14

National Fax Directory, 23

National Institute for Occupational Safety and Health, 97

National Institute of Standards and Technology, 89

National Institutes of Health, 94

National Libraries Catalogs Worldwide, 15

National Library of Medicine, 97, 227, 228

National Newspaper Index, 45

National Oceanic and Atmospheric Administration, 89-90

National Park Service, 99

National Science Foundation, 114

National Small Business Development Center Research Network, 159

National Technical Information Service, 83

National Trade Data Bank, 143

National Transportation Safety Board, 114-15

Native Americans, 97, 99

natural disasters, 80, 107

Natural Resource Library, 99

natural resources, 72, 80, 99

Navigator, Netscape, 181, 182

NEAR searches, 210-11, 213, 341

Nelson's Directory of Investment Research, 125-26

Net.Journal Directory, 221

Netscape Navigator, 181, 182

New Books, 85

New Competitor Intelligence, The (Fuld), 332

New Foreign Securities Offered in the United States 1952-1964, 150

New from CDS, 63

NewJour, 224

New Media Ethics, 340

Newsalert, 134, 136

NewsBank, 45

New School for Social Research, 340

newsgroups, online, 185, 217-20

NewsHunt, 221

NewsIndex, 221

newsletters, 337-38

directories, 23-27

Newsletters in Print, 23

Newspaper Abstracts, 45

Newspaper Index, 204, 222

newspapers, 327

on CD-ROM, 44, 45

databases online, 47, 204

feature editors, 20

library access to, 7

online, 184, 185, 186, 187

searchable archives online, 187, 222-23

Newspapers Fulltext, 45

newswires, xii, 47, 134, 185

New York Public Library, 11, 61, 64

New York Stock Exchange (NYSE), 154

Index